XENOPHON: SYMPOSIUM

Advisory Editor: M.M. Willcock

Xenophon

SYMPOSIUM

with an introduction, translation and commentary by

A.J. Bowen

ARIS & PHILLIPS LTD – WARMINSTER – ENGLAND

British Library Cataloguing-in-Publication Data
A catalogue record of this book is available from the British Library

ISBNS
0 85668 681 6   cloth
0 85668 682 4   limp

Printed and published in England by Aris & Phillips Ltd, Teddington House, Warminster, Wiltshire BA12 8PQ

Contents

Preface

'In this century Xenophon and his Socratic writings have been shamefully neglected': so Donald Morrison, in his *Bibliography of editions, translations, and commentary on Xenophon's Socratic writings, 1600 - present* (Pittsburgh 1988). His lists make the point starkly: of the *Symposium* in this century in English, no commentary, one edition (for the Loeb Library), and two translations (a third was published in 1996). Not since 1881 has there been a text with notes, and that heavily bowdlerised.

This translation and commentary have grown out of my work with the sort of Classics students who now increase by the year: they start their Greek at university. Between the end of beginners' courses and a reasonably fluent reading of the greatest of Greek literature there is room for texts like this, both to consolidate linguistic control and to enlarge the sense of Greek culture. In this context Xenophon's *Symposium* has three particular virtues: its Greek is clear, but not artless; its matter is a defining activity of upper class Greek society; and its hero Sokrates, himself a notable figure of that society, is presented as a person of easier sympathies and wider appeal than the more strictly intellectual person we find in Plato: the contrast is useful, and refreshing.

The translations which accompany the texts in this series are meant to let in Greekless readers; for them there is the usual commentary related to the translation. There is comment here on the Greek, however, to a greater extent than usual, for the sake of the readers whom I mentioned first; the level of linguistic comment has them chiefly in mind. For them also there is a generous vocabulary. In study they are recommended to keep the translation covered until they have worked out their own.

I have been much helped in preparing this edition by members of the Faculty of Classics at Cambridge, by the British School of Archaeology in Athens, and by the recent growth of interest in symposia; *Sympotica* (ed. O. Murray, Oxford 1990 hb and 1994 pb) marks it well: the paperback edition adds 146 items to the original bibliography, of which 43 are dated 1991 or later. But the best help has come first from students who have read parts of the work with me and second from three wise advisers. Professor Eric Handley read an early final draft and made many valuable comments and suggestions. So too did Paul Cartledge upon seeing a similar draft of the Introduction. Early and late I owe most to Professor Malcolm Willcock, editorial adviser to the series, whose shrewd comments and questions made me ponder again many a troublesome point. To all of them my thanks.

Jesus College, Cambridge   Anthony Bowen

Map of Southern Greece

Introduction

1. We know more of Xenophon than we do of most ancient authors. He and his contemporary Plato are the first of whom we know much. Most of our knowledge comes from their own writings, extensive in both cases, and in Xenophon's case very various. There are details to glean in later writers too, such as Diogenes Laertius.[1] Xenophon was a man of remarkable early achievement, but he wrote with modesty: in *Anabasis*, for instance, he writes of himself in the third person, as Thoukydides had done before him, and at the end of *Hellenika* he does not mention by name his own son Gryllos who died in a skirmish outside Mantineia in 362,[2] but says simply, 'Many brave men were killed' (ἀπέθανον πολλοὶ ἀγαθοί: VII 5.17).[3]

2. He was born in the early years of the Peloponnesian War, between 430 and 425.[4] His father's name was Gryllos (hence the name of the son, probably the elder of the two; it had perhaps been a nickname, meaning 'Grunter'), and the family had land in the deme of Erkhia in east Attica, good land (for Attica) then as now.[5] The invasions of the Peloponnesians may have interrupted its output, and after 413 their occupation of Dekeleia may have made it untenable. What happened to the estate, and to Xenophon's father, we do not know. In Athens Xenophon met Sokrates, around whom many of the richer and brighter young Athenians used to gather for stimulating debate on things moral and intellectual; Diogenes Laertius gives an attractive account of their first meeting: "They say that Sokrates met him in an alley; he stretched out his stick to prevent him passing while enquiring where this and that item of food could be bought. Xenophon answered him till the question 'And where

---

1   D. L. II 48-59. He wrote probably in the third century A.D., and drew his material from a lost biography by Demetrios Magnes, for whom see U. von Wilamowitz-Moellendorf, *Antigonos von Karystos* (Berlin 1885), 330-5.

2   All dates henceforward are B.C.

3   We know that Gryllos was one of the brave thanks to D. L. II 54 citing Aristotle and to Pausanias VIII 9.5. Xenophon's modesty (if that is what it is) also appears in his penchant for concealing himself under a pseudonym when in action in his own narrative. See *An.* 1.12 for the youth Theopompos, *HG* III 1.2 for Themistogenes the Syracusan, supposed writer of an *Anabasis*, and ὁ τῶν Κυρείων προεστηκώς at *HG* III 2.7. The youth at *An.* II 4.19 may be yet another persona for Xenophon himself. For discussion see M. MacLaren, 'Xenophon and Themistogenes', *TAPA* LXV (1934), 240-247, who distinguishes between Xenophon the man in history and Xenophon the historian; as historian Xenophon uses the first person happily, as Herodotos and Thoukydides had done.

4   The calculation depends upon putting together information in *An.* III 1.25, II 6.20, III 1.4 and V 3.5. Xenophon's friend Proxenos is the measure: he was probably a little older than Xenophon and he died aged 30 in 401.

5   For Erkhia see E. Vanderpool, 'The Location of the Attic deme Erchia', *BCH* 89 (1965), 21-26.

do men become gentlemen?'[6] He could not say. 'Follow me then,' said Sokrates, 'and start learning.'" It is appropriate that Xenophon's attention was caught by a question on manners and morals, rather than by one on something more narrowly intellectual.

3. He probably served in the Athenian cavalry.[7] Those who did so were among the top few in Athens socially, financially and often politically. Not all such men were unhappy when in 404 the Athenians lost the war and their democracy; some at least stuck by the ensuing régime of the 30 tyrants to its bitter end in 403. We do not know how long or how firmly Xenophon gave them his support, but it was long enough for him to be out in the cold when the democracy was restored. In 401 he accepted without apparent regret and with some determination[8] the invitation of a Theban friend Proxenos to join an overseas adventure of undisclosed aim, to be led by Kyros prince of Persia. Kyros' financial support for the Peloponnesian navy had played an important part in the recent defeat of Athens.

4. The adventure failed; Kyros was killed in battle, the senior Greek officers were trapped and murdered, and the surviving Greeks, led by Xenophon amongst others, had even greater adventures escaping. He later published their story. It reveals him as an excellent leader of men, sound in tactics, shrewd in psychology, brisk of tongue and meticulous in detail. When he was back in the Aegean world, in 399, he did not return home, despite at first intending to (An. VII 7.57), but committed his fortunes to the Spartans who were then campaigning against the Persians in Ionia and Aiolis, first under Thibron and Derkylidas and eventually under king Agesilaos. Xenophon returned to mainland Greece only in 394 (An. V 3.6 gives the occasion, the recall of Agesilaos to help deal with Sparta's enemies in Greece), and he was on the Spartan side at the battle of Koroneia, but probably did not fight. The Athenians were on the other side.

5. Xenophon had burnt his boats. The Athenians sentenced him to exile.[9] He was rescued by his Spartan friends. They had just made him their 'proxenos' at Athens,[10] a position of no use to them once he was an exile; now they gave him

---

6   'Gentlemen' represents the Greek καλοὶ κάγαθοί. See Commentary on I 1.

7   Much of HG. II 4, which records actions of the Athenian cavalry in the winter of 404/3, reads like an eye-witness account, and the work The Cavalry Commander (see 8 below) was written by an expert.

8   Xenophon tells the story against himself (An. III 1. 4-7) of consulting Sokrates about the project. Sokrates, perceiving the political risk to an Athenian in working with Kyros so soon after Athens' defeat, recommended he consult Delphi. Xenophon asked the oracle not whether he should go but to which gods he should sacrifice for a successful outcome.

9   Both date and grounds are disputed. The arguments of P. J. Rahn, 'The Date of Xenophon's Exile', in G. S. Shrimpton and D. J. McCargar edd. Classical Contributions: Studies in honour of M. F. McGregor (New York 1981), 103-119, for 394 or soon thereafter are accepted here.

10   A 'proxenos' was a citizen of one state appointed by another to represent its interests in his community as he saw fit. He might speak for it publicly in his own political assemblies, and he would entertain in his home any of its important citizens who came

land at Skillous in Triphylia, which they had recently taken from the Eleans. Skillous is close to Olympia, on the south side of the river Alpheios. Some think the village of Makríssia is the site; the name Skilloúntia has recently been bestowed on the village of Mázi, however, where a Doric temple of Zeus has been excavated.[11] It is an attractive area, well watered and green; there he settled. He was to be there for the next two decades, his middle age, managing the estate, establishing a shrine and festival of Artemis of Ephesos with booty from his time in Ionia (*An.* V 3.7-13), and raising a family of two boys, Gryllos and Diodoros.[12] There too much writing was done.

6. In 371 the Spartans marched into Boiotia and were defeated at Leuktra. They never recovered. The Eleans regained Triphylia, and Xenophon was homeless again. His family took refuge in Lepreon, south of Skillous, where he soon joined them, and then in Corinth. One political consequence of Leuktra was a reconciliation between Athens and Sparta. Xenophon's sentence of exile was rescinded (how soon is not known) and his sons were made citizens and served in the Athenian cavalry. In 362 came Gryllos' death, and his father's Kiplingesque reticence mentioned above. Others wrote encomia.[13] The last datable event to which Xenophon refers is the Sacred War declared late in 356 (*Vect.* V 9). Some time after that he died, aged at least 70, perhaps in Athens.[14] He was well aware of the situation in Athens, as *de*

---

to his state on business. Herodotos (VIII 136 and 143) notes the προξενία (proxeny might be the English word) of Alexander of Macedon on behalf of the Athenians, and (IX 85) that of Kleades of Plataiai for the state of Aigina. The practice harks back to an age when leading men of different states would meet each other at great Greek gatherings like the Olympic games, and establish guest-friendships between their families.

11   Pausanias V 6.4 and Strabo 343-4; N. Yaloúris, Πρακτικὰ τῆς Ἀρχαιολογικῆς Ἑταιρείας 1954 and later, esp. 1960, and A. Triándi *ibid.* 1979; E. Meyer, *Neue Peloponnesische Wanderungen*, Berne 1957; G. Daux, *BCH* 86 (1962); and P. Thémelis, Ἀρχαιολογικὸν Δελτίον 1968 pt. 1.

12   His wife's name was Philesia. Her nationality and the date of the marriage are not known. If they were married before Xenophon left to join Kyros, then she probably was Athenian; their sons' eventual legitimation as Athenian citizens may support that (Athenian citizenship had been conditional since 451/0 on both parents being Athenian); but a marriage after his return to Greece seems likelier, in which case perhaps she was not. The boys were, at the invitation of Agesilaos himself (Plu. *Ages.* 20.2), put through the Spartan system of education, a signal mark of the esteem in which their father was held.

13   Aristotle (D. L. II 55) said that they were written in part to please Xenophon: clearly he was a man well known in many quarters and worth pleasing.

14   D. L. II 56, citing Demetrios, says Corinth. Pausanias V 6.6 reports a grave just outside the sanctuary at Olympia bearing a portrait bust of Pentelic marble said by the Eleans to be Xenophon's, but that probably marks a belated Elean attempt to claim a famous man. A portrait bust of Xenophon does exist, in the Museum in Alexandria: see G.M.A.Richter, The Portraits of the Greeks vol. II (London 1965), 157-8 or R. R. R. Smith's revised edition in one vol. (Oxford 1984), 217.

Vectigalibus shows. We do not know if the land in Erkhia ever returned to the family.

7. Xenophon the busy country squire, riding round the estate, replete with memories of soldiering, highly esteemed by the king of the Spartans, presents a picture well able to fill its frame. But Xenophon was a literary squire: he wrote about horses and estates, he wrote about his deeds and times, he wrote about Agesilaos and Sparta. What made him take up pen?

8. He had models for some of what he wrote. For works like *Anabasis* (to some extent) and *Hellenica* there were the historians Herodotos and Thoukydides. Thoukydides' work had been left unfinished, and Xenophon started his *Hellenica* as if to complete it (the manner of writing as far as II 3.10 shows the debt);[15] in *Anabasis,* however, there is an apologetic element: the expedition was a dubious enterprise, and it fell at the first fence, but Xenophon's rescue of the survivors was a fine achievement, and its narration might have restored his credit in Athens. Historical also (though not certainly his) is the *Constitution of Sparta*, but a model for it is hard to see; the pamphlet on Athens now usually called the *Old Oligarch,* anciently included among Xenophon's works, might have served. At the end of his life he wrote a study of Athens' sources of income, *de Vectigalibus*; with it could be put *Oeconomicus,* a pamphlet on household and estate management, but because that was written as a dialogue led by Socrates, it is counted among the Socratic works. *The Cavalry Commander, On Hunting* and *The Art of Horsemanship* are further specialised studies, whose models could be early works in the Hippocratic corpus, or essays of the kind called *tekhnai* (the nearest English is 'handbook': authors we know of include Iktinos architect of the Parthenon, on architecture, and Sophokles, on the chorus). For *Hiero,* a dialogue about monarchy, for the *Education of Cyrus,* a long fable on the upbringing of a monarch, and for *Agesilaus,* a laudation of the Spartan king, the practice of encomia may have helped. Leadership was in any case a topic of interest to Xenophon.[16]

9. The variety recalls the versatility of the early sophists. But Diogenes Laertius remarked on Xenophon's originality, and mention of models may be misleading. Xenophon was not in thrall to other men's works. He wrote partly to satisfy himself, partly for a variety of other audiences, and partly, we may reckon, to earn and sustain that attention, particularly in Athens, which was denied him by exile. Publication kept him known, and the proximity of his residence to Olympia[17] made

---

15   See M. MacLaren, 'On the composition of Xenophon's Hellenica', *AJP* LV (1934), 121-139. Dillery, 255 note 10, gives a selection of leading discussions of the topic, and A.Andrewes and K.J.Dover, A Historical Commentary on Thucydides vol. 5 (Oxford 1981), 437-44 is well balanced; Gray, Introduction 1-9, has a different approach.

16   Dillery has recently explored it.

17   The temple of Artemis which he built on his estate at Skillous was on a site about 20 stades (two and a half miles) from Olympia (*An.* V 3.11).

for easy communication with leading Greeks, if they wished, when the games were on. Out of Athens did not have to mean out of mind.

10. There are four works of Xenophon devoted to Sokrates, *Apologia Socratis, Oeconomicus, Memorabilia,* and *Symposium.* The *Symposium,* which is divided into nine unequal sections, goes as follows:

I. I write this work to show gentlemen in playful mood, because their playful moments are as worthy of record as their serious ones. Kallias son of Hipponikos, admirer of Autolykos, victor in the boys' pankration, was taking the boy, together with his father Lykon, home for a party, accompanied by a friend, Nikeratos. On their way to the house they meet Sokrates together with Kritoboulos, Hermogenes, Antisthenes and Kharmides. After polite resistance, all agree to be Kallias' guests. The eight adults recline to eat, and Autolykos sits. His beauty reduces them all to silence. A known wag called Philippos knocks and Kallias invites him in. His first jokes fail, but eventually he relaxes the mood.

II. After the meal an entertainment of music, dancing and singing is provided by a small professional troupe. Sokrates praises it, but refuses Kallias' offer of scent: not for men among men. Lykon asks what men of his age should smell of: Gentlemanliness, says Sokrates, and in quoting Theognis develops a compliment to Lykon and his son. Some seek a discussion of personal excellence (such as might develop in a dialogue of Plato), but Sokrates restores his host's programme. The girl dancer demonstrates her skill and nerve, causing Sokrates to commend the teachability of women. Antisthenes asks why Sokrates fails to train his own wife, but Sokrates parries the thrust with wit. The boy of the troupe dances, and Sokrates praises him, expressing a wish to learn the steps. All laugh, but he justifies himself vigorously, appealing to Kharmides for confirmation of his seriousness. Philippos then dances in grotesque imitation of both girl and boy till exhausted. All refresh themselves with wine, which Sokrates commends if taken as plants best take rain, little and often; Philippos requests frequent service.

III. The boy sings to his lyre. Kharmides, half-quoting Sokrates, says sexual feelings are being stirred, but Sokrates suggests that they now talk; he takes up their host's earlier promise, to demonstrate how well the sophists had educated him. Kallias agrees to do so if they will all declare what they are most proud of. All do so, with a few jests as they go. A competitive theme for the symposium is thus set up.

IV. Kallias leads off by boasting of his ability to make men good with his money, and though challenged by Antisthenes holds his own, after a fashion, till Sokrates rescues him. Nikeratos is also challenged, but turns his boast, of being able to recite all Homer, into a joke anyway. Kritoboulos talks at length

about his passion for Kleinias, and Sokrates challenges him to a beauty competition, with the boy and girl of the dance troupe to judge between them. Hermogenes expresses surprise at Kritoboulos' state of infatuation; Sokrates says it was worse before the youth came to him for counsel. Kharmides starts to tease Sokrates, but is invited by Kritoboulos to justify his boast of poverty. After him, Antisthenes develops his boast of wealth: it turns out to be the wealth of the poor man contented with his lot. Hermogenes then explains his own pride in the concern that gods and friends show for his welfare, and Philippos justifies his rôle of laughter-maker. Kharmides turns to the troupe-owner, a Syracusan, and invites him to make his boast (Lykon and Autolykos, who had expressed their pride in each other earlier, are not asked to expand on it). Lastly Kallias invites Sokrates to justify his declared pride in procuring. Sokrates defines his terms as Plato often shows him doing, explains what a good procurer would do to bring the right people together, and suddenly claims Antisthenes as a perfect example. Antisthenes' initial anger fades as Sokrates says that he was speaking metaphorically: for Antisthenes has brought Kallias and sophists together, to the advantage of both.

V. Kallias revives Sokrates' challenge of Kritoboulos to a beauty contest. In argument Sokrates easily shows that he must be the better: his protruding eyes are better to see with, his fat lips are better to kiss with, his flaring nostrils are better to smell with, and his big mouth is better to bite with. But when the votes are counted, Kritoboulos wins.

VI. Hermogenes has been silent; Sokrates rallies him quite sharply, but then begs his host to rescue him when Hermogenes defends himself. The Syracusan meantime has been chafing at the neglect of his troupe, and attacks Sokrates, using jibes from Aristophanes' *Clouds* (produced the previous year). Some of the company want to attack the Syracusan, but Sokrates firmly dissuades them.

VII. He starts a song, and then chides the Syracusan for not providing entertainment appropriate to the occasion. He suggests a dance of Graces, Seasons and Nymphs. The Syracusan goes out to prepare.

VIII. In his absence, Sokrates develops the occasion with a long speech on passionate relationships. He himself, he says, is for ever in love with someone; so is Kharmides, so is Kritoboulos; Nikeratos has his wife, and Hermogenes is in love with gentlemanliness; what about Antisthenes? Antisthenes claims his passion is Sokrates. Pretending embarrassment, Sokrates comes to his point, the relationship of Kallias and Autolykos. He distinguishes between a physical and a spiritual passion, preferring the latter as likely to develop a relationship of lasting mutual pride and of encouragement towards goodness; he is scathing about a physical passion physically satisfied. He draws on myth and history in support of his case, and

imagines Autolykos' potential pride in having a worthy admirer: Kallias must learn from the great statesmen of Athens, justify his own high birth, and seek a rôle in politics. Kallias expresses a hope that Sokrates will assist him.

IX. It is time for Autolykos to move. Lykon, departing with him, pauses to express his approval of Sokrates. The Syracusan announces a mime of the passion of Ariadne and Dionysos. The girl and boy present it so convincingly that the married men hasten home to their wives and the bachelors swear to get married. Sokrates and a few others go with Kallias to join Autolykos and Lykon.

11. All the Socratic works, both of Xenophon and of others, are essentially apologetic.[18] The word needs to be understood in its ancient sense. It was not enough to put the record on Sokrates straight, with a decent dispassion. The man was thought by his apologists to be not merely innocent of the charges brought against him, but better than innocent. Plato's words about him at the end of *Phaedo* make the point very clearly: 'our friend, the best man of his time, we can say, that we knew, and the most sensible and fair-minded man too.' The picture they wanted of their hero had to be wholly to his moral credit. Such a picture may, however, reflect the painter more than the sitter. That is one reason, and a very good one among several, why we cannot establish the 'real' Sokrates; although the ancient literature on him is plentiful, it is mostly compromised to some degree by its apologetic purpose.

12. The work of vindication was under way soon after Sokrates' death.[19] The four principal apologists known to the ancient world were Antisthenes, Aiskhines, Plato and Xenophon.[20] The first to write was probably Antisthenes, but it is impossible to give the sort of dates to the Socratic writings that would enable us to establish a sequence, and there is some danger of circularity in the discussion. Xenophon could have compiled his works over time, as he clearly did *Hellenica*; the form of *Memorabilia* is notably episodic. But for the date of *Symposium* we appear to have some control: Plato also wrote a *Symposium*, there are signs that one or other of them read the other's work and was influenced by it, and Plato's works can to some extent be ordered and dated.[21]

---

18 Xenophon's apologetic stance is well revealed in the episode he recorded not in his Socratic works but in *An.* III 1. 4-7 (cited in note 8). The stance is explicit in the opening both of his *Apologia* and of *Memorabilia*.

19 It was probably provoked by one Polykrates, who wrote a *Prosecution of Sokrates* (which has not survived). It was issued not earlier than 394, and may have started a flood of apologetic literature. See E. R. Dodds ed. Plato *Gorgias* (Oxford 1959), 28-29, and P. Treves, *RE* xxi2 (Stuttgart 1952) 1736-1752.

20 D. L. II 64 quoting Panaetius. On the evidence of X. *Ap.* 2, Hermogenes was also one.

21 See Guthrie IV, 41-54.

13. Scholars have usually seen Xenophon's *Symposium* as poorer than Plato's intellectually and artistically. This accords with a general judgment of the two surviving Socratics, which may be summarised as follows: Socrates was a clever man, and Plato was a very clever man and a great stylist to boot, but Xenophon was not so clever; hence, in understanding and recording what Socrates said, Plato is bound to have done better than Xenophon.[22] The comparison of Plato and Xenophon we may accept, but opinion upon the fidelity of either writer to the character and ideas of Socrates has swung to and fro for many years.[23] How clever was he? From study of the Sokrates offered to us, we could quite reasonably call him a man of earthy moral shrewdness and an uncommon sense of justice; this seems to be what impressed contemporaries most, and it is close to what Plato has Phaedo say in the passage quoted above. Xenophon, we might reckon, has depicted such a man very well, whereas Plato took the intellectual implications of the morality far beyond any point of analysis that Sokrates himself might ever have reached.

14. Neither *Symposium* contains much that is intellectual, and each is a special piece within its author's works, with its own content and purpose: the emphasis in Xenophon's work is first and last on Socrates' social example, and Plato's *Symposium* has the same base. Ancient commentators liked to detect a rivalry between Plato and Xenophon, confirmed in their view by the fact that though each was aware of the other, neither mentioned the other.[24] But each also failed to mention other Socratics, friendly or hostile; Plato, who used Sokrates in almost everything he wrote, had more occasion than Xenophon to mention them: his failure to do so may mark simply the steady divergence of his own aims from apologia as he continued to write and think. His own apologetic phase was soon over; Xenophon's lasted longer, and it may have influenced his memories.

15. So which wrote first? Scholars taking Xenophon as inferior to Plato have assumed that Plato wrote first and that Xenophon palely imitated him. In 1978 Thesleff argued[25] that first Xenophon wrote a *Symposium* much like the existing one, Plato then saw it and was stirred to write his, and finally Xenophon saw that and partly rewrote his own. I find the argument convincing. In particular it caters for the fact that Xenophon's apparent dependence on Plato is confined almost entirely to VIII, which contains Socrates' long speech on passion. Remove that speech (it is not

---

22 To a considerable extent this view is due to the strictly philosophical interest in Sokrates for which Plato is responsible. Xenophon's contribution to that is tiny; hence the disparagement of him. Guthrie III2, 19, speaks of 'features .. at the trial .. blunted and coarsened by Xenophon's less sensitive mind.'

23 Pomeroy, 23-24, takes the debate back to 1767.

24 Xenophon does mention Plato's name at *Mem.* III 6.1, but casually. There is gentle exploration of the supposed hostility in Aulus Gellius XIV 3.

25 Holger Thesleff, 'The Interrelation and Date of the *Symposia* of Plato and Xenophon', *BICS* 25, 157-70.

wholly consistent with its context), and 'it could quite safely be argued that it is Plato who is dependent on Xenophon.' Dependent does not mean inferior. Thesleff shows that Plato took detail after detail in Xenophon's work and transformed them with a sharp and brilliant wit; refinement and improvement must come second: hence Xenophon's basic priority. Xenophon's reaction on reading Plato's *Symposium* we can only guess; he clearly thought that a climactic speech for Socrates was a good idea, on apologetic as well as on literary grounds: a clearer moral stance would enhance and confirm the man's merit, even if it hardly fulfilled the author's original intention to show Sokrates in relaxed mood. What it replaced we cannot tell; the troupe's mime of a physical and heterosexual passion in IX is in unresolved contrast with it.

16. Plato's *Symposium* was written not earlier than 384 and not later than 378.[26] Xenophon could have written his first version at almost any time, but it is a work of mature social understanding and fair literary control; he probably wrote it not long before 384, when he was already settled at Skillous. The revised version is very unlikely to be later than 371: after the Spartan disaster at Leuktra it would be hard to make the comparison between the Spartans on the one hand and the Boeotians and Eleans on the other (VIII 34-5)[27] which Sokrates does to the advantage of the Spartans. Closer dating is not possible.[28]

17. The dramatic date of the work is easy to establish. It celebrates an athletic victory at the Great Panathenaia. The festival occurred every year, but a Great Panathenaia only every fourth year, in the middle of the Olympic cycle.[29] The relationship between Kallias and Autolykos was mocked by Eupolis the comic poet in 421 in his *Flatterers* and in 420 in his *Autolykos*.[30] Clearly, Autolykos was victor in 422, between the Olympic games of 424 and 420.

18. In 422 Xenophon himself was eight years old at most. How sound is what he says, in fact and spirit, thirty and forty years after the event? How sound was he trying to be? Did he consult survivors? Perhaps the party was no more than a cue for

---

26   See Dover PS, 10, where he summarises his more detailed discussion in *Phronesis* 10 (1965), 1-20.

27   References in this form are to Xenophon's *Symposium*.

28   Thesleff thinks that Xenophon was also influenced by Plato's *Phaedrus*. Dates for that work have varied greatly: its latest editor C. J. Rowe says (*PCPS* 212 (1986), *The Argument and Structure of Plato's Phaedrus*, 106-125) that Plato wrote it 'at a time relatively close to, but still some distance from, the end of his life.' In 371 Plato was about 55, and had 25 years still to live.

29   The arrangement was deliberate, to enable other Greeks to come to the Athenian festival, but it never attained the panHellenic status of the great four, the Olympic, Pythian, Isthmian and Nemean games. See Parke, 33-50.

30   See Athen. V 218bc and 216d who dates by the eponymous archons of the years concerned. For the surviving fragments of the plays and other *testimonia* see K-A V.

a picture of Sokrates assembled from various occasions; even so, and despite the revision mentioned above, Xenophon has written a work of considerable coherence in itself which is consistent with what we know both of the people concerned and of their lifestyle and times.

19. At least eight of the nine main people at the party were alive and in Athens when Xenophon came to manhood; he could well have known them all. We know very different amounts about them. Sokrates, at nearly 50 years of age, was probably the oldest man present. We know more about him than we do about any other Greek of the classical period; he avoided a political career, but he had more impact on those who met him than any other Athenian. His father Sophroniskos was probably a master-mason and sculptor, and a man of some standing: no less a person than Lysimakhos son of Aristeides said that Sophroniskos and he had always been friends and companions.[31] That social standing is confirmed not only by the company that Plato and Xenophon consistently show him keeping but also by the fact that Sokrates served in time of war as a hoplite: hoplites were responsible for arming themselves, at no small expense. His intellectual activities were also noteworthy enough for him to be presented by Aristophanes in *Clouds* in 423 as the archetypal sophist. Other comic poets did likewise. In 406 he found himself a councillor, one of 500 (50 per tribe) selected by lot to manage the state's affairs for a year. His tribe presided over assembly at a moment when six of Athens' ten generals, accused of dereliction of duty, were to be tried as one; despite great popular pressure, to which his colleagues capitulated, he refused his assent to the illegal proposal. Two years later, the war lost, he similarly resisted the 30 tyrants, quietly walking home when they sent for him to help seize the wealthy Leon of Salamis. In 399, after the democracy had been restored, he was brought to trial aged 70, accused of acknowledging novel deities instead of the city's gods and of corrupting the young. He was found guilty and accepted the penalty of death. At the time he had three children, the eldest in his teens. His impact abides; whole books continue to be written on the man. The most judicious survey in English, to which I refer my readers for more, is that by W. K. C. Guthrie, in volume III of his 'History of Greek Philosophy' (Cambridge 1969), published separately two years later as 'Socrates'.

20. Next oldest was Lykon, father of Autolykos: if Autolykos was about 16 (if he was much older he would have been classified at the games as a beardless youth, and if much younger he would not have won), then Lykon was at least in his forties. His precise social status is obscure: Eupolis in his *Autolykos* (17 above) mocked not only Kallias and Autolykos but also both Autolykos' parents; some anomaly may be suspected. Otherwise, we know nothing about him.[32] Autolykos is known for his

---

31   Pl. *La.* 180e.
32   Some have assumed that he was one of Sokrates' three prosecutors in 399. If so, his comment at IX 1 would be deeply ironical on Xenophon's part, which is not how it reads. The name Lykon is not unique. The prosecutor is surely a different man.

death.[33] Athens endured a Spartan garrison after her defeat in 404; Autolykos meeting Kallibios, the Spartan governor, at a muddy place on a road failed to give way. Kallibios struck at him with his staff. Autolykos picked him up in a wrestler's hold and dumped him in the mud. Kallibios, enraged, appealed to Lysander, commander of the Spartan troops. Lysander dismissed the protest, chiding him for not knowing how to govern free men. But a little later Autolykos was murdered, probably by pro-Spartan Athenians to gratify Kallibios.

21. Nikeratos was also eliminated in the same period.[34] The family held land in the silver-mining area of Laureion in south-east Attica; Nikias his father, who was executed by the Syracusans in Sicily in 413 (Th. VII 86.2), had been making 10 talents a year out of the 1000 mining slaves he owned. The family spent heavily in the service of Athens. After 413, when the Spartans occupied Dekeleia, income from Laureion was cut off; Nikeratos, one of three brothers, left estate to his own son Nikias, then still a minor, worth 14 talents.[35] In 409/8 he served as a trierarch; like his father he aligned himself with the democracy (despite *HG* II 3.39), and paid for it under the 30 tyrants. In 422 he was probably in his early twenties, and married (II 3); he had already found his way to Sokrates.[36] Xenophon shows him a little rueful about the education that his father had procured for him, but well able to be humorous about it and about himself (IV 6-7, 45 and 51).

22. Kharmides son of Glaukon was a cousin of the Kritias who became chief of the 30 tyrants.[37] In 430 or so he was of Autolykos' age and condition, the beauty of his generation;[38] presumably he was born a little after 450. His only attempt at public service brought his death: he was one of the 30 tyrants' ten commissioners for the Peiraieus, and was killed in the fighting at Mounykhia in 403 (*HG* II 4.19). Most of his contributions to the conversation have a homosexual dimension (see III 1 and IV 8-9, 27 and 52), which is consistent with Plato's information about him; his claim to be poor, however, may be at least in part anachronistic (see note on IV 30).

23. Three of the symposiasts were thus dead when Xenophon was in his early twenties. Between what we learn elsewhere of Autolykos, Nikeratos and Kharmides[39] and what Xenophon says here, no quarrels emerge; Nikeratos and

---

33   Plu. *Lys.* 15.
34   See Plu. *Lys.* 18.6 and 24. For his family see Davies, 10808.
35   Lysias 19.47.
36   Pl. *La.* 200cd.
37   For the family see Davies, 8792.
38   He was old enough to appear in Plato's *Protagoras* (315a), whose dramatic date is about 433; in the dialogue named after him Socrates, on leave from the siege of Poteidaia which lasted from 432 to 429, reckons he is no longer παῖς, a boy, but μειράκιον, a youth (154b). Plato is not free of anachronisms, but the dates fit. As for Kharmides' looks, he was so striking as a youth that even younger boys gazed at him in admiration (Pl. *Chrm.* 154c).
39   Some risk of circularity has to be accepted here: Xenophon's work may have influenced later sources.

Kharmides are portrayed with plausibility. Soon Sokrates too was dead. But the other four lived on, and could all have been consulted; if any one of them was consulted, it was probably Hermogenes.[40]

24. Despite being Kallias' half-brother, he had no part in the inheritance; he was probably therefore his father's bastard.[41] He was devoted to Socrates, as is attested in several places.[42] Indeed, devotion to the powers for good seems to have been his guiding principle (III 14 and IV 47-49); in VI 1-4 it even sounds priggish, but in *Memorabilia* (II 10) he wins high commendation. In VIII 12 he shows some concern for his half-brother, and it is certainly attractive to think that he may have made representations to Xenophon about the portrayal of Kallias, whose life-style needed some apologia.[43] He was present when Sokrates drank the hemlock, as were Kritoboulos and Antisthenes.

25. Kritoboulos' interest in Sokrates followed his father Kriton's, who was a firm friend and contemporary; if Kritoboulos was newly wed in 422 like Nikeratos (II 3), then they were an early-marrying family.[44] In recording a pederastic passion which lasted past the marriage, Xenophon makes him seem rather young for his years. He was a very suitable recipient of the advice which Sokrates gives him about marriage in *Oeconomicus*.[45] If Sokrates' sums are right (*Oec.* II 5), Kritoboulos had an estate worth at least 8 talents.

26. Antisthenes in his devotion to Sokrates (*Mem.* III 11.17) was different from the others. First, he was older. Sokrates observes that Kallias had been introduced to the sophists Prodikos and Hippias by Antisthenes. Kallias was born not later than 450;[46] for Antisthenes a date of birth in 455 has been suggested, and 460 is not impossible. He was still alive in 366. Second, he was a sophist and leader of thought himself. Unfortunately, 'very little is known about Antisthenes from first-rate sources' and there has been 'an immense amount of conjecture and hypothesis about him'.[47] In Xenophon's depiction of him there is a persistent waspishness, as well as strong indications of the line of thought which, inspired by Sokrates' own superiority

40   See *Ap.* 2.
41   See Davies, 7826 XVIB. Xenophon's reference to him at *Ap.* 2 as son of Hipponikos could be added to Davies' discussion of his paternity.
42   Pl. *Phd.* 59b, X. *Ap.* 2ff, *Mem.* I 2.48, II 10.3 and IV 8.4ff.
43   See Ollier, 25.
44   See Davies, 8823.
45   See IV 12-22 and *Mem.* I 3.8ff, together with *Oec.* III 12-13.
46   His younger son, child of his third marriage, was old enough to be marriageable in 399 (see note 48).
47   The quotations, from Popper and Field respectively, are made by Guthrie; see his III1, 304-311, together with 209-219 and 247-9, for a sober attempt to set out his life, his thinking and his place among his contemporaries. His social status is not clear. Davies, 1194, identifies an Antisthenes amongst the liturgical class (to which at least Kallias, Nikeratos and Kritoboulos of the company belonged) who may be the man of that name in *Mem.* III 4; his view that the man there is not this Antisthenes is accepted here.

over ordinary human needs, later led to Antisthenes and not Diogenes being called the founder of the Cynic school of philosophy. He and Plato did not see eye to eye: Xenophon's relationship with him is not clear, but we may reckon that each knew the other's writings (about 74 items are recorded for Antisthenes).

27. Last the host, Kallias son of Hipponikos.[48] The family was old: the senior male was torch-bearer at the Eleusinian Mysteries. It was also very rich: they held land fit for horses in the deme of Alopeke, just south of the city walls, and also land in the silver-mining area of Laureion, which Kallias' grandfather first exploited, with huge profit. There was a town house west of the Agora in the deme of Melite, where Themistokles had had his house,[49] and a house in the Peiraieus, the scene of the party. Grandfather Kallias had lived long; right at the end of his life in the 440s he did notable service for Athens as ambassador both to Persia and then to Sparta, establishing terms of peace; the Spartans made him their proxenos in Athens (Sokrates mentions the honour at VIII 39). Hipponikos his son served as general in 426/5. Kallias honoured family tradition in both respects, serving as general in 391/0 (*HG* IV 5.13) and as ambassador to Sparta (for the third time) in 371 (*HG* VI 3.2-6), at an age which matched his grandfather's. But both Xenophon's comment on Kallias as ambassador and the speech he reports him making show a vain and shallow man. At the time of the party Kallias was nearly 30 and almost certainly a father, well beyond the age and state at which courtship of a youth was seemly; yet the affair according to Sokrates (VIII 7) was known all over the city. Hipponikos was probably still alive at the time, but he was dead before the next spring, when Eupolis' *Flatterers* showed Kallias in possession of the inheritance.[50] Grandfather left a fortune of 200 talents; grandson reduced it to fewer than 2.[51] The comic poets had at least two decades of fun at his expense, from Eupolis' *Flatterers* to Aristophanes' *Frogs*. His family life was also unseemly, as Andokides revealed (1 117-131); to marry a young widow, to replace her with her mother, and then to repudiate his son by the older woman was indeed scandalous behaviour. It is significant that the ancient office of torch-bearer did not pass to either son.[52] In 422 much was still expected of him, but little was forthcoming; Xenophon's

---

48 For a thorough analysis of the evidence for this remarkable family, attested through more generations than any other in classical Athens, see Davies, 7826; the family tree in D. M. McDowell ed. Andocides, *On the Mysteries* (Oxford 1962), appendix L, differs slightly, and is followed by M. J. E. Edwards ed. Andocides (Warminster 1995).

49 Ar. *Frogs* scholion on 428, and Plu. *Them.* 22.

50 See Athen. V 218bc, where inconsistency with Pl. *Prt.* is plain but unexplored.

51 Lys. 19.48. Two may seem too small to be credible, but in the preceding sentence Lysias mentions Nikeratos' 14 talents, a figure not to be doubted.

52 Aristotle's suggestion (*Rh.* 1405a19/20) that Kallias did not have the means to sustain the duty is difficult to reconcile with the fact that Xenophon calls him 'torch-bearer' at *HG* VI 3.3 in introducing his speech, and has Kallias refer to the office in the speech clearly Kallias himself was still δᾳδοῦχος in his old age.

understanding of the man's ambiguous position is to be found in Kallias' own words
of himself at I 6, and is particularly clear in Sokrates' words to him at VIII 39-41.

28. Both in their characters and in their circumstances Xenophon seems to
present his cast as they were. There are a few external references from which we
may judge further the soundness of his picture. Some of them are references that
anyone acquainted with Athens in the last two or three decades of the fifth century
should get right: mention of the sophists Protagoras, Gorgias and Prodikos at I 5,
picked up at IV 62-3 (Gorgias is also mentioned at II 26); mention of two others,
Stesimbrotos and Anaximander, at III 6; and of Kleinias as Kritoboulos' beloved at
IV 9. Nikostratos the actor, mentioned at VI 3, is not someone we can date
accurately enough to use in argument at all. Mention of Sokrates' wife at II 10 could
be significant if we could answer certain questions explored by Guthrie (see note *ad
loc.*). The dates of marriage of Nikeratos and Kritoboulos are also critical (perhaps
Xenophon attended the weddings as a boy). Kharmides' impoverishment (IV 31,
mentioned in 22 above) could have come as early as the 420s, but it was events of
415 that undid him for sure; Xenophon may have misremembered the timing. The
reference to Peisander, in 415 a comparative moderate in politics but in II 14 called
a demagogue by Philippos (perhaps to flatter the company), argues a good
awareness of the politics of the time, but that could have come from study of the
comic poets (see note *ad loc.*). The only reference clearly wrong, that to Pausanias
and Agathon in VIII 32, is of a different sort. Though their relationship was long-
standing, and could have been mentioned without probable anachronism for itself,
the reference is in fact to something Pausanias says in Plato's *Symposium*. The
probable secondary nature of this part of the work was noted in 15 above. Despite
Xenophon's poor reputation as a narrative historian,[53] the historical references in
this work, for what they are worth, are mostly sound.

29. There is also Xenophon's truth to contemporary society, especially to young
men's parties and pederastic relationships. Circular argument here can scarcely be
avoided, for Xenophon's *Symposium* is a *locus classicus* for both. Just as readers
were referred to Guthrie for information on Sokrates, so now they are referred to
Sympotica (ed. O. Murray) for drinking parties. Xenophon's party comes in Murray's
fourth and last category, the *'symposion* for pleasure'.[54] The invitations to it are
casual, their number is not large, the purpose is social, the guests come as they are,
control of the drinking is divided between the invited and senior guest Sokrates and
the uninvited Philippos, Kallias' hosting duties are lightly exercised, his servants
pour the wine, paid performers play the music and sing, and the guests have little to
do but talk and tease. Some politics slips in at the end but to little effect; if Kallias'
aims were serious, he would have invited the sort of guests he rejects with some

---

53   See Anderson, 62ff, for a standard view, and Dillery, 4 and 253, for glossing of it.
54   See Murray 5.

relief at I 4, and at the end he might have led them tipsy into the streets to parade his importance.[55] We may note that there is nothing for Autolykos to do but be there: in an earlier generation he might have sung to the lyre and served the wine.[56] There is no playing, almost no singing (apart from the paean at II 1 and Sokrates' deliberate singing at VII 1), and only scraps of poetry: there is Sokrates' quotation of a well-known couplet of Theognis at II 5 and interpretation of some Homer at VIII 30, and Nikeratos' quotation of Homer at IV 6 and 45. The Syracusan's quotation (VI 6-8) of Aristophanes, a contemporary poet, is different: he is not demonstrating his education.

30. Kallias' party is the occasion at which, within conventions that Xenophon takes largely as read, a lover introduces his chosen beloved to friends, and they accept the relationship, demonstrating in the variety and nature of their converse how gentlemen behave, both implicitly and (especially when Sokrates speaks in VIII) explicitly. Xenophon's purposes in the work are several, but the relationship between lover and beloved eventually shares prime position with Sokrates. Acknowledgement of the relationship is the cause of the party, and the impact of the beloved is established at once (I 8-10); contrasts with it occur, of different sorts;[57] references are made to the sexual side of such relationships, not only indirectly at III 1 and IV 52-54, but directly and deliberately by Sokrates himself (VIII 19-23). Thanks largely to Dover's 'Greek Homosexuality' the topic of close relationships between young men which was so notable a feature of classical Greek society can now be studied seriously. In his book Dover analyses a variety of evidence for a pattern of behaviour peculiar, it seems, to upper class society; it was probably developed in a military context and was sustained at least in part by the absence of young women acceptable socially. The men married, on the whole, in their twenties, but girls were married in their teens, often in their early teens, more or less at puberty: they passed from father's care into husband's care without emerging into society at all. The young men, forming a society to some extent on its own, expressed their desire for appreciation and affection in each other. A youth of good family could expect to be taken up by one a little older who would introduce him to society. In due course the older one, ὁ ἐραστής, the admirer, would take a wife, without necessarily abandoning the earlier relationship or forgetting its enduring social obligations, and the younger one, ὁ ἐρώμενος, the beloved, could look about for a youth to do him credit in his turn. Some sexual activity between them may be assumed; but the evidence of Aristophanic comedy, of vase paintings and of graffiti should be taken with a fairly large pinch of salt: elements of fantasy are obvious in

---

55   See Murray 150, rightly citing the final scenes of Aristophanes' *Wasps*.
56   See Murray 135-145; NB 141 in connection with VIII 30.
57   See III 12 for the father and son relationship of Lykon and Autolykos, IV 10-28 for the relationship between Kritoboulos and Kleinias, 52-54 for the Syracusan and his boy, V for the beauty contest between Kritoboulos and Sokrates, and VIII 4-6 for Antisthenes' idolisation of Sokrates.

it. sexual activity is notoriously a field where exaggeration is frequent and some element of social pose may be suspected, born of a need to conform to fashion.[58] Xenophon observes in his *Symposium* the conventional decencies that his class would expect. Kallias' age and marital status are not mentioned; other embarrassing features of the party's host, such as his enthusiasm for sophists and his evasion of politics, are touched upon lightly.

31. In the ancient world Xenophon was read at first for his content. Interest in his Greek developed in the early Empire, at the rise of the Second Sophistic, when there was a significant attempt to revive Attic Greek.[59] He was then seen as a model of ἀφέλεια, of smoothness; the Greek word is a negative, meaning 'unpebbledness': no lumps and bumps. Where the writing of ancient Greek is still practised, he remains the best first model.

32. Ancient interest was limited to labelling him, to praising him in general terms (with occasional note of faults) and to close examination of his vocabulary.[60] To exemplify the smoothness is difficult precisely because of the smoothness. Not for him the experiments of Thoukydides[61] or the mannerisms of Plato; not for him the careful niceties of Lysias and Isokrates. At the risk of observing the obvious,[62] we may note that his word order is matched to his meaning and that though there is a less vigorous variety in it than in, for instance, Herodotos,[63] there is gain in lucidity; that participles are in wide and various use; that the structure of long sentences is more likely to be repetitive than complex;[64] that in historic sequence finite verbs in subordinate clauses are mostly optative in mood; that the full range of connecting particles is to be seen, including some combinations almost peculiar to Xenophon,[65] and that the talk is marked with a full range of emphatic particles.[66]

33. To call Xenophon's style smooth may serve in summary of his narrative, but in the case of *Symposium* it overlooks both the variety of wit and certain shifts in the

---

58   Both Plato and Xenophon, as Malcolm Willcock reminds me, show a Sokrates who claims to be perpetually in love with some beautiful youth, but in fact make it pretty plain that he does not do anything physical about it.

59   See Horrocks, 79-88.

60   For all of this see Breitenbach 1895-98. There is also a discussion with references in Pomeroy (9-15).

61   *HG* I-II 3.10, written in continuation of Thoukydides' work, is a special case. See note 15 above.

62   Pomeroy's comment (14) is pertinent: 'Modern analysis of Xenophon's prose has not essentially progressed beyond the observations of the ancient critics.' This is not the place to take them further.

63   See Denniston GPS 5-8 and Dover GWO 67-8.

64   See II 17-18, for instance.

65   See GP lxxx.

66   Yves Duhoux, in NAGP 15-48, has studied the use of particles in a variety of works and authors including X. *Smp*. His summarising paragraph on this work (47) should raise our estimation of X.'s linguistic skill and sensitivity.

speeches: Sokrates changes register as well as topic in VIII, and his capacity to do so is foreshadowed in II 26; the speeches of Kritoboulos, Antisthenes and Hermogenes in IV all show rhetorical traits of various sorts (Antisthenes, together with Kharmides, is a model of antitheses expressed with μέν and δέ). Xenophon knew the arts of speech. The essence of a symposium is talk. Xenophon's part was to set the context and to let the speakers speak. They do so, inevitably, in his words; equally inevitably, they all speak with a case to put: symposia were competitive. Hence rhetoric, within the smoothness.

34. Ancient critics searching Xenophon's vocabulary noted his unAttic words. That reveals their pre-occupation. We may note rather a certain catholicity in it and some innovation.[67] Like most writers, Xenophon has words of his own, perhaps of his own invention;[68] more interesting are the words first recorded in this work which only recur some time later, in writers with a nose for such words like Plutarch and Lucian[69] or in other late and post-Hellenistic authors.[70] The breadth of his vocabulary is partly shown in the words he shares with Aristophanes, and more thoroughly in those he shares with Herodotos and the Hippocratic corpus. When Xenophon shares a word with Aristophanes,[71] there is nothing poetical in it; each is simply using a word of common Attic stock. Words shared with Herodotos[72] point to a similar Ionic stock and also to Xenophon's reading; so too words shared with the

---

67   In notes 67-72 the details, after initial work in L-G, are derived from LSJ, whose evidence is not exhaustive. Some inaccuracy therefore is likely, but I think the general picture to be sound.

68   There are nine words recorded only in this work: ἀντιπεριλαμβάνειν, ἀντιπροσφέρειν, ἀξιάκουστος, ἐνιδροῦν, ἡδυγνώμων, ἡδυσώματος, σπουδαρχίας (if correctly conjectured), συγκυλινδεῖσθαι and χλιδαίνεσθαι. None of these is notable: four are verbs unique by prefix and one unique by suffix; the three adjectives and the noun are compounds of a common pattern. In addition κυνοδρομεῖν and προσκαίεσθαι are uniquely used metaphorically and συνιστάναι is unique to Xenophon but not to this work.

69   For instance ἀντερᾶν, ἀξιέραστος, γελωτοποιία, διαστρέφειν (active), καταθεᾶσθαι, καταδυναστεύειν, λαμυρός, μαστροπεία, ὄρχημα, παιγνιώδης, περίμεστος and ὑπερασπάζεσθαι.

70   For instance ἀντιστοιχεῖν, ἀξιοπρεπής, γοργός, ἐθελούσιος, ἐμπνεῖν (trans.), μορφάζειν, πολυχρηματία, ὑπερσεμνύνειν, χρῦμα and ψηλάφημα.

71   For instance ἀνεγείρειν, θαλλοφόρος and (with some qualification) καθέρπειν. συνεραστής occurs in an unattributed comic fragment. A. Körte, Aufbau und Ziel von Xenophons Symposion, Leipzig 1927, 44-48, argues for a considerable acquaintance with Old Comedy in Xenophon.

72   For instance ἀρματηλατεῖν, περιέπειν and σχίζεσθαι (used of γνῶμαι). To these could be added ἄμορφος, ἀναστενάζειν, ἀξιοθέατος, and χειρονομεῖν which resurface in later Hellenistic writers. Xenophon's contact with Herodotos is well explored by Gray.

Hippocratic corpus,[73] which mark his taste for technicalities.[74] The ancients in accounting for this broadness noted his varied experience of serving as a soldier alongside Thessalians, Boeotians[75] and Arcadians, of campaigning in Ionia and Aiolis with Spartans, and of then passing twenty years in the western Peloponnese. The sort of Greek he probably least heard for most of his writing life was Attic, in the period in which it became virtually the only sort of Greek in which to write.[76] How much he noticed his own innovations, so slight anyway, is a good question; in context it is remarkable how faithful he was to the Attic in which he had grown up.[77]

35. It remains to consider the work as literature. In it Xenophon was trying to catch the mood of a party where topics of conversation could come and go in casual succession, and where people could contribute for a while and be silent in between times, reacting to the moment according to their disposition; hence in considerable part the contrast with Plato, who set out to write a piece of rising drive and focus. The episodic form is set early, in the chance encounter of Kallias and Sokrates out of which the party is made, and in the addition of Philippos to the group. The transition to his noise from the silence of the rest in I 11 is made through a narrative device common in Herodotos (and in Homer before him) of a summarising sentence with μέν or μὲν δή which gives way to the new event marked with δέ. So too at VIII 1, where Socrates' new theme is set up. But the summary sentences are often more heavily marked even than that: the author's voice is audible, not only closing the topic and stressing its nature, particularly its exemplary nature (οὕτω is common), but also pausing before moving off on another tack.[78]

---

73 ἄλγος, ἀνάριστος, λεπτύνειν and ὀδάξειν are all worth study in LSJ, but none is confined to Xenophon and the Hippocratic corpus alone. I have not attempted to distinguish early works in the corpus from late.

74 See 8 above.

75 Speaking with a Boeotian accent is noted at An. III 1.26.

76 Xenophon's proximity to Olympia (see 5 and 9 above) should be remembered: there was competitive speech-making at Olympia as well as competitive athletics, and the new Attic, developing into the Attic-based Koine, would be the competitors' language. To borrow from Horrocks (see ch. 3), I would call Xenophon's Greek 'literary Attic', but without pretentiousness; Quintilian's word (X 1.82) 'inaffectata' comes to mind.

77 For instance, he stuck by -ττ- and -ρρ- where most other dialects and in due course the Koiné had -σσ- and -ρσ-; in the 2nd and 3rd person sing. weak aor. opt. active he has -σαις twice and -σαι once in this work but -σειε four times. On the other hand he has ναός, not νεώς, ἄν for ἐάν, not ἤν, and though he keeps σύν (see note on VIII 40), it is σύν, not ξύν.

78 See II 10, III 1, IV 6, 10, 28, 50, 64, VI 1, 6, 10 and IX 1. At IV 52 and 56 εἶεν, 'All right', marks discontinuity. At II 10 Xenophon continues μετὰ δὲ τοῦτο, 'after this', merely temporal, but at II 15 and often thereafter he continues ἐκ τούτου, 'next'. Ἐκ τούτου means 'from then', or 'as a result': he is suggesting a more than merely chronological link, but usually without much substance. Guthrie goes much too far in

36. It was remarked earlier (9) that in writing this work Xenophon was in thrall to no one. As a literary form the Symposium has been traced back to Xenophanes and Ion of Khios, and to supposed meetings of the Seven Sages such as Plutarch later composed.[79] Plato's *Protagoras* is not far from being such a composition, and Antisthenes' *Protreptikos* may have contributed,[80] as perhaps did some comedies, Ameipsias' *Konnos,* for instance, as well as those of Eupolis mentioned above (17) and Aristophanes' *Banqueters.*[81] The banquet of Attaginos at Thebes of which Herodotos reports an episode (IX 15.4-16.5) may have provided a hint. But none of this should detract from the originality of what Xenophon did. Best mark of his achievement is the flattering perception of Plato in almost instantly borrowing the idea to improve it; Xenophon's own pride and lack of pride is well revealed in the revision he then made of his own work. Despite its episodic form, despite the rewriting and certain loose ends,[82] the overall unity of the work is striking. Drama is one genre that Xenophon did not attempt, but there is singular skill in the author's handling of his large cast: all take part as appropriate, and none is long overlooked or forgotten. Much of the work's considerable wit lies in the precise selection and placement of individual words, as was to be expected of such company. The ultimate host at Kallias' party, receiving and giving as a gentleman should, as inwardly firm in his own views as he was courteously accommodating of others, is the author himself.

---

saying (III2 22) 'Structurally the composition creaks at every joint'; rather, Xenophon in achieving his own aim has not minded such incidental noise.

79   Breitenbach 1872-3 discusses the topic and gives references.
80   See Thesleff 157 for references.
81   For Ameipsias' *Konnos* see K-A II 200-202 and for Ar. *Banqueters* K-A III2 122-148.
82   For instance, was Kallias really going to entertain only Autolykos, Lykon and Nikeratos had he not met Sokrates? Is Hermogenes the speaker at the start of III 9? What is the relationship of the homosexual focus of VIII as we now have it to the heterosexual mime in IX? What of the mention of Pausanias and Agathon in VIII 32? How were the symposiasts divided into the three groups of IX 7?

Select bibliography

Books

Anderson   J.K.Anderson, *Xenophon*, London 1974

Bartlett: R.C.Bartlett, *The Shorter Socratic Writings*, New York 1996

Breitenbach   H.R.Breitenbach, *Xenophon von Athen* (*RE* ix A^2), Stuttgart 1967

Chantraine   P. Chantraine, *Dictionnaire Etymologique de la langue grecque* (2 vols), Paris 1968-80

Davies   J.K.Davies, *Athenian Propertied Families*, Oxford 1971

Delebecque   E.Delebecque, *Essai sur la vie de Xénophon*, Paris 1957

Denniston GPS J.D.Denniston, *Greek Prose Style*, Oxford 1952

Dillery   John Dillery, *Xenophon and the History of his Times*, London 1995

Dittmar   H.Dittmar, *Aiskhines von Sphettos*, Berlin 1912

Dover GWO   K.J.Dover, *Greek Word Order*, Cambridge 1960

Dover GH   K.J.Dover, *Greek Homosexuality*, London 1978

Dover PS   K.J.Dover, ed. *Plato: Symposium*, Cambridge 1980

Gauthier   Ph.Gauthier, *Commentaire historique des Πόροι de Xénophon*, Geneva/Paris 1976

GMT   W.W.Goodwin, *Syntax of the Moods and Tenses of the Greek Verb*, London 1889

GP   J.D.Denniston, *The Greek Particles*, Oxford 1954 (second edition)

Gray   Vivienne Gray, *The Character of Xenophon's Hellenica*, London 1989

Guthrie III1   W.K.C.Guthrie, *The Sophists*, Cambridge 1971

———— III2   W.K.C.Guthrie, *Socrates*, Cambridge 1971

———— IV   W.K.C.Guthrie, *A History of Greek Philosophy* vol. IV, Cambridge 1975

Handley   E.W.Handley, ed. Menander *Dyskolos*, London 1965 and 1992

Harris   H.A.Harris, *Greek Athletes and Athletics*, London 1964

Henry   W.P.Henry, *Greek Historical Writing*, Chicago 1966

Higgins   W.E.Higgins, *Xenophon the Athenian*, New York 1977

Hirsch   S.W.Hirsch, *Friendship of the Barbarians*, London 1985

Horrocks   G.C.Horrocks, *Greek: A History of the Language and its Speakers*, London 1997

K-A II   R.Kassel & C.Austin, edd. *Poetae Comici Graeci* vol. II, Berlin 1991

——— III2   R.Kassel & C.Austin, edd. *Poetae Comici Graeci* vol. III2, Berlin 1984

——— V   R.Kassel & C.Austin, edd. *Poetae Comici Graeci* vol. V, Berlin 1986

L-G   A.R.López & F.M.García, *Index Socraticorum Xenophontis Operum*, Hildesheim 1995

22 BIBLIOGRAPHY

LSJ   H.G.Liddell & R.Scott, *A Greek-English Lexicon*, revised by H.S.Jones, Oxford 1940 (ninth edition)

Marchant   E.C.Marchant, ed. *Xenophon* vol. II, Oxford 1921

Murray   O.Murray, ed. *Sympotica*, Oxford 1994 (pb)

NAGP   A.Rijksbaron, ed. *New Approaches to Greek Particles*, Amsterdam 1997

Ollier   F.Ollier, ed. *Xénophon Banquet*, Paris 1961 (Budé Library)

Parke   H.W.Parke, *Festivals of the Athenians*, London 1977

Pomeroy   Sarah B.Pomeroy, ed. Xenophon *Oeconomicus*, Oxford 1994

Strauss   Leo Strauss, *Xenophon's Socrates*, New York 1972

Thalheim   Th.Thalheim, ed. Xenophon *scripta minora* II, Leipzig 1915

Todd   O.J.Todd, tr. Xenophon *Symposium*, London 1923 (Loeb Library)

Tredennick   H. Tredennick, tr. Xenophon *Symposium*, Harmondsworth 1970

West   M.L.West, *Ancient Greek Music*, Oxford 1992

Articles

Fritz   K. von Fritz, 'Antisthenes und Socrates in Xenophons Symposion', *Rheinisches Museum für Philologie* LXXXIV (1935) 19-45

Thesleff   Holger Thesleff, 'The Interrelationship and Date of the *Symposia* of Plato and Xenophon', *BICS* 25 (1978) 157-70

Note on text and translation.

A good dozen manuscripts of value exist for Xenophon's Symposium, dating from the thirteenth to the fifteenth centuries. There is also a tiny quantity of papyrus evidence. The author has been very adequately served by his copyists, and his intent is seldom seriously obscured. The text printed here is based on E. C. Marchant's, made for the Oxford Classical text series in 1901. In 1921 a second edition was issued; addenda and corrigenda were put in a preface and not incorporated into the text. I have consulted the texts of Thalheim, produced for the Teubner series in 1915, of Todd, for the Loeb library in 1923, and of Ollier, for the Budé library in 1961.

   Of the 41 differences between this and Marchant's printed text, 8 come from his second preface (noted as M^2), 5 are differences of punctuation (all trivial except one already made by Thalheim and Ollier), 4 of accent, and 3 of spelling; 5, including one new lacuna, occur where I follow the text of Thalheim (Th) or Ollier (O) or both. In 1 I follow Todd. The remaining 15 are eliminations of daggers (1) and of square and angled brackets (14: not listed below); where square brackets have gone, so have the contents. Thus, apart from two lacunae, a clean text has been printed.

   I have done no work on the manuscripts and the tradition myself. The record (Ollier's is the most recent discussion of it) appears to me consistent enough for an apparatus criticus not to be worth printing. Comment on textual problems has been kept to a minimum, but I have occasionally voiced a suspicion that the text available is not sound.

   In translation I have tried, with some exceptions noted below, to write English that will read as English. I spend enough time teaching the art of translation to regret the version published by Bartlett, but I recognise that for some things there are no happy versions. For instance, vocatives and oaths: I think there is no natural English of Ὦ Συρακόσιε, 'O Syracusan', and 'By Zeus' and 'By Hera' seem better left as they are than converted into 'Gosh' or 'Bless my soul'. Certain words or phrases of cultural importance are notoriously difficult, like καλὸς κἀγαθός, 'gentleman', and may give rise to another problem: if certain words occur frequently, are they always to be translated the same way? English taste is to vary by synonyms, and I have done so without qualm when it seemed appropriate. Those who need to know whether one and the same Greek word or phrase was being used consistently will learn enough Greek to find out. At a trivial level this occurs with ἔφη, 'said he'; Xenophon does not even avail himself of Plato's archaism ἦ δ' ὅς, 'quoth he'. English dialogue is usually conducted with variety: 'he said', 'observed', 'asked', 'interrupted' *et sim.* Xenophon's Greek is usually clear, precise and unforced. I have

tried not to tidy up occasional obscurities or infelicities, as for instance at III 9 or IV 9, where it is not clear who is speaking; I hope I have imported none.

Differences (apart from the elimination of brackets noted above) between Marchant's OCT text and this text:

I	8	after τι add τὸ (M²)
	10	for πρᾳοτέραν read πραοτέραν
	15	for ἀλλ᾽ ἤ read ἀλλ᾽ ἦ (Denniston: GP 28)
II	5	for ... read < ... >
	10	for ἄπο read ἀπὸ
IV	2	for βαλαντ- read βαλλαντ- (twice)
	12	for τᾶλλα read τἄλλα
		for δεξαίμην ἂν read ἂν δεξαίμην (M²)
	14	for Κλεινίᾳ τὰ ὄντα read τὰ ὄντα Κλεινίᾳ (M²)
	19	for κομπάζεις. read κομπάζεις;
	27	after εἶδον add ,
	35	for πλείω read πλείονα (M²)
	45	for προσδεῖσθαι, οὕτω read προσδεῖσθαι· οὕτω δὲ (M²)
	49	for ἔφη, ὁ Σωκράτης read ἔφη ὁ Σωκράτης,
	64	delete daggers
V	6	for ἕνεκεν ἐποίησαν read ἕνεκ᾽ ἐνεποίησαν (Th, after Richards)
VI	9	for πάντ᾽ αὐτοῦ βελτίων read πάντα τὰ αὐτοῦ βελτίω and delete daggers
VII	2	for ᾖσεν read ᾖσαν (O,Th)
VIII	2	delete νῦν (M²)
	9	for τε καὶ ναοί εἰσι read τέ εἰσι καὶ ναοὶ (M²)
	17	for παρά τι ποιήσῃ read παρανοήσῃ and delete daggers (M²)
	18	for ὁπότερος οὖν read ὁποτεροσοῦν
	26	for τᾶλλα read τἄλλα
	32	for ἐγκαλινδουμένων read συγκυλινδουμένων (O,Th)
	40	for , ἱερεὺς θεῶν τῶν ἀπ᾽ Ἐρεχθέως, read τῶν ἀπ᾽ Ἐρεχθέως, ἱερεὺς θεῶν (Todd)
IX	6	after Διόνυσον add < ... > (O,Th)

SYMPOSIUM
ΣΥΜΠΟΣΙΟΝ

ΣΥΜΠΟΣΙΟΝ

Ἀλλ' ἐμοὶ δοκεῖ τῶν καλῶν κἀγαθῶν ἀνδρῶν ἔργα οὐ μόνον **1**
τὰ μετὰ σπουδῆς πραττόμενα ἀξιομνημόνευτα εἶναι, ἀλλὰ καὶ
τὰ ἐν ταῖς παιδιαῖς. οἷς δὲ παραγενόμενος ταῦτα γιγνώσκω
δηλῶσαι βούλομαι. ἦν μὲν γὰρ Παναθηναίων τῶν μεγάλων **2**
ἱπποδρομία, Καλλίας δὲ ὁ Ἱππονίκου ἐρῶν ἐτύγχανεν
Αὐτολύκου παιδὸς ὄντος, καὶ νενικηκότα αὐτὸν παγκράτιον
ἧκεν ἄγων ἐπὶ τὴν θέαν. ὡς δὲ ἡ ἱπποδρομία ἔληξεν, ἔχων
τόν τε Αὐτόλυκον καὶ τὸν πατέρα αὐτοῦ ἀπῄει εἰς τὴν ἐν
Πειραιεῖ οἰκίαν· συνείπετο δὲ αὐτῷ καὶ Νικήρατος.

ἰδὼν δὲ ὁμοῦ ὄντας Σωκράτην τε καὶ Κριτόβουλον καὶ **3**
Ἑρμογένην καὶ Ἀντισθένην καὶ Χαρμίδην, τοῖς μὲν ἀμφ'
Αὐτόλυκον ἡγεῖσθαί τινα ἔταξεν, αὐτὸς δὲ προσῆλθε τοῖς
ἀμφὶ Σωκράτην, καὶ εἶπεν· Εἰς καλόν γε ὑμῖν συντετύχηκα· **4**
ἑστιᾶν γὰρ μέλλω Αὐτόλυκον καὶ τὸν πατέρα αὐτοῦ. οἶμαι οὖν
πολὺ ἂν τὴν κατασκευήν μοι λαμπροτέραν φανῆναι εἰ
ἀνδράσιν ἐκκεκαθαρμένοις τὰς ψυχὰς ὥσπερ ὑμῖν ὁ ἀνδρῶν
κεκοσμημένος εἴη μᾶλλον ἢ εἰ στρατηγοῖς καὶ ἱππάρχοις καὶ
σπουδαρχίαις.

καὶ ὁ Σωκράτης εἶπεν· Ἀεὶ σὺ ἐπισκώπτεις ἡμᾶς **5**
καταφρονῶν, ὅτι σὺ μὲν Πρωταγόρᾳ τε πολὺ ἀργύριον δέδωκας
ἐπὶ σοφίᾳ καὶ Γοργίᾳ καὶ Προδίκῳ καὶ ἄλλοις πολλοῖς, ἡμᾶς
δ' ὁρᾷς αὐτουργούς τινας τῆς φιλοσοφίας ὄντας.

καὶ ὁ Καλλίας, Καὶ πρόσθεν μέν γε, ἔφη, ἀπεκρυπτόμην **6**
ὑμᾶς ἔχων πολλὰ καὶ σοφὰ λέγειν, νῦν δέ, ἐὰν παρ' ἐμοὶ ἦτε,
ἐπιδείξω ὑμῖν ἐμαυτὸν πάνυ πολλῆς σπουδῆς ἄξιον ὄντα.

οἱ οὖν ἀμφὶ τὸν Σωκράτην πρῶτον μέν, ὥσπερ εἰκὸς ἦν, **7**
ἐπαινοῦντες τὴν κλῆσιν οὐχ ὑπισχνοῦντο συνδειπνήσειν· ὡς
δὲ πάνυ ἀχθόμενος φανερὸς ἦν, εἰ μὴ ἔψοιντο, συνηκολού-
θησαν. ἔπειτα δὲ αὐτῷ οἱ μὲν γυμνασάμενοι καὶ χρισάμενοι,
οἱ δὲ καὶ λουσάμενοι παρῆλθον. Αὐτόλυκος μὲν οὖν παρὰ τὸν **8**
πατέρα ἐκαθέζετο, οἱ δ' ἄλλοι, ὥσπερ εἰκός, κατεκλίθησαν.

εὐθὺς μὲν οὖν ἐννοήσας τις τὰ γιγνόμενα ἡγήσατ' ἂν
φύσει βασιλικόν τι τὸ κάλλος εἶναι, ἄλλως τε καὶ ἂν μετ'
αἰδοῦς καὶ σωφροσύνης, καθάπερ Αὐτόλυκος τότε, κεκτῆταί
τις αὐτό. πρῶτον μὲν γάρ, ὥσπερ ὅταν φέγγος τι ἐν νυκτὶ **9**
φανῇ, πάντων προσάγεται τὰ ὄμματα, οὕτω καὶ τότε τοῦ

SYMPOSIUM

I Well, what gentlemen do in their serious moments is very much worth recording, but so too, in my view, are the activities of their lighter moments, and I want to show you the people I was with when I came to this conclusion. 2 It was horse-race day at the Great Panathenaia. Kallias son of Hipponikos happened to be courting Autolykos, a boy who had just won the pankration, and Kallias had brought him to see the race. When it was over, he set off for his house in the Peiraieus taking both Autolykos and the boy's father with him, and Nikeratos went with him as well.

3 Then Kallias noticed Sokrates, Kritoboulos, Hermogenes, Antisthenes and Kharmides in a group together. He arranged for someone to take the Autolykos party on and then went across to the Sokrates group himself, and said, 4 "What a lucky meeting! I'm just about to entertain Autolykos and his father at my house. I think my arrangements would seem much more glamorous if the dining-room were graced by men like you, men of purified souls, than it would be by generals and cavalry commanders and political hopefuls."

5 "You're always making fun of us in that superior way of yours," said Sokrates, "just because you've paid big money for lessons in knowledge to Protagoras and Gorgias and Prodikos and strings of others, while you look upon us as do-it-yourself philosophers."

6 "In the old days, well, yes," said Kallias, "I did conceal from you my ability to say plenty of clever things. If you come to me now, however, I shall display myself to you as someone worth very serious attention."

7 So Sokrates and his friends politely declined his invitation at first, as was to be expected, and did not promise to join him at dinner; but when Kallias was plainly getting cross if they would not come, they did go along with him, and finally he had his guests, some freshly oiled after their exercise and some fresh from a wash as well. 8 Autolykos went and sat beside his father, and the rest reclined as normal.

Anyone reflecting on what was happening would have reckoned at once that beauty is something naturally regal, especially if its possessor combines it with modesty and good sense, as Autolykos did there. 9 In the first place, just like a beacon shining in the night which draws the eyes of all towards it, so on that occasion the good looks of Autolykos forced

Αὐτολύκου τὸ κάλλος πάντων εἷλκε τὰς ὄψεις πρὸς αὐτόν· (I)
ἔπειτα τῶν ὁρώντων οὐδεὶς οὐκ ἔπασχέ τι τὴν ψυχὴν ὑπ'
ἐκείνου. οἱ μέν γε σιωπηρότεροι ἐγίγνοντο, οἱ δὲ καὶ
ἐσχηματίζοντό πως. πάντες μὲν οὖν οἱ ἐκ θεῶν του 10
κατεχόμενοι ἀξιοθέατοι δοκοῦσιν εἶναι· ἀλλ' οἱ μὲν ἐξ ἄλλων
πρὸς τὸ γοργότεροί τε ὁρᾶσθαι καὶ φοβερώτερον φθέγγεσθαι
καὶ σφοδρότεροι εἶναι φέρονται, οἱ δ' ὑπὸ τοῦ σώφρονος
ἔρωτος ἔνθεοι τά τε ὄμματα φιλοφρονεστέρως ἔχουσι καὶ τὴν
φωνὴν πραοτέραν ποιοῦνται καὶ τὰ σχήματα εἰς τὸ
ἐλευθεριώτερον ἄγουσιν. ἃ δὴ καὶ Καλλίας τότε διὰ τὸν
ἔρωτα πράττων ἀξιοθέατος ἦν τοῖς τετελεσμένοις τούτῳ τῷ
θεῷ.

ἐκεῖνοι μὲν οὖν σιωπῇ ἐδείπνουν, ὥσπερ τοῦτο 11
ἐπιτεταγμένον αὐτοῖς ὑπὸ κρείττονός τινος. Φίλιππος δ' ὁ
γελωτοποιὸς κρούσας τὴν θύραν εἶπε τῷ ὑπακούσαντι
εἰσαγγεῖλαι ὅστις τε εἴη καὶ δι' ὅ τι κατάγεσθαι βούλοιτο,
συνεσκευασμένος τε παρεῖναι ἔφη πάντα τὰ ἐπιτήδεια ὥστε
δειπνεῖν τἀλλότρια, καὶ τὸν παῖδα δὲ ἔφη πάνυ πιέζεσθαι διά
τε τὸ φέρειν μηδὲν καὶ διὰ τὸ ἀνάριστον εἶναι. ὁ οὖν 12
Καλλίας ἀκούσας ταῦτα εἶπεν· Ἀλλὰ μέντοι, ὦ ἄνδρες,
αἰσχρὸν στέγης γε φθονῆσαι· εἰσίτω οὖν. καὶ ἅμα ἀπέβλεψεν
εἰς τὸν Αὐτόλυκον, δῆλον ὅτι ἐπισκοπῶν τί ἐκείνῳ δόξειε τὸ
σκῶμμα εἶναι.

ὁ δὲ στὰς ἐπὶ τῷ ἀνδρῶνι ἔνθα τὸ δεῖπνον ἦν εἶπεν· 13
Ὅτι μὲν γελωτοποιός εἰμι ἴστε πάντες· ἥκω δὲ προθύμως
νομίσας γελοιότερον εἶναι τὸ ἄκλητον ἢ τὸ κεκλημένον ἐλθεῖν
ἐπὶ τὸ δεῖπνον.

Κατακλίνου τοίνυν, ἔφη ὁ Καλλίας. καὶ γὰρ οἱ παρόντες
σπουδῆς μέν, ὡς ὁρᾷς, μεστοί, γέλωτος δὲ ἴσως ἐνδεέστεροι.

δειπνούντων δὲ αὐτῶν ὁ Φίλιππος γελοῖόν τι εὐθὺς 14
ἐπεχείρει λέγειν, ἵνα δὴ ἐπιτελοίη ὧνπερ ἕνεκα ἐκαλεῖτο
ἑκάστοτε ἐπὶ τὰ δεῖπνα. ὡς δ' οὐκ ἐκίνησε γέλωτα, τότε μὲν
ἀχθεσθεὶς φανερὸς ἐγένετο. αὖθις δ' ὀλίγον ὕστερον ἄλλο τι
γελοῖον ἐβούλετο λέγειν. ὡς δὲ οὐδὲ τότε ἐγέλασαν ἐπ' αὐτῷ,
ἐν τῷ μεταξὺ παυσάμενος τοῦ δείπνου συγκαλυψάμενος
κατέκειτο.

καὶ ὁ Καλλίας, Τί τοῦτ', ἔφη, ὦ Φίλιππε; ἀλλ' ἦ ὀδύνη σε 15
εἴληφε; καὶ ὃς ἀναστενάξας εἶπε· Ναὶ μὰ Δί', ἔφη, ὦ Καλλία,
μεγάλη γε· ἐπεὶ γὰρ γέλως ἐξ ἀνθρώπων ἀπόλωλεν, ἔρρει τὰ

the gaze of everyone towards him; in the second place, not one of those who gazed failed to be stirred to the core by him. Some fell silent, and others reacted by gesture. 10 All people who are possessed by one of the gods do seem to be worth contemplation; but those in the grip of other gods tend to go goggle-eyed and to talk rather alarmingly and to be over-emphatic, while those possessed of sober passion keep their eyes looking friendly, and pitch their voice soothingly, and moderate their gestures like free men. Such was the behaviour of Kallias then, under the influence of his passion; for the initiates of Eros he was well worth contemplation.

11 Their dinner thus began in silence, as if that was the injunction upon them from some greater power. But Philippos the laughter-maker knocked at the door. He told the man who answered it to announce who he was and say why he wanted to come in; he had come fully equipped, he said, with everything necessary to dine at someone else's expense, and he added that his slave was under great pressure too, both from having nothing to carry and from lack of breakfast. 12 Kallias listened and said, "Well, gentlemen, it's a poor thing to deny a chap a roof: so let's have him in." At the same time he glanced at Autolykos, obviously looking to see what he thought of the fellow's joke.

13 Philippos halted on the threshold of the room where the feast was and said, "I'm a laughter-maker. You all know that. I've come in the firm conviction that it is funnier to come to the dinner without an invitation than with."

"Take a couch then," said Kallias. "As you can see, the company is amply fed on seriousness but is perhaps rather short on merriment."

14 As they went on with the meal Philippos attempted to say something funny at once, in order to satisfy the terms on which he always used to be invited to dinners, but when he failed to arouse laughter he became visibly cross. A little later he tried something else meant to be funny, but when they did not laugh at him then either, he promptly stopped eating, covered his head, and lay full length.

15 "What's this, Philippos?" said Kallias. "Are you in pain?" Philippos groaned and said, "By Zeus I am, Kallias, big pain: now that laughter has

ἐμὰ πράγματα. πρόσθεν μὲν γὰρ τούτου ἕνεκα ἐκαλούμην ἐπὶ
τὰ δεῖπνα, ἵνα εὐφραίνοιντο οἱ συνόντες δι' ἐμὲ γελῶντες·
νῦν δὲ τίνος ἕνεκα καὶ καλεῖ μέ τις; οὔτε γὰρ ἔγωγε
σπουδάσαι ἂν δυναίμην μᾶλλον ἤπερ ἀθάνατος γενέσθαι, οὔτε
μὴν ὡς ἀντικληθησόμενος καλεῖ μέ τις, ἐπεὶ πάντες ἴσασιν
ὅτι ἀρχὴν οὐδὲ νομίζεται εἰς τὴν ἐμὴν οἰκίαν δεῖπνον
προσφέρεσθαι. καὶ ἅμα λέγων ταῦτα ἀπεμύττετό τε καὶ τῇ
φωνῇ σαφῶς κλαίειν ἐφαίνετο. πάντες μὲν οὖν παρεμυθοῦντό 16
τε αὐτὸν ὡς αὖθις γελασόμενοι καὶ δειπνεῖν ἐκέλευον,
Κριτόβουλος δὲ καὶ ἐξεκάγχασεν ἐπὶ τῷ οἰκτισμῷ αὐτοῦ. ὁ δ'
ὡς ᾔσθετο τοῦ γέλωτος, ἀνεκαλύψατό τε καὶ τῇ ψυχῇ
παρακελευσάμενος θαρρεῖν, ὅτι ἔσονται συμβολαί, πάλιν
ἐδείπνει.

Ὡς δ' ἀφῃρέθησαν αἱ τράπεζαι καὶ ἔσπεισάν τε καὶ II
ἐπαιάνισαν, ἔρχεται αὐτοῖς ἐπὶ κῶμον Συρακόσιός τις
ἄνθρωπος, ἔχων τε αὐλητρίδα ἀγαθὴν καὶ ὀρχηστρίδα τῶν τὰ
θαύματα δυναμένων ποιεῖν, καὶ παῖδα πάνυ γε ὡραῖον καὶ
πάνυ καλῶς κιθαρίζοντα καὶ ὀρχούμενον. ταῦτα δὲ καὶ
ἐπιδεικνὺς ὡς ἐν θαύματι ἀργύριον ἐλάμβανεν. ἐπεὶ δὲ αὐτοῖς 2
ἡ αὐλητρὶς μὲν ηὔλησεν, ὁ δὲ παῖς ἐκιθάρισε, καὶ ἐδόκουν
μάλα ἀμφότεροι ἱκανῶς εὐφραίνειν, εἶπεν ὁ Σωκράτης· Νὴ Δί',
ὦ Καλλία, τελέως ἡμᾶς ἑστιᾷς. οὐ γὰρ μόνον δεῖπνον
ἄμεμπτον παρέθηκας, ἀλλὰ καὶ θεάματα καὶ ἀκροάματα
ἥδιστα παρέχεις.

καὶ ὃς ἔφη· Τί οὖν εἰ καὶ μύρον τις ἡμῖν ἐνέγκαι, ἵνα 3
καὶ εὐωδίᾳ ἑστιώμεθα;

Μηδαμῶς, ἔφη ὁ Σωκράτης. ὥσπερ γάρ τοι ἐσθὴς ἄλλη
μὲν γυναικί, ἄλλη δὲ ἀνδρὶ καλή, οὕτω καὶ ὀσμὴ ἄλλη μὲν
ἀνδρί, ἄλλη δὲ γυναικὶ πρέπει. καὶ γὰρ ἀνδρὸς μὲν δήπου
ἕνεκα ἀνὴρ οὐδεὶς μύρῳ χρίεται. αἱ μέντοι γυναῖκες ἄλλως τε
καὶ ἂν νύμφαι τύχωσιν οὖσαι, ὥσπερ ἡ Νικηράτου τοῦδε καὶ
ἡ Κριτοβούλου, μύρου μὲν τί καὶ προσδέονται; αὐταὶ γὰρ 4
τούτου ὄζουσιν· ἐλαίου δὲ τοῦ ἐν γυμνασίοις ὀσμὴ καὶ
παροῦσα ἡδίων ἢ μύρου γυναιξὶ καὶ ἀποῦσα ποθεινοτέρα. καὶ
γὰρ δὴ μύρῳ μὲν ὁ ἀλειψάμενος καὶ δοῦλος καὶ ἐλεύθερος
εὐθὺς ἅπας ὅμοιον ὄζει· αἱ δ' ἀπὸ τῶν ἐλευθερίων μόχθων
ὀσμαὶ ἐπιτηδευμάτων τε πρῶτον χρηστῶν καὶ χρόνου πολλοῦ
δέονται, εἰ μέλλουσιν ἡδεῖαί τε καὶ ἐλευθέριοι ἔσεσθαι.

perished among men, my occupation's gone. Previously, you see, I used to be invited to dinners to make the company laugh and enjoy themselves, but why will anyone invite me now? I couldn't be serious any more than turn immortal, and no one will invite me out in order to get an invitation back, since it's common knowledge that to begin with, there's no practice in my house of even sending out for dinner." As he spoke, he wiped his nose, and his voice went all weepy. 16 So they all began to talk him round, promising to start laughing again, and they urged him to carry on dining, and Kritoboulos actually broke into a guffaw at Philippos' self-pity. When he heard the laughter, he uncovered his head and returned to the dinner, bidding his heart be brave: there would be contributions!

II When the tables had been removed and they had made libation and paean, they were joined by a Syracusan, with a view to some entertainment. He had with him a girl who was a good aulos-player, and a dancing-girl who was one of the top stunt-artistes, and a very comely boy who was particularly good on the kithara and at dancing. The Syracusan made a prodigious living by exhibiting them. 2 The aulos-player played her aulos for them, and the boy played his kithara, and they both appeared to be making a good contribution to people's enjoyment when Sokrates said, "By Zeus, Kallias, you are entertaining us perfectly. You've not only served up an impeccable feast, but you are also providing delights for the eye and ear."

3 Kallias said, "What if we were brought some scent, so that we can be entertained by sweet smells as well?"

"No, no," said Sokrates. "There are clothes that are good for women to wear and clothes that are good for men, and in the same way there's one scent appropriate for men and another for women. No man surely goes putting on scent for the sake of a man, and as for women, especially if they're newly married, like the wife of Nikeratos here, and Kritoboulos' wife, what do they want with scent in addition? 4 They're perfumed as they are. And women like the smell of gymnasium oil better than scent when it's on, and they miss it more than scent when it isn't. You see, when a man has put scent on, immediately, slave or free, everyone smells the same, whereas the smells that come from the work that free men do need first of all good exercise and plenty of time if they are going to be sweet smells, proper to a free man."

καὶ ὁ Λύκων εἶπεν· Οὐκοῦν νέοις μὲν ἂν εἴη ταῦτα· ἡμᾶς **(II)**
δὲ τοὺς μηκέτι γυμναζομένους τίνος ὄζειν δεήσει;
Καλοκἀγαθίας νὴ Δί', ἔφη ὁ Σωκράτης.
Καὶ πόθεν ἄν τις τοῦτο τὸ χρῖμα λάβοι;
Οὐ μὰ Δί', ἔφη, οὐ παρὰ τῶν μυροπωλῶν.
᾿Αλλὰ πόθεν δή;
Ὁ μὲν Θέογνις ἔφη·
  Ἐσθλῶν μὲν γὰρ ἀπ' ἐσθλὰ διδάξεαι· ἢν δὲ κακοῖσι
  συμμίσγῃς, ἀπολεῖς καὶ τὸν ἐόντα νόον.
καὶ ὁ Λύκων εἶπεν· ᾿Ακούεις ταῦτα, ὦ υἱέ;   5
Ναὶ μὰ Δί', ἔφη ὁ Σωκράτης, καὶ χρῆταί γε. ἐπεὶ γοῦν
νικηφόρος ἐβούλετο τοῦ παγκρατίου γενέσθαι, σὺν σοὶ
σκεψάμενος < ... > αὖ, ὃς ἂν δοκῇ αὐτῷ ἱκανώτατος εἶναι εἰς
τὸ ταῦτα ἐπιτηδεῦσαι, τούτῳ συνέσται.
ἐνταῦθα δὴ πολλοὶ ἐφθέγξαντο· καὶ ὁ μέν τις αὐτῶν 6
εἶπε· Ποῦ οὖν εὑρήσει τούτου διδάσκαλον; ὁ δέ τις ὡς οὐδὲ
διδακτὸν τοῦτο εἴη, ἕτερος δέ τις ὡς εἴπερ τι καὶ ἄλλο καὶ
τοῦτο μαθητόν. ὁ δὲ Σωκράτης ἔφη· Τοῦτο μὲν ἐπειδὴ 7
ἀμφίλογόν ἐστιν, εἰς αὖθις ἀποθώμεθα· νυνὶ δὲ τὰ προκείμενα
ἀποτελῶμεν. ὁρῶ γὰρ ἔγωγε τήνδε τὴν ὀρχηστρίδα
ἐφεστηκυῖαν καὶ τροχούς τινα αὐτῇ προσφέροντα.
ἐκ τούτου δὴ ηὔλει μὲν αὐτῇ ἡ ἑτέρα, παρεστηκὼς δέ 8
τις τῇ ὀρχηστρίδι ἀνεδίδου τοὺς τροχοὺς μέχρι δώδεκα. ἡ δὲ
λαμβάνουσα ἅμα τε ὠρχεῖτο καὶ ἀνερρίπτει δονουμένους
συντεκμαιρομένη ὅσον ἔδει ῥιπτεῖν ὕψος ὡς ἐν ῥυθμῷ
δέχεσθαι αὐτούς. καὶ ὁ Σωκράτης εἶπεν· Ἐν πολλοῖς μέν, ὦ 9
ἄνδρες, καὶ ἄλλοις δῆλον καὶ ἐν οἷς δ' ἡ παῖς ποιεῖ ὅτι ἡ
γυναικεία φύσις οὐδὲν χείρων τῆς τοῦ ἀνδρὸς οὖσα τυγχάνει,
γνώμης δὲ καὶ ἰσχύος δεῖται. ὥστε εἴ τις ὑμῶν γυναῖκα ἔχει,
θαρρῶν διδασκέτω ὅ τι βούλοιτ' ἂν αὐτῇ ἐπισταμένη χρῆσθαι.
καὶ ὁ ᾿Αντισθένης, Πῶς οὖν, ἔφη, ὦ Σώκρατες, οὕτω 10
γιγνώσκων οὐ καὶ σὺ παιδεύεις Ξανθίππην, ἀλλὰ χρῇ γυναικὶ
τῶν οὐσῶν, οἶμαι δὲ καὶ τῶν γεγενημένων καὶ τῶν ἐσομένων
χαλεπωτάτῃ;
Ὅτι, ἔφη, ὁρῶ καὶ τοὺς ἱππικοὺς βουλομένους γενέσθαι
οὐ τοὺς εὐπειθεστάτους ἀλλὰ τοὺς θυμοειδεῖς ἵππους
κτωμένους. νομίζουσι γάρ, ἂν τοὺς τοιούτους δύνωνται
κατέχειν, ῥᾳδίως τοῖς γε ἄλλοις ἵπποις χρήσεσθαι. κἀγὼ δὴ
βουλόμενος ἀνθρώποις χρῆσθαι καὶ ὁμιλεῖν ταύτην κέκτημαι,

Lykon observed, "That would be for the young ones, then. What's the proper smell for the likes of us, who don't any longer take exercise?"

"Essence of gentleman, of course!" said Sokrates.

"And where can you get that particular brand?"

"Not from the perfume-sellers," said Sokrates, "oh no."

"Well, where then?" said Lykon.

"Theognis said, 'Good men will teach you good: the bad
                    will e'en destroy the sense you had.'"

5 "You hear that, my son?" said Lykon.

"He does indeed," said Sokrates, "and he goes by it too. At any rate, when he wanted to be the prize-winner at all-in wrestling, upon examining it with you < ... > in turn, he will go with the man who seems to him the best at giving that sort of instruction."

6 At that point many of them spoke. "Where will he find a teacher of that?" said one; a second remarked that it was not a teachable thing anyway, while another said it was as learnable a thing as there was. 7 Sokrates said, "Since it's an arguable question, let's put it aside for another occasion; for the moment let's finish the programme. I can see the dancing-girl here in position and someone bringing in hoops for her."

8 The other girl then began playing the aulos for her, and someone stood by to give her the hoops, until there were a dozen of them. As she took them she continued to dance, and threw them up with a whirr, calculating how great a height she had to throw them to get them back in steady sequence. 9 Sokrates observed, "It's really very obvious, gentlemen, particularly in terms of what the girl is actually doing, that a woman's nature is not inferior to a man's at all, though there is a shortfall in power of decision and in physique. So any of you with a wife can instruct her in full confidence in whatever he'd like to have her know."

10 Antisthenes inquired, "If that is your perception, Sokrates, how come you don't teach Xanthippe, instead of having as your wife the most difficult woman not just of this generation, in my view, but of all generations past and yet to come?"

"It's because I can see that people who want to be horse-trainers pick not the most docile animals but the most spirited. They reckon that if they can establish control of them, they'll easily manage the rest. I chose my wife because of my desire for human society and conversation,

εὖ εἰδὼς ὅτι εἰ ταύτην ὑποίσω, ῥᾳδίως τοῖς γε ἄλλοις (II)
ἅπασιν ἀνθρώποις συνέσομαι. καὶ οὗτος μὲν δὴ ὁ λόγος οὐκ
ἀπὸ τοῦ σκοποῦ ἔδοξεν εἰρῆσθαι.

μετὰ δὲ τοῦτο κύκλος εἰσηνέχθη περίμεστος ξιφῶν ὀρθῶν. 11
εἰς οὖν ταῦτα ἡ ὀρχηστρὶς ἐκυβίστα τε καὶ ἐξεκυβίστα ὑπὲρ
αὐτῶν. ὥστε οἱ μὲν θεώμενοι ἐφοβοῦντο μή τι πάθῃ, ἡ δὲ
θαρρούντως τε καὶ ἀσφαλῶς ταῦτα διεπράττετο. καὶ ὁ 12
Σωκράτης καλέσας τὸν Ἀντισθένην εἶπεν· Οὗτοι τούς γε
θεωμένους τάδε ἀντιλέξειν ἔτι οἴομαι, ὡς οὐχὶ καὶ ἡ ἀνδρεία
διδακτόν, ὁπότε αὕτη καίπερ γυνὴ οὖσα οὕτω τολμηρῶς εἰς
τὰ ξίφη ἵεται.

καὶ ὁ Ἀντισθένης εἶπεν· Ἆρ᾽ οὖν καὶ τῷδε τῷ Συρακοσίῳ 13
κράτιστον ἐπιδείξαντι τῇ πόλει τὴν ὀρχηστρίδα εἰπεῖν, ἐὰν
διδῶσιν αὐτῷ Ἀθηναῖοι χρήματα, ποιήσειν πάντας Ἀθηναίους
τολμᾶν ὁμόσε ταῖς λόγχαις ἰέναι;

καὶ ὁ Φίλιππος, Νὴ Δί᾽, ἔφη, καὶ μὴν ἔγωγε ἡδέως ἂν 14
θεώμην Πείσανδρον τὸν δημηγόρον μανθάνοντα κυβιστᾶν εἰς
τὰς μαχαίρας, ὃς νῦν διὰ τὸ μὴ δύνασθαι λόγχαις ἀντιβλέπειν οὐδὲ συστρατεύεσθαι ἐθέλει.

ἐκ τούτου ὁ παῖς ὠρχήσατο. καὶ ὁ Σωκράτης εἶπεν· 15
Εἴδετ᾽, ἔφη, ὡς καλὸς ὁ παῖς ὢν ὅμως σὺν τοῖς σχήμασιν ἔτι
καλλίων φαίνεται ἢ ὅταν ἡσυχίαν ἔχῃ;

καὶ ὁ Χαρμίδης εἶπεν· Ἐπαινοῦντι ἔοικας τὸν ὀρχηστοδιδάσκαλον.

Ναὶ μὰ τὸν Δί᾽, ἔφη ὁ Σωκράτης· καὶ γὰρ ἄλλο τι προσ- 16
ενενόησα, ὅτι οὐδὲν ἀργὸν τοῦ σώματος ἐν τῇ ὀρχήσει ἦν,
ἀλλ᾽ ἅμα καὶ τράχηλος καὶ σκέλη καὶ χεῖρες ἐγυμνάζοντο,
ὥσπερ χρὴ ὀρχεῖσθαι τὸν μέλλοντα εὐφορώτερον τὸ σῶμα
ἕξειν. καὶ ἐγὼ μέν, ἔφη, πάνυ ἂν ἡδέως, ὦ Συρακόσιε,
μάθοιμι τὰ σχήματα παρὰ σοῦ.

καὶ ὅς, Τί οὖν χρήσῃ αὐτοῖς; ἔφη.

Ὀρχήσομαι νὴ Δία. ἐνταῦθα δὴ ἐγέλασαν ἅπαντες. 17

καὶ ὁ Σωκράτης μάλα ἐσπουδακότι τῷ προσώπῳ, Γελᾶτε,
ἔφη, ἐπ᾽ ἐμοί; πότερον ἐπὶ τούτῳ εἰ βούλομαι γυμναζόμενος
μᾶλλον ὑγιαίνειν ἢ εἰ ἥδιον ἐσθίειν καὶ καθεύδειν ἢ εἰ
τοιούτων γυμνασίων ἐπιθυμῶ, μὴ ὥσπερ οἱ δολιχοδρόμοι τὰ
σκέλη μὲν παχύνονται, τοὺς ὤμους δὲ λεπτύνονται, μηδ᾽
ὥσπερ οἱ πύκται τοὺς μὲν ὤμους παχύνονται, τὰ δὲ σκέλη
λεπτύνονται, ἀλλὰ παντὶ διαπονῶν τῷ σώματι πᾶν ἰσόρροπον

knowing very well that if I can endure her, I can easily get along with everyone else." And these words seemed to be not far off the mark.

11 After this a ring was brought in with swords close together on it, fixed point up, and the girl began diving in and out of them. The spectators were scared she might get hurt, but she kept going with confidence as well as safety. 12 Sokrates called to Antisthenes and said, "At least the people watching this won't object any more, I take it, that bravery too isn't a teachable thing, when this girl keeps launching herself into the swords so boldly, despite being a female."

13 Antisthenes replied, "Would it then actually be a very good thing for this Syracusan to display his dancing-girl to the people and say that if the Athenians will pay him he'll make all of them brave enough to charge the enemy spearpoints?"

14 "By Zeus," said Philippos, "I'd love to see that demagogue Peisander learning to jump into the knives; because he can't look a spearpoint in the face at the moment, so he doesn't even want to go on campaign!"

15 Then the boy did a dance. Sokrates said, "Did you notice? He's a good-looking boy, but he looks even better when he's dancing than when he's at rest."

Kharmides observed, "You might as well praise the dancing-master."

16 "Yes by Zeus," said Sokrates; "I had another point in mind as well, that in the dancing no part of his body was idle: his neck and legs and arms were all getting exercise together, the way you need to dance if you mean to be fitter. Personally," he said to the Syracusan, "I should be delighted to learn the movements from you."

"And what will you do with them?" said the Syracusan.

17 "I shall dance by Zeus!" At that everybody burst out laughing.

Sokrates' face took on a very earnest look, and he said, "You're laughing at me, are you? Why? Is it because I want to improve my health by taking exercise rather than eat and sleep in comfort, or because I'm eager to use these exercises not as long-distance runners do, thickening their legs and reducing their shoulders, nor as wrestlers do, thickening their shoulders and reducing their legs, but to work at the whole of my

ποιεῖν; ἢ ἐπ' ἐκείνῳ γελᾶτε, ὅτι οὐ δεήσει με συγγυμναστὴν (II)18
ζητεῖν, οὐδ' ἐν ὄχλῳ πρεσβύτην ὄντα ἀποδύεσθαι, ἀλλ' ἀρκέσει
μοι οἶκος ἑπτάκλινος, ὥσπερ καὶ νῦν τῷδε τῷ παιδὶ ἤρκεσε
τόδε τὸ οἴκημα ἐνιδρῶσαι, καὶ χειμῶνος μὲν ἐν στέγῃ
γυμνάσομαι, ὅταν δὲ ἄγαν καῦμα ᾖ, ἐν σκιᾷ; ἢ τόδε γελᾶτε, 19
εἰ. μείζω τοῦ καιροῦ τὴν γαστέρα ἔχων μετριωτέραν βούλομαι
ποιῆσαι αὐτήν; ἢ οὐκ ἴστε ὅτι ἔναγχος ἕωθεν Χαρμίδης
οὑτοσὶ κατέλαβέ με ὀρχούμενον;

Ναὶ μὰ τὸν Δί', ἔφη ὁ Χαρμίδης· καὶ τὸ μέν γε πρῶτον
ἐξεπλάγην καὶ ἔδεισα μὴ μαίνοιο· ἐπεὶ δέ σου ἤκουσα ὅμοια
οἷς νῦν λέγεις, καὶ αὐτὸς ἐλθὼν οἴκαδε ὠρχούμην μὲν οὔ, οὐ
γὰρ πώποτε τοῦτ' ἔμαθον, ἐχειρονόμουν δέ· ταῦτα γὰρ
ἠπιστάμην.

Νὴ Δί', ἔφη ὁ Φίλιππος, καὶ γὰρ οὖν οὕτω τὰ σκέλη τοῖς 20
ὤμοις φαίνει ἰσοφόρα ἔχειν ὥστε δοκεῖς ἐμοί, κἂν εἰ τοῖς
ἀγορανόμοις ἀφισταίης ὥσπερ ἄρτους τὰ κάτω πρὸς τὰ ἄνω,
ἀζήμιος ἂν γενέσθαι.

καὶ ὁ Καλλίας εἶπεν· Ὦ Σώκρατες, ἐμὲ μὲν παρακάλει,
ὅταν μέλλῃς μανθάνειν ὀρχεῖσθαι, ἵνα σοι ἀντιστοιχῶ τε καὶ
συμμανθάνω.

Ἄγε δή, ἔφη ὁ Φίλιππος, καὶ ἐμοὶ αὐλησάτω, ἵνα καὶ 21
ἐγὼ ὀρχήσωμαι. ἐπειδὴ δ' ἀνέστη, διῆλθε μιμούμενος τήν τε
τοῦ παιδὸς καὶ τὴν τῆς παιδὸς ὄρχησιν. καὶ πρῶτον μὲν ὅτι 22
ἐπήνεσαν ὡς ὁ παῖς σὺν τοῖς σχήμασιν ἔτι καλλίων ἐφαίνετο,
ἀνταπέδειξεν ὅ τι κινοίη τοῦ σώματος ἅπαν τῆς φύσεως
γελοιότερον· ὅτι δ' ἡ παῖς εἰς τοὔπισθεν καμπτομένη τροχοὺς
ἐμιμεῖτο, ἐκεῖνος ταὐτὰ εἰς τὸ ἔμπροσθεν ἐπικύπτων
μιμεῖσθαι τροχοὺς ἐπειρᾶτο. τέλος δ' ὅτι τὸν παῖδ' ἐπήνουν
ὡς ἐν τῇ ὀρχήσει ἅπαν τὸ σῶμα γυμνάζοι, κελεύσας τὴν
αὐλητρίδα θάττονα ῥυθμὸν ἐπάγειν ἵει ἅμα πάντα καὶ σκέλη
καὶ χεῖρας καὶ κεφαλήν. ἐπειδὴ δὲ ἀπειρήκει, κατακλινόμενος 23
εἶπε· Τεκμήριον, ὦ ἄνδρες, ὅτι καλῶς γυμνάζει καὶ τὰ ἐμὰ
ὀρχήματα. ἐγὼ γοῦν διψῶ· καὶ ὁ παῖς ἐγχεάτω μοι τὴν
μεγάλην φιάλην.

Νὴ Δί', ἔφη ὁ Καλλίας, καὶ ἡμῖν γε, ἐπεὶ καὶ ἡμεῖς
διψῶμεν ἐπὶ σοὶ γελῶντες.

ὁ δ' αὖ Σωκράτης εἶπεν· Ἀλλὰ πίνειν μέν, ὦ ἄνδρες, καὶ 24
ἐμοὶ πάνυ δοκεῖ· τῷ γὰρ ὄντι ὁ οἶνος ἄρδων τὰς ψυχὰς τὰς
μὲν λύπας, ὥσπερ ὁ μανδραγόρας τοὺς ἀνθρώπους, κοιμίζει,

body and so get it all into balance? 18 Or are you laughing because I won't have to look for a wrestling-partner, or strip off in a crowd at my advanced age, but I can get away with a seven-couch room, the way this boy here just now found this room was fine to work up a sweat in? In winter I can exercise indoors, and when it's very hot, I'll be in the shade. 19 Or are you laughing because I've got a belly larger than it should be and I want to make it more modest? Don't you know that Kharmides there caught me dancing, early the other day?"

"By Zeus I did," said Kharmides. "At first I was astounded, and I was afraid you were going mad. But when I heard you say more or less what you're saying now, I went off home myself and didn't exactly dance - I've never learnt that - but I did do some arm movements. That I did know."

20 "Yes by Zeus," said Philippos, "and in consequence your legs look so well matched for strength with your shoulders that in my view, even if you were weighing out upper limbs against lower like loaves of bread for the market-inspectors, you'd escape being fined!"

Kallias said, "Do invite me, Sokrates, when you propose to learn dancing, so that I can stand opposite and share the lessons with you."

21 "Come on," said Philippos, "let her play the aulos for me too, so that I can dance as well," and he stood up and proceeded to mimic the dancing of both the boy and the girl. 22 Because they had praised the way the boy looked even better when he moved, Philippos in response first made every bit of his body that he moved look unnaturally comical; and because the girl had been bending over backwards to look like hoops, he tried to imitate hoops too, but by bending over forwards. Finally, because they had been praising the boy for exercising the whole of his body in his dancing, he told the aulos-girl to set up a quicker tempo and he let everything go at once, legs and arms and head. 23 When he was exhausted he went back to his couch and said, "Proof, gentlemen, that my dancing is good exercise too. At any rate, I'm thirsty: and the boy can pour me out the big bowl."

"By Zeus," said Kallias, "he can do it for us too, because we're thirsty too, from laughing at you."

24 Sokrates said, "Actually, gentlemen, drinking is something I very much approve of. Wine irrigates the spirit; it soothes irritability as

38

τὰς δὲ φιλοφροσύνας, ὥσπερ ἔλαιον φλόγα, ἐγείρει. δοκεῖ 25
μέντοι μοι καὶ τὰ τῶν ἀνδρῶν σώματα ταὐτὰ πάσχειν ἅπερ
καὶ τὰ τῶν ἐν γῇ φυομένων. καὶ γὰρ ἐκεῖνα, ὅταν μὲν ὁ θεὸς
αὐτὰ ἄγαν ἀθρόως ποτίζῃ, οὐ δύναται ὀρθοῦσθαι οὐδὲ ταῖς
αὔραις διαπνεῖσθαι· ὅταν δ' ὅσῳ ἥδεται τοσοῦτον πίνῃ, καὶ
μάλα ὀρθά τε αὔξεται καὶ θάλλοντα ἀφικνεῖται εἰς τὴν
καρπογονίαν. οὕτω δὲ καὶ ἡμεῖς ἂν μὲν ἀθρόον τὸ ποτὸν 26
ἐγχεώμεθα, ταχὺ ἡμῖν καὶ τὰ σώματα καὶ αἱ γνῶμαι
σφαλοῦνται, καὶ οὐδὲ ἀναπνεῖν, μὴ ὅτι λέγειν τι δυνησόμεθα·
ἂν δὲ ἡμῖν οἱ παῖδες μικραῖς κύλιξι πυκνὰ ἐπιψακάζωσιν, ἵνα
καὶ ἐγὼ ἐν Γοργιείοις ῥήμασιν εἴπω, οὕτως οὐ βιαζόμενοι
μεθύειν ὑπὸ τοῦ οἴνου ἀλλ' ἀναπειθόμενοι πρὸς τὸ
παιγνιωδέστερον ἀφιξόμεθα. ἐδόκει μὲν δὴ ταῦτα πᾶσι· 27
προσέθηκε δὲ ὁ Φίλιππος ὡς χρὴ τοὺς οἰνοχόους μιμεῖσθαι
τοὺς ἀγαθοὺς ἁρματηλάτας, θᾶττον περιελαύνοντας τὰς
κύλικας. οἱ μὲν δὴ οἰνοχόοι οὕτως ἐποίουν.

Ἐκ δὲ τούτου συνηρμοσμένῃ τῇ λύρᾳ πρὸς τὸν αὐλὸν III
ἐκιθάρισεν ὁ παῖς καὶ ᾖσεν. ἔνθα δὴ ἐπήνεσαν μὲν ἅπαντες·
ὁ δὲ Χαρμίδης καὶ εἶπεν· Ἀλλ' ἐμοὶ μὲν δοκεῖ, ὦ ἄνδρες,
ὥσπερ Σωκράτης ἔφη τὸν οἶνον, οὕτως καὶ αὕτη ἡ κρᾶσις
τῶν τε παίδων τῆς ὥρας καὶ τῶν φθόγγων τὰς μὲν λύπας
κοιμίζειν, τὴν δ' ἀφροδίτην ἐγείρειν.

ἐκ τούτου δὲ πάλιν εἶπεν ὁ Σωκράτης· Οὗτοι μὲν δή, ὦ 2
ἄνδρες, ἱκανοὶ τέρπειν ἡμᾶς φαίνονται· ἡμεῖς δὲ τούτων οἶδ'
ὅτι πολὺ βελτίονες οἰόμεθα εἶναι· οὐκ αἰσχρὸν οὖν εἰ μηδ'
ἐπιχειρήσομεν συνόντες ὠφελεῖν τι ἢ εὐφραίνειν ἀλλήλους;

Ἐντεῦθεν εἶπαν πολλοί· Σὺ τοίνυν ἡμῖν ἐξηγοῦ ποίων
λόγων ἁπτόμενοι μάλιστ' ἂν ταῦτα ποιοῖμεν.

Ἐγὼ μὲν τοίνυν, ἔφη, ἥδιστ' ἂν ἀπολάβοιμι παρὰ Καλλίου 3
τὴν ὑπόσχεσιν. ἔφη γὰρ δήπου, εἰ συνδειπνοῖμεν, ἐπιδείξειν
τὴν αὑτοῦ σοφίαν.

Καὶ ἐπιδείξω γε, ἔφη, ἐὰν καὶ ὑμεῖς ἅπαντες εἰς μέσον
φέρητε ὅ τι ἕκαστος ἐπίστασθε ἀγαθόν.

Ἀλλ' οὐδείς σοι, ἔφη, ἀντιλέγει τὸ μὴ οὐ λέξειν ὅ τι
ἕκαστος ἡγεῖται πλείστου ἄξιον ἐπίστασθαι.

Ἐγὼ μὲν τοίνυν, ἔφη, λέγω ὑμῖν ἐφ' ᾧ μέγιστον φρονῶ. 4
ἀνθρώπους γὰρ οἶμαι ἱκανὸς εἶναι βελτίους ποιεῖν.

mandragora soothes people, and it rouses thoughts of friendliness as oil does a fire. 25 I think, however, that it's the same for the bodies of men as it is for plants in the ground: when god gives plants too much to drink all at once, they can't keep upright and have the air blow through them; but when they can drink to their pleasure and no more, then they grow tall and come to their fruiting in fine condition. 26 So it is with us: if we pour in all the drink at once, both our bodies and our brains will soon start stumbling, and we shan't even be able to breathe, never mind talk sense. But if your boys 'besprinkle us with little cups and oft', if I may use the language of Gorgias, then we shall arrive at comparative merriness from a persuasion rather than from a compulsion to get drunk on the wine." 27 Everyone agreed, with Philippos adding that the wine-waiters should copy good charioteers and drive round the cups at good speed. And so they did.

III After this the boy tuned his lyre to the aulos, and played and sang. There was unanimous applause, and Kharmides added, "It seems to me, gentlemen, as Sokrates remarked of wine, that this mixture of the beauty of the youngsters and of the sounds they make soothes our irritability and rouses thoughts of sex."

2 Sokrates intervened again. "These people are clearly competent to give us enjoyment, but I'm sure we think we are much their betters. Won't it be a shame, then, if we don't even attempt to give each other some benefit or pleasure now we are together?"

Then several people said, "In that case you tell us what sort of talk we should go for to do that best."

3 "Well," said he, "I should be happiest to take up the promise that Kallias made. He said, I think, that if we came to dinner with him, he would display his own learning."

"Yes, and I will," he said, "provided you too contribute, all of you, what you each know about that's good."

"No one can protest against declaring what he thinks most worth knowing about."

4 "Then," said Kallias, "I will tell you what I most pride myself on. I think I have the ability to make people better."

καὶ ὁ Ἀντισθένης εἶπε· Πότερον τέχνην τινὰ βαναυσικὴν (III) ἢ καλοκἀγαθίαν διδάσκων;

Εἰ καλοκἀγαθία ἐστὶν ἡ δικαιοσύνη.

Νὴ Δί᾽, ἔφη ὁ Ἀντισθένης, ἥ γε ἀναμφιλογωτάτη· ἐπεί τοι ἀνδρεία μὲν καὶ σοφία ἔστιν ὅτε βλαβερὰ καὶ φίλοις καὶ πόλει δοκεῖ εἶναι, ἡ δὲ δικαιοσύνη οὐδὲ καθ᾽ ἓν συμμίγνυται τῇ ἀδικίᾳ.

Ἐπειδὰν τοίνυν καὶ ὑμῶν ἕκαστος εἴπῃ ὅ τι ὠφέλιμον 5 ἔχει, τότε κἀγὼ οὐ φθονήσω εἰπεῖν τὴν τέχνην δι᾽ ἧς τοῦτο ἀπεργάζομαι. ἀλλὰ σὺ αὖ, ἔφη, λέγε, ὦ Νικήρατε, ἐπὶ ποίᾳ ἐπιστήμῃ μέγα φρονεῖς.

καὶ ὃς εἶπεν· Ὁ πατὴρ ὁ ἐπιμελούμενος ὅπως ἀνὴρ ἀγαθὸς γενοίμην ἠνάγκασέ με πάντα τὰ Ὁμήρου ἔπη μαθεῖν· καὶ νῦν δυναίμην ἂν Ἰλιάδα ὅλην καὶ Ὀδύσσειαν ἀπὸ στόματος εἰπεῖν.

Ἐκεῖνο δ᾽, ἔφη ὁ Ἀντισθένης, λέληθέ σε, ὅτι καὶ οἱ 6 ῥαψῳδοὶ πάντες ἐπίστανται ταῦτα τὰ ἔπη;

Καὶ πῶς ἄν, ἔφη, λελήθοι ἀκροώμενόν γε αὐτῶν ὀλίγου ἀν᾽ ἑκάστην ἡμέραν;

Οἶσθά τι οὖν ἔθνος, ἔφη, ἠλιθιώτερον ῥαψῳδῶν;

Οὐ μὰ τὸν Δί᾽, ἔφη ὁ Νικήρατος, οὔκουν ἔμοιγε δοκῶ.

Δῆλον γάρ, ἔφη ὁ Σωκράτης, ὅτι τὰς ὑπονοίας οὐκ ἐπίστανται. σὺ δὲ Στησιμβρότῳ τε καὶ Ἀναξιμάνδρῳ καὶ ἄλλοις πολλοῖς πολὺ δέδωκας ἀργύριον, ὥστε οὐδέν σε τῶν πολλοῦ ἀξίων λέληθε. τί γὰρ σύ, ἔφη, ὦ Κριτόβουλε, ἐπὶ τίνι 7 μέγιστον φρονεῖς;

Ἐπὶ κάλλει, ἔφη.

Ἦ οὖν καὶ σύ, ἔφη ὁ Σωκράτης, ἕξεις λέγειν ὅτι τῷ σῷ κάλλει ἱκανὸς εἶ βελτίους ἡμᾶς ποιεῖν;

Εἰ δὲ μή, δῆλόν γε ὅτι φαῦλος φανοῦμαι.

Τί γὰρ σύ, εἶπεν, ἐπὶ τίνι μέγα φρονεῖς, ὦ Ἀντίσθενες; 8 Ἐπὶ πλούτῳ, ἔφη.

ὁ μὲν δὴ Ἑρμογένης ἀνήρετο εἰ πολὺ εἴη αὐτῷ ἀργύριον. ὁ δὲ ἀπώμοσε μηδὲ ὀβολόν.

Ἀλλὰ γῆν πολλὴν κέκτησαι;

Ἴσως ἄν, ἔφη, Αὐτολύκῳ τούτῳ ἱκανὴ γένοιτο ἐγκονίσασθαι.

Ἀκουστέον ἂν εἴη καὶ σοῦ. τί γὰρ σύ, ἔφη, ὦ Χαρμίδη, 9 ἐπὶ τίνι μέγα φρονεῖς;

Antisthenes asked, "By teaching them some craft skill, or by teaching them 'essence of gentleman'?"

"If that's what justice is, yes."

"It certainly is," said Antisthenes; "it's the most indisputable form of it: braveness and intelligence sometimes appear damaging both to friends and to country, but justice can have no part in injustice at all."

5 "In that case, as soon as all of you say what each one sees as useful, then I too shall be happy to tell you the means by which I achieve my good. Come on you, Nikeratos," he said, "tell us what you pride yourself on."

"My father," said Nikeratos, "who minded very much about my being a brave man, compelled me to learn the whole of Homer. I could at this moment recite the whole of the Iliad and the Odyssey straight off."

6 "Has it escaped your observation," said Antisthenes, "that those verses are also known to all the rhapsodes?"

"How could it, when I listened to them virtually every day?"

"Do you know of any set of people sillier than rhapsodes?"

"No by Zeus," said Nikeratos, "not in my view."

"Plainly," said Sokrates, "they don't comprehend the deep meaning. You, however, have paid considerable sums to Stesimbrotos and Anaximander and lots of others, and so you've missed none of the important bits. 7 What about you, Kritoboulos?" he continued. "What are you most proud of?"

"Good looks," he said.

"So will you be able to say," said Sokrates, "that you have the capacity to improve us by your good looks?"

"If not, I'm bound to seem futile."

8 "What about you, Antisthenes? What do you set store by?" he said.

"Wealth," said Antisthenes.

Hermogenes asked him whether he had a lot of money, and he declared on oath that he hadn't an obol.

"Do you own a lot of land then?"

"It would probably be enough for Autolykos there to dust himself with."

9 "You certainly need a hearing. What about you, Kharmides? What do you make boast of?"

Ἐγὼ αὖ, ἔφη, ἐπὶ πενίᾳ μέγα φρονῶ. (III)

Νὴ Δί᾽, ἔφη ὁ Σωκράτης, ἐπ᾽ εὐχαρίτῳ γε πράγματι. τοῦτο γὰρ δὴ ἥκιστα μὲν ἐπίφθονον, ἥκιστα δὲ περιμάχητον, καὶ ἀφύλακτον ὂν σώζεται καὶ ἀμελούμενον ἰσχυρότερον γίγνεται.

Σὺ δὲ δή, ἔφη ὁ Καλλίας, ἐπὶ τίνι μέγα φρονεῖς, ὦ 10 Σώκρατες;

καὶ ὃς μάλα σεμνῶς ἀνασπάσας τὸ πρόσωπον, Ἐπὶ μαστροπείᾳ, εἶπεν. ἐπεὶ δὲ ἐγέλασαν ἐπ᾽ αὐτῷ, Ὑμεῖς μὲν γελᾶτε, ἔφη, ἐγὼ δὲ οἶδ᾽ ὅτι καὶ πάνυ ἂν πολλὰ χρήματα λαμβάνοιμι, εἰ βουλοίμην χρῆσθαι τῇ τέχνῃ.

Σύ γε μὴν δῆλον, ἔφη ὁ Λύκων τὸν Φίλιππον προσειπών, 11 ὅτι ἐπὶ τῷ γελωτοποιεῖν μέγα φρονεῖς.

Δικαιότερόν γ᾽, ἔφη, οἶμαι, ἢ Καλλιππίδης ὁ ὑποκριτής, ὃς ὑπερσεμνύνεται ὅτι δύναται πολλοὺς κλαίοντας καθίζειν.

Οὐκοῦν καὶ σύ, ἔφη ὁ Ἀντισθένης, λέξεις, ὦ Λύκων, ἐπὶ 12 τίνι μέγα φρονεῖς;

καὶ ὃς ἔφη· Οὐ γὰρ ἅπαντες ἴστε, ἔφη, ὅτι ἐπὶ τούτῳ τῷ υἱεῖ;

Οὗτός γε μήν, ἔφη τις, δῆλον ὅτι ἐπὶ τῷ νικηφόρος εἶναι.

καὶ ὁ Αὐτόλυκος ἀνερυθριάσας εἶπε· Μὰ Δί᾽ οὐκ ἔγωγε.

ἐπεὶ δὲ ἅπαντες ἡσθέντες ὅτι ἤκουσαν αὐτοῦ φωνήσαντος 13 προσέβλεψαν, ἤρετό τις αὐτόν· Ἀλλ᾽ ἐπὶ τῷ μήν, ὦ Αὐτόλυκε;

ὁ δ᾽ εἶπεν· Ἐπὶ τῷ πατρί, καὶ ἅμα ἐνεκλίθη αὐτῷ.

καὶ ὁ Καλλίας ἰδών, Ἆρ᾽ οἶσθα, ἔφη, ὦ Λύκων, ὅτι πλουσιώτατος εἶ ἀνθρώπων;

Μὰ Δί᾽, ἔφη, τοῦτο μέντοι ἐγὼ οὐκ οἶδα.

Ἀλλὰ λανθάνει σε ὅτι οὐκ ἂν δέξαιο τὰ βασιλέως χρήματα ἀντὶ τοῦ υἱοῦ;

Ἐπ᾽ αὐτοφώρῳ εἴλημμαι, ἔφη, πλουσιώτατος, ὡς ἔοικεν, ἀνθρώπων ὤν.

Σὺ δέ, ἔφη ὁ Νικήρατος, ὦ Ἑρμόγενες, ἐπὶ τίνι μάλιστα 14 ἀγάλλῃ;

καὶ ὅς, Ἐπὶ φίλων, ἔφη, ἀρετῇ καὶ δυνάμει, καὶ ὅτι τοιοῦτοι ὄντες ἐμοῦ ἐπιμέλονται. ἐνταῦθα τοίνυν πάντες προσέβλεψαν αὐτῷ, καὶ πολλοὶ ἅμα ἤροντο εἰ καὶ σφίσι δηλώσοι αὐτούς. ὁ δὲ εἶπεν ὅτι οὐ φθονήσει.

"I make boast of poverty," he said.

"By Zeus," said Sokrates, "and a very agreeable thing too. It causes least envy and fewest fights; it needs no protection to preserve it, and it grows stronger by neglect."

10 "What about you, Sokrates?" said Kallias. "What do you make boast of?"

Sokrates pulled a very solemn face and said, "Procuring." When they had laughed at him, he said, "You may laugh, but I know I could be making a great deal of money if I were willing to use my skill."

11 "You," said Lykon, addressing Philippos, "obviously pride yourself on your laughter-making."

"Yes," he said, "and with more justice, I reckon, than Kallippides the actor, who gives himself extraordinary airs because he can get thousands weeping in their seats."

12 "Won't you also tell us, Lykon," said Antisthenes, "what you are proud of?"

"Don't you all know," said Lykon, "that it's my son here?"

"And he," said someone, "is obviously proud of being a champion."

Autolykos blushed, and said, "By Zeus I'm not."

13 Everyone was delighted they had heard him speak, and they looked in his direction, and someone asked, "Well, what are you proud of then, Autolykos?"

"My father," he said, and leant up against him as he spoke.

Kallias was watching. "Do you realise, Lykon," he said, "that you are the richest man on earth?"

"By Zeus," he said, "I certainly don't."

"You mean you don't realise that you wouldn't take the wealth of the king of Persia in exchange for your son?"

"Caught red-handed," he said. "Obviously I am the richest of men."

14 "Now you, Hermogenes," said Nikeratos. "What's your particular glory?"

"The quality and power of my friends," he replied, "and the fact that they are who they are and yet mind about me." At that, everybody looked at him, and many asked him, all at the same time, if he would point them out, and he said he would be happy to.

44

Ἐκ τούτου ἔλεξεν ὁ Σωκράτης· Οὐκοῦν λοιπὸν ἂν εἴη IV
ἡμῖν ἃ ἕκαστος ὑπέσχετο ἀποδεικνύναι ὡς πολλοῦ ἄξιά ἐστιν.
Ἀκούοιτ' ἄν, ἔφη ὁ Καλλίας, ἐμοῦ πρῶτον. ἐγὼ γὰρ ἐν
τῷ χρόνῳ ᾧ ὑμῶν ἀκούω ἀπορούντων τί τὸ δίκαιον, ἐν τούτῳ
δικαιοτέρους τοὺς ἀνθρώπους ποιῶ.
καὶ ὁ Σωκράτης, Πῶς, ὦ λῷστε; ἔφη.
Διδοὺς νὴ Δί' ἀργύριον.
καὶ ὁ Ἀντισθένης ἐπαναστὰς μάλα ἐλεγκτικῶς αὐτὸν 2
ἐπήρετο· Οἱ δὲ ἄνθρωποι, ὦ Καλλία, πότερον ἐν ταῖς ψυχαῖς
ἢ ἐν τῷ βαλλαντίῳ τὸ δίκαιόν σοι δοκοῦσιν ἔχειν;
Ἐν ταῖς ψυχαῖς, ἔφη.
Κᾆπειτα σὺ εἰς τὸ βαλλάντιον διδοὺς ἀργύριον τὰς ψυχὰς
δικαιοτέρους ποιεῖς;
Μάλιστα.
Πῶς;
Ὅτι διὰ τὸ εἰδέναι ὡς ἔστιν ὅτου πριάμενοι τὰ
ἐπιτήδεια ἕξουσιν οὐκ ἐθέλουσι κακουργοῦντες κινδυνεύειν.
Ἦ καί σοι, ἔφη, ἀποδιδόασιν ὅ τι ἂν λάβωσι; 3
Μὰ τὸν Δί', ἔφη, οὐ μὲν δή.
Τί δέ, ἀντὶ τοῦ ἀργυρίου χάριτας;
Οὐ μὰ τὸν Δί', ἔφη, οὐδὲ τοῦτο, ἀλλ' ἔνιοι καὶ ἐχθιόνως
ἔχουσιν ἢ πρὶν λαβεῖν.
Θαυμαστά γ', ἔφη ὁ Ἀντισθένης ἅμα εἰσβλέπων ὡς
ἐλέγχων αὐτόν, εἰ πρὸς μὲν τοὺς ἄλλους δύνασαι δικαίους
ποιεῖν αὐτούς, πρὸς δὲ σαυτὸν οὔ.
Καὶ τί τοῦτ', ἔφη ὁ Καλλίας, θαυμαστόν; οὐ καὶ τέκτονάς 4
τε καὶ οἰκοδόμους πολλοὺς ὁρᾷς οἳ ἄλλοις μὲν πολλοῖς
ποιοῦσιν οἰκίας, ἑαυτοῖς δὲ οὐ δύνανται ποιῆσαι, ἀλλ' ἐν
μισθωταῖς οἰκοῦσι; καὶ ἀνάσχου μέντοι, ὦ σοφιστά,
ἐλεγχόμενος.
Νὴ Δί', ἔφη ὁ Σωκράτης, ἀνεχέσθω μέντοι· ἐπεὶ καὶ οἱ 5
μάντεις λέγονται δήπου ἄλλοις μὲν προαγορεύειν τὸ μέλλον,
ἑαυτοῖς δὲ μὴ προορᾶν τὸ ἐπιόν. οὗτος μὲν δὴ ὁ λόγος 6
ἐνταῦθα ἔληξεν.
ἐκ τούτου δὲ ὁ Νικήρατος, Ἀκούοιτ' ἄν, ἔφη, καὶ ἐμοῦ ἃ
ἔσεσθε βελτίονες, ἂν ἐμοὶ συνῆτε. ἴστε γὰρ δήπου ὅτι
Ὅμηρος ὁ σοφώτατος πεποίηκε σχεδὸν περὶ πάντων τῶν
ἀνθρωπίνων. ὅστις ἂν οὖν ὑμῶν βούληται ἢ οἰκονομικὸς ἢ
δημηγορικὸς ἢ στρατηγικὸς γενέσθαι ἢ ὅμοιος Ἀχιλλεῖ ἢ

IV Then Sokrates said, "Well, it remains for us to demonstrate that what each man promised is so very important."

"You shall hear me first," said Kallias. "I listen to you people wondering what justice is, and even as I listen, all the while I am making men more just."

"Brilliant," said Sokrates. "How do you do it?"

"By giving them money, by Zeus."

2 Antisthenes rose at the answer and asked him, in best cross-examining fashion, "Kallias, do these people appear to you to keep their sense of justice in their hearts or in their pockets?"

"In their hearts," he said.

"And you make their hearts more just by putting money in their pockets?"

"Certainly."

"How?"

"Because once they know they can have what they need and pay for it, they stop wanting to risk committing crimes."

3 "And do they actually pay you back what they get?" he asked.

"No by Zeus," he said, "they certainly don't!"

"You mean you get thanked instead of repaid?"

"No by Zeus," he said, "not even thanked. Some of them are even more aggressive than before they got the money."

"Extraordinary," said Antisthenes, gazing at him all the while as if in mid-refutation; "extraordinary, if you can make them behave justly towards everyone else and not towards yourself."

4 "What's extraordinary about it?" said Kallias. "Aren't there craftsmen and builders in plenty who produce houses for lots of other people, but can't do it for themselves, and they live in rented accommodation instead? You put up with being cross-examined yourself, mister sophist!"

5 "By Zeus," said Sokrates, "let him! After all, even soothsayers, I think, are said to tell others the future but not to foresee what's coming their way." 6 And there that discussion came to an end.

Next Nikeratos spoke. "You shall now hear from me about the improvement that association with me can give you. I'm sure you all know that Homer, that ultimate expert, has dealt with virtually every human circumstance. Anyone keen on estate management or politics or

Αἴαντι ἢ Νέστορι ἢ Ὀδυσσεῖ, ἐμὲ θεραπευέτω. ἐγὼ γὰρ **(IV)**
ταῦτα πάντα ἐπίσταμαι.

Ἦ καὶ βασιλεύειν, ἔφη ὁ Ἀντισθένης, ἐπίστασαι, ὅτι
οἶσθα ἐπαινέσαντα αὐτὸν τὸν Ἀγαμέμνονα ὡς βασιλεύς τε
εἴη ἀγαθὸς κρατερός τ᾽ αἰχμητής;

Καὶ ναὶ μὰ Δί᾽, ἔφη, ἔγωγε ὅτι ἁρματηλατοῦντα δεῖ
ἐγγὺς μὲν τῆς στήλης κάμψαι,
    αὐτὸν δὲ κλινθῆναι ἐϋξέστου ἐπὶ δίφρου
    ἦκ᾽ ἐπ᾽ ἀριστερὰ τοῖιν, ἀτὰρ τὸν δεξιὸν ἵππον
    κένσαι ὁμοκλήσαντ᾽ εἶξαί τέ οἱ ἡνία χερσί.

καὶ πρὸς τούτοις γε ἄλλο οἶδα, καὶ ὑμῖν αὐτίκα μάλ᾽ ἔξεστι 7
πειρᾶσθαι. εἶπε γάρ που Ὅμηρος· Ἐπὶ δὲ κρόμυον ποτῷ
ὄψον. ἐὰν οὖν ἐνέγκῃ τις κρόμμυον, αὐτίκα μάλα τοῦτό γε
ὠφελημένοι ἔσεσθε· ἥδιον γὰρ πιεῖσθε.

καὶ ὁ Χαρμίδης εἶπεν· Ὦ ἄνδρες, ὁ Νικήρατος κρομμύων 8
ὄζων ἐπιθυμεῖ οἴκαδε ἐλθεῖν, ἵν᾽ ἡ γυνὴ αὐτοῦ πιστεύῃ μηδὲ
διανοηθῆναι μηδένα ἂν φιλῆσαι αὐτόν.

Νὴ Δί᾽, ἔφη ὁ Σωκράτης, ἀλλ᾽ ἄλλην που δόξαν γελοίαν
κίνδυνος ἡμῖν προσλαβεῖν. ὄψον μὲν γὰρ δὴ ὄντως ἔοικεν
εἶναι, ὡς κρόμμυόν γε οὐ μόνον σῖτον ἀλλὰ καὶ ποτὸν ἡδύνει.
εἰ δὲ δὴ τοῦτο καὶ μετὰ δεῖπνον τρωξόμεθα, ὅπως μὴ φήσῃ
τις ἡμᾶς πρὸς Καλλίαν ἐλθόντας ἡδυπαθεῖν.

Μηδαμῶς, ἔφη, ὦ Σώκρατες. εἰς μὲν γὰρ μάχην ὁρμωμένῳ 9
καλῶς ἔχει κρόμμυον ὑποτρώγειν, ὥσπερ ἔνιοι τοὺς
ἀλεκτρυόνας σκόροδα σιτίσαντες συμβάλλουσιν· ἡμεῖς δὲ ἴσως
βουλευόμεθα ὅπως φιλήσομέν τινα μᾶλλον ἢ μαχούμεθα. καὶ 10
οὗτος μὲν δὴ ὁ λόγος οὕτω πως ἐπαύσατο.

ὁ δὲ Κριτόβουλος, Οὐκοῦν αὖ ἐγὼ λέξω, ἔφη, ἐξ ὧν ἐπὶ
τῷ κάλλει μέγα φρονῶ.

Λέγε, ἔφασαν.

Εἰ μὲν τοίνυν μὴ καλός εἰμι, ὡς οἴομαι, ὑμεῖς ἂν
δικαίως ἀπάτης δίκην ὑπέχοιτε· οὐδενὸς γὰρ ὁρκίζοντος ἀεὶ
ὀμνύοντες καλόν μέ φατε εἶναι. κἀγὼ μέντοι πιστεύω. καλοὺς
γὰρ καὶ ἀγαθοὺς ὑμᾶς ἄνδρας νομίζω. εἰ δ᾽ εἰμί τε τῷ ὄντι 11
καλὸς καὶ ὑμεῖς τὰ αὐτὰ πρὸς ἐμὲ πάσχετε οἷάπερ ἐγὼ πρὸς
τὸν ἐμοὶ δοκοῦντα καλὸν εἶναι, ὄμνυμι πάντας θεοὺς μὴ
ἑλέσθαι ἂν τὴν βασιλέως ἀρχὴν ἀντὶ τοῦ καλὸς εἶναι. νῦν 12
γὰρ ἐγὼ Κλεινίαν ἥδιον μὲν θεῶμαι ἢ τἆλλα πάντα τὰ ἐν
ἀνθρώποις καλά· τυφλὸς δὲ τῶν ἄλλων ἁπάντων μᾶλλον ἂν

strategy, or who wants to be like Akhilleus or Aias or Nestor or Odysseus, should cultivate me: I understand it all."

"You understand kingship too, do you?" said Antisthenes. "You know, of course, that he praises Agamemnon as a 'good king and sturdy spearman.'"

"Oh yes by Zeus," he said, "and I know he also says that a charioteer must turn close to the post, 'and lean across upon his well-planed chariot, a little to the left of them, goading the right-hand horse with cries, and slackening his hold on its reins.' 7 I know another thing too, and you can try it out here and now. Homer said, if I remember, 'An onion adds relish to a drink.' So if someone brings in an onion, you can have the profit of that on the spot: you'll drink with extra delight!"

8 "Gentlemen," said Kharmides, "Nikeratos is eager to get home smelling of onions so that his wife can be sure that no one would even have thought of kissing him."

"Yes by Zeus," said Sokrates, "and I think there's the chance of a further comic possibility. Onion really does seem to be a relish, since it can season drink as well as food; but if we're really going to munch onion after dinner as well, mind nobody says we had a fine time of it coming to Kallias!"

9 "Certainly not, Sokrates," he said. "Nibbling a bit of onion is fine when you're going into battle, just as some people feed their fighting cocks on garlic before a bout. We perhaps are planning a kiss or two, however, rather than a fight." 10 And so that conversation ended more or less.

"I'll speak next," said Kritoboulos, "and tell you the reason why I'm proud of my good looks."

"Speak," they said.

"If I'm not good-looking, as I think I am, you lot would all deserve to be up on a charge of deception: no one puts you on oath, and yet you keep swearing that I am good-looking. And for my part I trust you. I consider you to be gentlemen. 11 If I really am good-looking, and if you get the same sort of feelings about me that I get about someone I think good-looking, then I swear by all the gods that I wouldn't choose the empire of the king of Persia in preference to good looks. 12 These days I gaze upon Kleinias with more delight than on anything else at all that men think beautiful. I could take being blind to all the rest of the world

δεξαίμην εἶναι ἢ Κλεινίου ἑνὸς ὄντος· ἄχθομαι δὲ καὶ νυκτὶ (IV)
καὶ ὕπνῳ ὅτι ἐκεῖνον οὐχ ὁρῶ, ἡμέρᾳ δὲ καὶ ἡλίῳ τὴν
μεγίστην χάριν οἶδα ὅτι μοι Κλεινίαν ἀναφαίνουσιν. ἄξιόν γε 13
μὴν ἡμῖν τοῖς καλοῖς καὶ ἐπὶ τοῖσδε μέγα φρονεῖν, ὅτι τὸν
μὲν ἰσχυρὸν πονοῦντα δεῖ κτᾶσθαι τάγαθὰ καὶ τὸν ἀνδρεῖον
κινδυνεύοντα, τὸν δέ γε σοφὸν λέγοντα· ὁ δὲ καλὸς καὶ
ἡσυχίαν ἔχων πάντ' ἂν διαπράξαιτο. ἐγὼ γοῦν καίπερ εἰδὼς 14
ὅτι χρήματα ἡδὺ κτῆμα ἥδιον μὲν ἂν τὰ ὄντα Κλεινίᾳ
διδοίην ἢ ἕτερα παρ' ἄλλου λαμβάνοιμι, ἥδιον δ' ἂν
δουλεύοιμι ἢ ἐλεύθερος εἴην, εἴ μου Κλεινίας ἄρχειν ἐθέλοι.
καὶ γὰρ πονοίην ἂν ῥᾷον ἐκείνῳ ἢ ἀναπαυοίμην, καὶ
κινδυνεύοιμ' ἂν πρὸ ἐκείνου ἥδιον ἢ ἀκίνδυνος ζῴην.

ὥστε εἰ σύ, ὦ Καλλία, μέγα φρονεῖς ὅτι δικαιοτέρους 15
δύνασαι ποιεῖν, ἐγὼ πρὸς πᾶσαν ἀρετὴν δικαιότερος σοῦ εἰμι
ἄγων ἀνθρώπους. διὰ γὰρ τὸ ἐμπνεῖν τι ἡμᾶς τοὺς καλοὺς
τοῖς ἐρωτικοῖς ἐλευθεριωτέρους μὲν αὐτοὺς ποιοῦμεν εἰς
χρήματα, φιλοπονωτέρους δὲ καὶ φιλοκαλωτέρους ἐν τοῖς
κινδύνοις, καὶ μὴν αἰδημονεστέρους τε καὶ ἐγκρατεστέρους, οἵ
γε καὶ ὧν δέονται μάλιστα ταῦτ' αἰσχύνονται. μαίνονται δὲ 16
καὶ οἱ μὴ τοὺς καλοὺς στρατηγοὺς αἱρούμενοι. ἐγὼ γοῦν μετὰ
Κλεινίου κἂν διὰ πυρὸς ἰοίην· οἶδα δ' ὅτι καὶ ὑμεῖς μετ'
ἐμοῦ. ὥστε μηκέτι ἀπόρει, ὦ Σώκρατες, εἴ τι τοὐμὸν κάλλος
ἀνθρώπους ὠφελήσει. ἀλλ' οὐδὲ μέντοι ταύτῃ γε ἀτιμαστέον 17
τὸ κάλλος ὡς ταχὺ παρακμάζον, ἐπεὶ ὥσπερ γε παῖς γίγνεται
καλός, οὕτω καὶ μειράκιον καὶ ἀνὴρ καὶ πρεσβύτης. τεκμήριον
δέ· θαλλοφόρους γὰρ τῇ Ἀθηνᾷ τοὺς καλοὺς γέροντας
ἐκλέγονται, ὡς συμπαρομαρτοῦντος πάσῃ ἡλικίᾳ τοῦ κάλλους.
εἰ δὲ ἡδὺ τὸ παρ' ἑκόντων διαπράττεσθαι ὧν τις δέοιτο, εὖ 18
οἶδ' ὅτι καὶ νυνὶ θᾶττον ἂν ἐγὼ καὶ σιωπῶν πείσαιμι τὸν
παῖδα τόνδε καὶ τὴν παῖδα φιλῆσαί με ἢ σύ, ὦ Σώκρατες, εἰ
καὶ πάνυ πολλὰ καὶ σοφὰ λέγοις.

Τί τοῦτο; ἔφη ὁ Σωκράτης· ὡς γὰρ καὶ ἐμοῦ καλλίων ὢν 19
ταῦτα κομπάζεις;

Νὴ Δί', ἔφη ὁ Κριτόβουλος, ἢ πάντων Σειληνῶν τῶν ἐν
τοῖς σατυρικοῖς αἴσχιστος ἂν εἴην.

Ἄγε νυν, ἔφη ὁ Σωκράτης, ὅπως μεμνήσῃ διακριθῆναι 20
περὶ τοῦ κάλλους, ἐπειδὰν οἱ προκείμενοι λόγοι περιέλθωσι.
κρινάτω δ' ἡμᾶς μὴ Ἀλέξανδρος ὁ Πριάμου, ἀλλ' αὐτοὶ οὗτοι
οὕσπερ σὺ οἴει ἐπιθυμεῖν σε φιλῆσαι.

rather than be blind to just Kleinias. I get angry with night and sleep because then I can't see him, whereas I'm hugely grateful to daytime and sun because they reveal me Kleinias. 13 It is right, moreover, for us good-lookers to be proud also of the fact that while the strong man must achieve his good by his energy, and the brave man by taking risks, and the clever man by his talk, the good-looking man will achieve all his object by doing absolutely nothing. 14 I know that money is a nice thing to have, but I'd be happier to offer what I've got to Kleinias than be given more by someone else, and I'd rather be a slave than free if Kleinias were willing to be my master. I'd find it easier to work on for him than take a break, and I'd run risks for him more gladly than live without risk at all.

15 If then you are proud, Kallias, because you can make men more just, I'm a more just man than you because I bring men to perfection. Because we good-lookers are an inspiration to our admirers, we make them more like free men as regards money, and keener on hard work and glory in moments of peril; what's more, we give them a greater sense of shame and self-control, since it's precisely what they want most that they are embarrassed about. 16 People who don't elect good-looking generals are mad! Anyway, in Kleinias' company I'd even go through fire, and I know that you all would in mine. So don't be doubtful any longer, Sokrates, whether my good looks will benefit mankind. 17 Good looks are certainly not to be disparaged on the grounds that they quickly go over, since young men and mature men and old men can all be as good-looking as boys can, and my proof is that they select good-looking old men to carry the olive shoots for Athena, because good looks can accompany every stage of life. 18 If it's nice to get people to do what you wanted of their own free will, then I'm very sure I could get this boy and girl here to kiss me right now, without my saying a word, more quickly than you could get them to kiss you, Sokrates, even if you said lots of clever things."

19 "What's this?" said Sokrates. "You make this boast because you are even better-looking than I am?"

"By Zeus I am," said Kritoboulos, "or else I'd be uglier than all the Seilenoi in the satyr plays."

20 "Now mind you remember to come to the judgment of beauty," said Sokrates, "when the present discussion is concluded, and our judge shall not be Alexander son of Priam, but exactly these people you think are so keen to kiss you."

Κλεινίᾳ δ', ἔφη, ὦ Σώκρατες, οὐκ ἂν ἐπιτρέψαις; (IV) 21
καὶ ὃς εἶπεν· Οὐ γὰρ παύσῃ σὺ Κλεινίου μεμνημένος;
"Αν δὲ μὴ ὀνομάζω, ἧττόν τί με οἴει μεμνῆσθαι αὐτοῦ;
οὐκ οἶσθα ὅτι οὕτω σαφὲς ἔχω εἴδωλον αὐτοῦ ἐν τῇ ψυχῇ ὡς
εἰ πλαστικὸς ἢ ζωγραφικὸς ἦν, οὐδὲν ἂν ἧττον ἐκ τοῦ
εἰδώλου ἢ πρὸς αὐτὸν ὁρῶν ὅμοιον αὐτῷ ἀπειργασάμην;
καὶ ὁ Σωκράτης ὑπέλαβε· Τί δῆτα οὕτως ὅμοιον εἴδωλον 22
ἔχων πράγματά μοι παρέχεις ἄγεις τε αὐτὸν ὅπου ὄψει;
"Οτι, ὦ Σώκρατες, ἡ μὲν αὐτοῦ ὄψις εὐφραίνειν δύναται,
ἡ δὲ τοῦ εἰδώλου τέρψιν μὲν οὐ παρέχει, πόθον δὲ ἐμποιεῖ.
καὶ ὁ Ἑρμογένης εἶπεν· Ἀλλ' ἐγώ, ὦ Σώκρατες, οὐδὲ 23
πρὸς σοῦ ποιῶ τὸ περιιδεῖν Κριτόβουλον οὕτως ὑπὸ τοῦ
ἔρωτος ἐκπλαγέντα.
Δοκεῖς γάρ, ἔφη ὁ Σωκράτης, ἐξ οὗ ἐμοὶ σύνεστιν οὕτω
διατεθῆναι αὐτόν;
Ἀλλὰ πότε μήν;
Οὐχ ὁρᾷς ὅτι τούτῳ μὲν παρὰ τὰ ὦτα ἄρτι ἴουλος
καθέρπει, Κλεινίᾳ δὲ πρὸς τὸ ὄπισθεν ἤδη ἀναβαίνει; οὗτος
οὖν συμφοιτῶν εἰς ταὐτὸ διδασκαλεῖον ἐκείνῳ τότε ἰσχυρῶς
προσεκαύθη. ἃ δὴ αἰσθόμενος ὁ πατὴρ παρέδωκέ μοι αὐτόν, εἴ 24
τι δυναίμην ὠφελῆσαι. καὶ μέντοι πολὺ βέλτιον ἤδη ἔχει.
πρόσθεν μὲν γάρ, ὥσπερ οἱ τὰς Γοργόνας θεώμενοι, λιθίνως
ἔβλεπε πρὸς αὐτὸν καὶ οὐδαμοῦ ἀπῄει ἀπ' αὐτοῦ· νῦν δὲ ἤδη
εἶδον αὐτὸν καὶ σκαρδαμύξαντα. καίτοι νὴ τοὺς θεούς, ὦ 25
ἄνδρες, δοκεῖ μοί γ', ἔφη, ὡς ἐν ἡμῖν αὐτοῖς εἰρῆσθαι, οὗτος
καὶ πεφιληκέναι τὸν Κλεινίαν· οὗ ἔρωτος οὐδέν ἐστι
δεινότερον ὑπέκκαυμα. καὶ γὰρ ἄπληστον καὶ ἐλπίδας τινὰς
γλυκείας παρέχει. οὗ ἕνεκα ἀφεκτέον ἐγώ φημι εἶναι 26
φιλημάτων ὡραίων τῷ σωφρονεῖν δυνησομένῳ.
καὶ ὁ Χαρμίδης εἶπεν· Ἀλλὰ τί δή ποτε, ὦ Σώκρατες, 27
ἡμᾶς μὲν οὕτω τοὺς φίλους μορμολύττῃ ἀπὸ τῶν καλῶν,
αὐτὸν δέ σε, ἔφη, ἐγὼ εἶδον, ναὶ μὰ τὸν Ἀπόλλω, ὅτε παρὰ
τῷ γραμματιστῇ ἐν τῷ αὐτῷ βιβλίῳ ἀμφότεροι ἐμαστεύετέ τι,
τὴν κεφαλὴν πρὸς τῇ κεφαλῇ καὶ τὸν ὦμον γυμνὸν πρὸς
γυμνῷ τῷ Κριτοβούλου ὤμῳ ἔχοντα.
καὶ ὁ Σωκράτης, Φεῦ, ἔφη, ταῦτ' ἄρα ἐγὼ ὥσπερ ὑπὸ 28
θηρίου τινὸς δεδηγμένος τόν τε ὦμον πλεῖν ἢ πέντε ἡμέρας
ὤδαξον καὶ ἐν τῇ καρδίᾳ ὥσπερ κνῆσμά τι ἐδόκουν ἔχειν.
ἀλλὰ νῦν τοί σοι, ἔφη, ὦ Κριτόβουλε, ἐναντίον τοσούτων

21 "Wouldn't you entrust the judgment to Kleinias, Sokrates?" he said.

"Can't you leave off mentioning Kleinias?" said Sokrates.

"Do you imagine I think of him any the less if I don't? Don't you realise I have so clear a picture of him in my mind that if I were a sculptor or a painter I could have made just as good a likeness of him from that as I could by looking at him for real?"

22 Sokrates retorted, "If you've got so perfect a picture of him, why ever be such a nuisance, trying to get him where you can see him?"

"Because it's the sight of him himself that has the power to make me happy, Sokrates, whereas the sight of my image of him only sets up a longing; there's no pleasure in that."

23 Hermogenes intervened. "But Sokrates, when Kritoboulos is as madly in love as this, I don't think it's at all like you to look on so complacently."

"You think he's only been like this since he joined me?" said Sokrates.

"Well, when did it start then?"

"Can't you see that whiskers have only just begun to move down past his ears, whereas Kleinias has them already climbing up behind? Anyway, Kritoboulos got into this excessive state when he first went to the same school as Kleinias. 24 His father noticed it, and sent him on to me to see if I could help. And things are much better already. Previously he used to gaze at him steady as a stone, like people who look at Gorgons, and never went away from him, but in the present state of affairs I've actually seen him blinking. 25 And yet by the gods, gentlemen," he said, "it does seem to me, and we're talking confidentially, that Kritoboulos has actually kissed Kleinias, and there's no fiercer tinder for passion than that: it's insatiable, and it sets up delicious hopes. 26 That's why I say anyone who's going to be capable of self-control must keep his distance from the kisses of good-lookers."

27 "But why," said Kharmides, "do you try to scare your friends away from beauty like this, Sokrates, when I've seen you in person, oh yes by Apollo I have," he said, "when the pair of you were at the schoolmaster's, searching for something in the same book, with your head beside his head and your shoulder bare beside Kritoboulos' bare shoulder."

28 "Help!" said Sokrates; "so that was the itch in my shoulder, was it, and more than five days of it, too, as if I'd been bitten by some beastie. I felt as if I had a scratch upon my heart. Now," he said, "in the presence of

μαρτύρων προαγορεύω μὴ ἅπτεσθαί μου πρὶν ἂν τὸ γένειον (IV)
τῇ κεφαλῇ ὁμοίως κομήσῃς. Καὶ οὗτοι μὲν δὴ οὕτως ἀναμὶξ
ἔσκωψάν τε καὶ ἐσπούδασαν.

ὁ δὲ Καλλίας, Σὸν μέρος, ἔφη, λέγειν, ὦ Χαρμίδη, δι' ὅ 29
τι ἐπὶ πενίᾳ μέγα φρονεῖς.

Οὐκοῦν τόδε μέν, ἔφη, ὁμολογεῖται, κρεῖττον εἶναι θαρρεῖν
ἢ φοβεῖσθαι καὶ ἐλεύθερον εἶναι μᾶλλον ἢ δουλεύειν καὶ
θεραπεύεσθαι μᾶλλον ἢ θεραπεύειν καὶ πιστεύεσθαι ὑπὸ τῆς
πατρίδος μᾶλλον ἢ ἀπιστεῖσθαι. ἐγὼ τοίνυν ἐν τῇδε τῇ πόλει 30
ὅτε μὲν πλούσιος ἦν πρῶτον μὲν ἐφοβούμην μή τίς μου τὴν
οἰκίαν διορύξας καὶ τὰ χρήματα λάβοι καὶ αὐτόν τί με κακὸν
ἐργάσαιτο· ἔπειτα δὲ καὶ τοὺς συκοφάντας ἐθεράπευον, εἰδὼς
ὅτι παθεῖν μᾶλλον κακῶς ἱκανὸς εἴην ἢ ποιῆσαι ἐκείνους. καὶ
γὰρ δὴ καὶ προσετάττετο μὲν ἀεί τί μοι δαπανᾶν ὑπὸ τῆς
πόλεως, ἀποδημῆσαι δὲ οὐδαμοῦ ἐξῆν. νῦν δ' ἐπειδὴ τῶν 31
ὑπερορίων στέρομαι καὶ τὰ ἔγγεια οὐ καρποῦμαι καὶ τὰ ἐκ
τῆς οἰκίας πέπραται, ἡδέως μὲν καθεύδω ἐκτεταμένος, πιστὸς
δὲ τῇ πόλει γεγένημαι, οὐκέτι δὲ ἀπειλοῦμαι, ἀλλ' ἤδη
ἀπειλῶ ἄλλοις, ὡς ἐλευθέρῳ τε ἔξεστί μοι καὶ ἀποδημεῖν καὶ
ἐπιδημεῖν· ὑπανίστανται δέ μοι ἤδη καὶ θάκων καὶ ὁδῶν
ἐξίστανται οἱ πλούσιοι. καὶ εἰμὶ νῦν μὲν τυράννῳ ἐοικώς, 32
τότε δὲ σαφῶς δοῦλος ἦν· καὶ τότε μὲν ἐγὼ φόρον ἀπέφερον
τῷ δήμῳ, νῦν δὲ ἡ πόλις τέλος φέρουσα τρέφει με. ἀλλὰ καὶ
Σωκράτει, ὅτε μὲν πλούσιος ἦν, ἐλοιδόρουν με ὅτι συνῆν, νῦν
δ' ἐπεὶ πένης γεγένημαι, οὐκέτι οὐδὲν μέλει οὐδενί. καὶ μὴν
ὅτε μέν γε πολλὰ εἶχον, ἀεί τι ἀπέβαλλον ἢ ὑπὸ τῆς πόλεως
ἢ ὑπὸ τῆς τύχης· νῦν δὲ ἀποβάλλω μὲν οὐδέν (οὐδὲ γὰρ ἔχω),
ἀεὶ δέ τι λήψεσθαι ἐλπίζω.

Οὐκοῦν, ἔφη ὁ Καλλίας, καὶ εὐχῇ μηδέποτε πλουτεῖν, καὶ 33
ἐάν τι ὄναρ ἀγαθὸν ἴδῃς, τοῖς ἀποτροπαίοις θύεις;

Μὰ Δία τοῦτο μέντοι, ἔφη, ἐγὼ οὐ ποιῶ, ἀλλὰ μάλα
φιλοκινδύνως ὑπομένω, ἄν ποθέν τι ἐλπίζω λήψεσθαι.

Ἀλλ' ἄγε δή, ἔφη ὁ Σωκράτης, σὺ αὖ λέγε ἡμῖν, ὦ 34
Ἀντίσθενες, πῶς οὕτω βραχέα ἔχων μέγα φρονεῖς ἐπὶ
πλούτῳ.

Ὅτι νομίζω, ὦ ἄνδρες, τοὺς ἀνθρώπους οὐκ ἐν τῷ οἴκῳ
τὸν πλοῦτον καὶ τὴν πενίαν ἔχειν ἀλλ' ἐν ταῖς ψυχαῖς. ὁρῶ 35
γὰρ πολλοὺς μὲν ἰδιώτας, οἳ πάνυ πολλὰ ἔχοντες χρήματα
οὕτω πένεσθαι ἡγοῦνται ὥστε πάντα μὲν πόνον, πάντα δὲ

all these witnesses, Kritoboulos, I forbid you to touch me until your chin has hair as long as your head has." And so they mixed it, in jest and in earnest.

29 "Your turn, Kharmides," said Kallias, "to say why you take pride in poverty."

"Well," he said, "there is agreement as follows, that it is better to be brave than fearful, to be free than a slave, to receive attentions than give them, and to be trusted by one's country than distrusted. 30 Now when I was a rich man in this town, first of all I was fearful that people might break into my house and take my property and do me some personal hurt. Second, I used to cultivate the sycophants, knowing that I was more likely to be hurt by them than vice versa. You see, I was always being required by the city to spend money, and I couldn't get away from the place, 31 whereas now, however, when I'm deprived of my foreign estates and I can't farm my Attic properties and my household goods have been sold, I lie full length and sleep sweetly, and I've become trusted by the city, and I don't get threats any more - I do that to others - and I can come and go like a free man. Rich men get up from their seats for me even, and make way for me in the streets. 32 I'm now a sort of tyrant, when once I was plainly a slave. In those days I used to pay my dues to the people, but now the state keeps me going with its contribution. Why, when I was rich they even abused me for associating with Sokrates, but now that I've become poor, no one bothers a scrap. What's more, when I had plenty, I was for ever losing some of it, because of the city or bad luck, whereas now I lose nothing because I've got nothing; instead, I expect to be for ever receiving."

33 "Do you actually pray then," asked Kallias, "never to be rich, and if you have a good dream do you sacrifice to the powers of aversion?"

"No by Zeus," he said, "that I don't do. But I do have a very foolhardy patience with my expectations of something turning up."

34 "Come on then, Antisthenes," said Sokrates. "Now you tell us how you think so highly of wealth when you own so little."

"It is because I think, gentlemen, that people don't keep wealth and poverty in their houses but in their hearts. 35 I see plenty of private citizens who have plenty of money but who are so poor in their own

κίνδυνον ὑποδύονται, ἐφ' ᾧ πλείονα κτήσονται, οἶδα δὲ καὶ (IV)
ἀδελφούς, οἳ τὰ ἴσα λαχόντες ὁ μὲν αὐτῶν τἀρκοῦντα ἔχει
καὶ περιττεύοντα τῆς δαπάνης, ὁ δὲ τοῦ παντὸς ἐνδεῖται·
αἰσθάνομαι δὲ καὶ τυράννους τινάς, οἳ οὕτω πεινῶσι 36
χρημάτων ὥστε ποιοῦσι πολὺ δεινότερα τῶν ἀπορωτάτων· δι'
ἔνδειαν μὲν γὰρ δήπου οἱ μὲν κλέπτουσιν, οἱ δὲ
τοιχωρυχοῦσιν, οἱ δὲ ἀνδραποδίζονται· τύραννοι δ' εἰσί τινες
οἳ ὅλους μὲν οἴκους ἀναιροῦσιν, ἀθρόους δ' ἀποκτείνουσι,
πολλάκις δὲ καὶ ὅλας πόλεις χρημάτων ἕνεκα ἐξ-
ανδραποδίζονται. τούτους μὲν οὖν ἔγωγε καὶ πάνυ οἰκτίρω 37
τῆς ἄγαν χαλεπῆς νόσου. ὅμοια γάρ μοι δοκοῦσι πάσχειν
ὥσπερ εἴ τις πολλὰ ἔχοι καὶ πολλὰ ἐσθίων μηδέποτε
ἐμπίμπλαιτο. ἐγὼ δὲ οὕτω μὲν πολλὰ ἔχω ὡς μόλις αὐτὰ καὶ
αὐτὸς εὑρίσκω· ὅμως δὲ περίεστί μοι καὶ ἐσθίοντι ἄχρι τοῦ
μὴ πεινῆν ἀφικέσθαι καὶ πίνοντι μέχρι τοῦ μὴ διψῆν καὶ
ἀμφιέννυσθαι ὥστε ἔξω μὲν μηδὲν μᾶλλον Καλλίου τούτου τοῦ
πλουσιωτάτου ῥιγοῦν· ἐπειδάν γε μὴν ἐν τῇ οἰκίᾳ γένωμαι, 38
πάνυ μὲν ἀλεεινοὶ χιτῶνες οἱ τοῖχοί μοι δοκοῦσιν εἶναι, πάνυ
δὲ παχεῖαι ἐφεστρίδες οἱ ὄροφοι, στρωμνήν γε μὴν οὕτως
ἀρκοῦσαν ἔχω ὥστ' ἔργον μέγ' ἐστὶ καὶ ἀνεγεῖραι. ἂν δέ
ποτε καὶ ἀφροδισιάσαι τὸ σῶμά μου δεηθῇ, οὕτω μοι τὸ
παρὸν ἀρκεῖ ὥστε αἷς ἂν προσέλθω ὑπερασπάζονταί με διὰ τὸ
μηδένα ἄλλον αὐταῖς ἐθέλειν προσιέναι. καὶ πάντα τοίνυν 39
ταῦτα οὕτως ἡδέα μοι δοκεῖ εἶναι ὡς μᾶλλον μὲν ἥδεσθαι
ποιῶν ἕκαστα αὐτῶν οὐκ ἂν εὐξαίμην, ἧττον δέ· οὕτω μοι
δοκεῖ ἔνια αὐτῶν ἡδίω εἶναι τοῦ συμφέροντος.

πλείστου δ' ἄξιον κτῆμα ἐν τῷ ἐμῷ πλούτῳ λογίζομαι 40
εἶναι ἐκεῖνο, ὅτι εἴ μού τις καὶ τὰ νῦν ὄντα παρέλοιτο,
οὐδὲν οὕτως ὁρῶ φαῦλον ἔργον ὁποῖον οὐκ ἀρκοῦσαν ἂν
τροφὴν ἐμοὶ παρέχοι. καὶ γὰρ ὅταν ἡδυπαθῆσαι βουληθῶ, οὐκ 41
ἐκ τῆς ἀγορᾶς τὰ τίμια ὠνοῦμαι (πολυτελῆ γὰρ γίγνεται),
ἀλλ' ἐκ τῆς ψυχῆς ταμιεύομαι. καὶ πολὺ πλέον διαφέρει πρὸς
ἡδονήν, ὅταν ἀναμείνας τὸ δεηθῆναι προσφέρωμαι ἢ ὅταν τινὶ
τῶν τιμίων χρῶμαι, ὥσπερ καὶ νῦν τῷδε τῷ Θασίῳ οἴνῳ
ἐντυχὼν οὐ διψῶν πίνω αὐτόν. ἀλλὰ μὴν καὶ πολὺ 42
δικαιοτέρους γε εἰκὸς εἶναι τοὺς εὐτέλειαν μᾶλλον ἢ
πολυχρηματίαν σκοποῦντας. οἷς γὰρ μάλιστα τὰ παρόντα
ἀρκεῖ ἥκιστα τῶν ἀλλοτρίων ὀρέγονται. ἄξιον δ' ἐννοῆσαι ὡς 43
καὶ ἐλευθερίους ὁ τοιοῦτος πλοῦτος παρέχεται. Σωκράτης τε

estimation that they undertake any task and any danger provided they can make more by it, and I know of brothers who receive an equal share of the inheritance, and one of them has plenty, more than he spends, while the other is short of everything. 36 I know of some tyrants, too, who are so hungry for money that they do things far worse than the poorest of men do, some turning to theft and some to burglary and some to the slave trade because of their neediness, presumably, and there are some tyrants who destroy whole households and kill the whole family and often enslave whole cities for the sake of money. 37 I really do pity these people; their disease must be so painful. I think they've got the same problem as a man who's got plenty and eats plenty and never gets to be full. I've got so much I can scarcely find it all myself; and yet the net result is that I can eat and reach a point of not being hungry, and I can drink and not be thirsty, and I can clothe myself so that I'm no colder out of doors than millionaire Kallias there, 38 and when I'm at home my walls are a warm tunic, my thatch is a thick mantle, and my bedding is so adequate that it's quite a task to rouse me. If ever my body wants sex, my present means are so adequate that because no one else is willing to approach the women I approach they greet me with enthusiasm. 39 All of this seems to me so pleasurable that in each bit of it I wouldn't pray for more pleasure but less: some of it seems so much more pleasurable than is appropriate.

40 "The most valuable piece in my wealth I reckon is this: even if my present possessions were taken away, there is no job I can see so awful that it wouldn't provide me with enough to live on. 41 When I want a fine time of it, I don't go to the market for its luxuries (they're expensive); I go instead to the cupboard of my soul. It makes a lot of difference to the enjoyment when I come to something after feeling the need for it, compared with the times when I get to taste something costly, like this Thasian wine, which I'm drinking now without being thirsty. 42 Frankly, people with an eye for thrift are likely to be much juster people than those with an eye for spending. The ones who are most content with what they've got are least excited by what belongs to others. 43 It is worth realising how wealth of this sort produces the people who are typically

γὰρ οὗτος παρ' οὗ ἐγὼ τοῦτον ἐκτησάμην οὔτ' ἀριθμῷ οὔτε (IV)
σταθμῷ ἐπήρκει μοι, ἀλλ' ὁπόσον ἐδυνάμην φέρεσθαι, τοσοῦτόν
μοι παρεδίδου· ἐγώ τε νῦν οὐδενὶ φθονῶ, ἀλλὰ πᾶσι τοῖς
φίλοις καὶ ἐπιδεικνύω τὴν ἀφθονίαν καὶ μεταδίδωμι τῷ
βουλομένῳ τοῦ ἐν τῇ ἐμῇ ψυχῇ πλούτου. καὶ μὴν καὶ τὸ 44
ἀβρότατόν γε κτῆμα, τὴν σχολὴν ἀεὶ ὁρᾶτέ μοι παροῦσαν,
ὥστε καὶ θεᾶσθαι τὰ ἀξιοθέατα καὶ ἀκούειν τὰ ἀξιάκουστα
καὶ ὃ πλείστου ἐγὼ τιμῶμαι, Σωκράτει σχολάζων συνδιημερεύειν. καὶ οὗτος δὲ οὐ τοὺς πλεῖστον ἀριθμοῦντας
χρυσίον θαυμάζει, ἀλλ' οἳ ἂν αὐτῷ ἀρέσκωσι τούτοις συνὼν
διατελεῖ. οὗτος μὲν οὖν οὕτως εἶπεν.

ὁ δὲ Καλλίας, Νὴ τὴν Ἥραν, ἔφη, τά τε ἄλλα ζηλῶ σε 45
τοῦ πλούτου καὶ ὅτι οὔτε ἡ πόλις σοι ἐπιτάττουσα ὡς δούλῳ
χρῆται οὔτε οἱ ἄνθρωποι, ἂν μὴ δανείσῃς, ὀργίζονται.

Ἀλλὰ μὰ Δί', ἔφη ὁ Νικήρατος, μὴ ζήλου· ἐγὼ γὰρ ἥξω
παρ' αὐτοῦ δανεισάμενος τὸ μηδενὸς προσδεῖσθαι· οὕτω δὲ
πεπαιδευμένος ὑπὸ Ὁμήρου ἀριθμεῖν
    ἕπτ' ἀπύρους τρίποδας, δέκα δὲ χρυσοῖο τάλαντα,
    αἴθωνας δὲ λέβητας ἐείκοσι, δώδεκα δ' ἵππους
σταθμῷ καὶ ἀριθμῷ, ὡς πλείστου πλούτου ἐπιθυμῶν οὐ
παύομαι· ἐξ ὧν ἴσως καὶ φιλοχρηματώτερός τισι δοκῶ εἶναι.
ἔνθα δὴ ἀνεγέλασαν ἅπαντες, νομίζοντες τὰ ὄντα εἰρηκέναι
αὐτόν.

ἐκ τούτου εἶπέ τις· Σὸν ἔργον, ὦ Ἑρμόγενες, λέγειν τε 46
τοὺς φίλους οἵτινές εἰσι καὶ ἐπιδεικνύναι ὡς μέγα τε
δύνανται καὶ σοῦ ἐπιμέλονται, ἵνα δοκῇς δικαίως ἐπ' αὐτοῖς
μέγα φρονεῖν.

Οὐκοῦν ὡς μὲν καὶ Ἕλληνες καὶ βάρβαροι τοὺς θεοὺς 47
ἡγοῦνται πάντα εἰδέναι τά τε ὄντα καὶ τὰ μέλλοντα εὔδηλον.
πᾶσαι γοῦν αἱ πόλεις καὶ πάντα τὰ ἔθνη διὰ μαντικῆς
ἐπερωτῶσι τοὺς θεοὺς τί τε χρὴ καὶ τί οὐ χρὴ ποιεῖν. καὶ
μὴν ὅτι νομίζομέν γε δύνασθαι αὐτοὺς καὶ εὖ καὶ κακῶς
ποιεῖν καὶ τοῦτο σαφές. πάντες γοῦν αἰτοῦνται τοὺς θεοὺς
τὰ μὲν φαῦλα ἀποτρέπειν, τἀγαθὰ δὲ διδόναι. οὗτοι τοίνυν οἱ 48
πάντα μὲν εἰδότες πάντα δὲ δυνάμενοι θεοὶ οὕτω μοι φίλοι
εἰσὶν ὥστε διὰ τὸ ἐπιμελεῖσθαί μου οὔποτε λήθω αὐτοὺς οὔτε
νυκτὸς οὔθ' ἡμέρας οὔθ' ὅποι ἂν ὁρμῶμαι οὔθ' ὅ τι ἂν μέλλω
πράττειν. διὰ δὲ τὸ προειδέναι καὶ ὅ τι ἐξ ἑκάστου
ἀποβήσεται σημαίνουσί μοι πέμποντες ἀγγέλους φήμας καὶ

free. Here's Sokrates, for instance, my source of this wealth: he never tried
to serve me by score or by weight, but just kept giving me as much as I
could carry away; and now here's me, envious of no one. Instead, I
display my generosity to all my friends and I share the wealth in my soul
with any who want it. 44 As for the most luxurious of my possessions,
that's the leisure you see me for ever enjoying: I can gaze at what's worth
gazing at, and I can listen to what's worth listening to, and (the thing that I
rate highest) I can spend all day at my leisure with Sokrates. He too fails
to be impressed by the people who can claim most gold; he spends all his
time with the people he likes." That was how Antisthenes spoke.

45 "By Hera," said Kallias, "I particularly envy you your wealth
because the city doesn't impose upon you and treat you as its slave, nor
do people get angry if you don't make them loans."

"No, don't go envying him by Zeus," said Nikeratos, "because I'm
going to be his debtor, for a loan of non-neediness; I've been taught by
Homer to count 'seven tripods unfired, ten talents of gold, twenty
gleaming ewers, and twelve horses' by weight and by score, and so I never
cease to want as much wealth as possible. Perhaps that's why some people
think I'm rather fond of money." At that, everybody burst into laughter,
reckoning he had told the truth.

46 Then someone said, "Your turn, Hermogenes, to say who your
friends are and to show how powerful they are and how they care for you,
so that your pride in them can appear justified."

47 "Greek and foreign belief in the omniscience of the gods about
things present and things to come is very plain. At any rate, all our
communities and all other peoples use oracles to ask the gods what
should and should not be done. It is clear, too, that we reckon they have
the power to do us good and to do us harm. Certainly, all people beseech
the gods to avert misery and to grant prosperity. 48 These omniscient and
omnipotent gods, then, are so much my friends that wherever I direct
myself and whatever I mean to do, night and day they never let me out of
their sight, because they care for me. Because of their foreknowledge of
all the consequences of everything, they tell me what I am and am not to

ἐνύπνια καὶ οἰωνοὺς ἅ τε δεῖ καὶ ἃ οὐ χρὴ ποιεῖν, οἷς ἐγὼ (IV) ὅταν μὲν πείθωμαι, οὐδέποτέ μοι μεταμέλει· ἤδη δέ ποτε καὶ ἀπιστήσας ἐκολάσθην.

καὶ ὁ Σωκράτης εἶπεν· ᾽Αλλὰ τούτων μὲν οὐδὲν ἄπιστον. 49 ἐκεῖνο μέντοι ἔγωγε ἡδέως ἂν πυθοίμην, πῶς αὐτοὺς θεραπεύων οὕτω φίλους ἔχεις.

Ναὶ μὰ τὸν Δί᾽, ἔφη ὁ Ἑρμογένης, καὶ μάλα εὐτελῶς. ἐπαινῶ τε γὰρ αὐτοὺς οὐδὲν δαπανῶν, ὧν τε διδόασιν ἀεὶ αὖ παρέχομαι, εὐφημῶ τε ὅσα ἂν δύνωμαι καὶ ἐφ᾽ οἷς ἂν αὐτοὺς μάρτυρας ποιήσωμαι ἑκὼν οὐδὲν ψεύδομαι.

Νὴ Δί᾽, ἔφη ὁ Σωκράτης, εἰ ἄρα τοιοῦτος ὢν φίλους αὐτοὺς ἔχεις, καὶ οἱ θεοί, ὡς ἔοικε, καλοκἀγαθίᾳ ἥδονται. οὗτος μὲν δὴ ὁ λόγος οὕτως ἐσπουδαιολογήθη. 50

ἐπειδὴ δὲ εἰς τὸν Φίλιππον ἧκον, ἠρώτων αὐτὸν τί ὁρῶν ἐν τῇ γελωτοποιίᾳ μέγα ἐπ᾽ αὐτῇ φρονοίη.

Οὐ γὰρ ἄξιον, ἔφη, ὁπότε γε πάντες εἰδότες ὅτι γελωτοποιός εἰμι, ὅταν μέν τι ἀγαθὸν ἔχωσι, παρακαλοῦσί με ἐπὶ ταῦτα προθύμως, ὅταν δέ τι κακὸν λάβωσι, φεύγουσιν ἀμεταστρεπτί, φοβούμενοι μὴ καὶ ἄκοντες γελάσωσι;

καὶ ὁ Νικήρατος εἶπε· Νὴ Δία, σὺ τοίνυν δικαίως μέγα 51 φρονεῖς. ἐμοὶ γὰρ αὖ τῶν φίλων οἳ μὲν εὖ πράττοντες ἐκποδὼν ἀπέρχονται, οἱ δ᾽ ἂν κακόν τι λάβωσι, γενεαλογοῦσι τὴν συγγένειαν καὶ οὐδέποτέ μου ἀπολείπονται.

Εἶεν· σὺ δὲ δή, ἔφη ὁ Χαρμίδης, ὦ Συρακόσιε, ἐπὶ τῷ 52 μέγα φρονεῖς; ἢ δῆλον ὅτι ἐπὶ τῷ παιδί;

Μὰ τὸν Δί᾽, ἔφη, οὐ μὲν δή· ἀλλὰ καὶ δέδοικα περὶ αὐτοῦ ἰσχυρῶς. αἰσθάνομαι γάρ τινας ἐπιβουλεύοντας διαφθεῖραι αὐτόν.

καὶ ὁ Σωκράτης ἀκούσας, Ἡράκλεις, ἔφη, τί τοσοῦτον 53 νομίζοντες ἠδικῆσθαι ὑπὸ τοῦ σοῦ παιδὸς ὥστε ἀποκτεῖναι αὐτὸν βούλεσθαι;

᾽Αλλ᾽ οὗτοι, ἔφη, ἀποκτεῖναι βούλονται, ἀλλὰ πεῖσαι αὐτὸν συγκαθεύδειν αὐτοῖς.

Σὺ δ᾽, ὡς ἔοικας, εἰ τοῦτο γένοιτο, νομίζεις ἂν διαφθαρῆναι αὐτόν;

Ναὶ μὰ Δί᾽, ἔφη, παντάπασί γε.

Οὐδ᾽ αὐτὸς ἄρ᾽, ἔφη, συγκαθεύδεις αὐτῷ; 54

Νὴ Δί᾽ ὅλας γε καὶ πάσας τὰς νύκτας.

do by sending me prophecies, omens and dreams as messages, and when I try to heed them I'm never sorry; whereas for acts of disobedience I've been punished."

49 "There's nothing to disbelieve in that," said Sokrates, "but I would like to know how you cultivate them so as to keep them friends."

"Very economically by Zeus," said Hermogenes. "I spend no money in giving them praise; their gifts to me I always return in part; I avoid ill words as much as I can; when I call them to witness I tell no lie wittingly."

"By Zeus," said Sokrates, "if you can keep them your friends by behaving like that, then it seems that the gods also take pleasure in a gentleman." 50 And that is how that serious conversation went.

When they arrived at Philippos, they asked him what he saw to be proud of in causing laughter.

"You mean I shouldn't be?" he said. "After all, everybody knows that I'm a laughter-maker, and that's why they press me to come along when they've got something good going, while they run away without a backward glance when they've got trouble, for fear of bursting into laughter despite themselves!"

51 "By Zeus," said Nikeratos, "then you're right to be proud. In my case, any of my friends who are prospering keep well out of my way, but the ones who are in trouble trace out their pedigree of kinship and never let me out of their sight."

52 "All right," said Kharmides. "What about you, man from Syracuse? What are you proud of? Your boy: that must be obvious."

"By Zeus no," he said. "though I am worried about him, very much so, because I can see that there are people plotting his ruin."

53 Sokrates had heard him. "Herakles," he said, "what great evil do they think they've been done by your boy to want to kill him?"

"Oh, they don't want to kill him," he said. "They want to get him to share their beds."

"If that were to happen, you think he'd be ruined, it seems?"

"Yes by Zeus," he said, "absolutely."

54 "Then you don't sleep with him either, of course?"

"By Zeus I do, all night and every night."

Νὴ τὴν Ἥραν, ἔφη ὁ Σωκράτης, εὐτύχημά γέ σου μέγα (IV)
τὸ τὸν χρῶτα τοιοῦτον φῦναι ἔχοντα ὥστε μόνον μὴ διαφθείρειν τοὺς συγκαθεύδοντας. ὥστε σοί γε εἰ μὴ ἐπ’ ἄλλῳ
ἀλλ’ ἐπὶ τῷ χρωτὶ ἄξιον μέγα φρονεῖν.

Ἀλλὰ μὰ Δί’, ἔφη, οὐκ ἐπὶ τούτῳ μέγα φρονῶ.   55

Ἀλλ’ ἐπὶ τῷ μήν;

Ἐπὶ νὴ Δία τοῖς ἄφροσιν. οὗτοι γὰρ τὰ ἐμὰ νευρόσπαστα θεώμενοι τρέφουσί με.

Ταῦτ’ ἄρ’, ἔφη ὁ Φίλιππος, καὶ πρώην ἐγώ σου ἤκουον
εὐχομένου πρὸς τοὺς θεοὺς ὅπου ἂν ᾖς διδόναι καρποῦ μὲν
ἀφθονίαν, φρενῶν δὲ ἀφορίαν.

Εἶεν, ἔφη ὁ Καλλίας· σὺ δὲ δή, ὦ Σώκρατες, τί ἔχεις 56
εἰπεῖν ὡς ἄξιόν σοί ἐστι μέγα φρονεῖν ἐφ’ ᾖ εἶπας οὕτως
ἀδόξῳ οὔσῃ τέχνῃ;

καὶ ὃς εἶπεν· Ὁμολογησώμεθα πρῶτον ποῖά ἐστιν ἔργα
τοῦ μαστροποῦ· καὶ ὅσα ἂν ἐρωτῶ, μὴ ὀκνεῖτε ἀποκρίνεσθαι,
ἵνα εἰδῶμεν ὅσα ἂν συνομολογῶμεν. καὶ ὑμῖν οὕτω δοκεῖ; ἔφη.

Πάνυ μὲν οὖν, ἔφασαν. ὡς δ’ ἅπαξ εἶπαν Πάνυ μὲν οὖν,
τοῦτο πάντες ἐκ τοῦ λοιποῦ ἀπεκρίναντο.

Οὐκοῦν ἀγαθοῦ μέν, ἔφη, ὑμῖν δοκεῖ μαστροποῦ ἔργον 57
εἶναι ἢν ἂν ᾖ ὃν ἂν μαστροπεύῃ ἀρέσκοντα τοῦτον ἀποδεικνύναι οἷς ἂν συνῇ;

Πάνυ μὲν οὖν, ἔφασαν.

Οὐκοῦν ἓν μέν τί ἐστιν εἰς τὸ ἀρέσκειν ἐκ τοῦ
πρέπουσαν ἔχειν σχέσιν καὶ τριχῶν καὶ ἐσθῆτος;

Πάνυ μὲν οὖν, ἔφασαν.

Οὐκοῦν καὶ τόδε ἐπιστάμεθα, ὅτι ἔστιν ἀνθρώπῳ τοῖς 58
αὐτοῖς ὄμμασι καὶ φιλικῶς καὶ ἐχθρῶς πρός τινας βλέπειν;

Πάνυ μὲν οὖν.

Τί δέ, τῇ αὐτῇ φωνῇ ἔστι καὶ αἰδημόνως καὶ θρασέως
φθέγγεσθαι;

Πάνυ μὲν οὖν.

Τί δέ, λόγοι οὐκ εἰσὶ μέν τινες ἀπεχθανόμενοι, εἰσὶ δέ
τινες οἳ πρὸς φιλίαν ἄγουσι;

Πάνυ μὲν οὖν.

Οὐκοῦν τούτων ὁ ἀγαθὸς μαστροπὸς τὰ συμφέροντα εἰς 59
τὸ ἀρέσκειν διδάσκοι ἄν;

Πάνυ μὲν οὖν.

"By Hera," said Sokrates, "it's a great piece of luck on your part to be born with the sort of skin that keeps you alone from ruining your bedfellows. In your case you ought at least to be proud of your skin, if nothing else."

55 "By Zeus," he said, "that's not what I'm proud of."

"Well, what then?"

"Idiots by Zeus! They make me my living by watching my puppets."

"So that's what I heard you praying to the gods for the other day," said Philippos, "that wherever you were they'd give you abundance of harvest and dearth of wits."

56 "All right," said Kallias. "Sokrates: what can you say to justify your pride in the skill you mentioned when it's such an unseemly one?"

"Let us first agree," he said, "what sort of things a procurer does. Do not shrink from answering any of my questions; then we can know how much we do agree on. Is that all right by you?" he said.

"Absolutely," they said. And when they had once said Absolutely, that was the universal answer thereafter.

57 "Is it your view then," he said, "that it's the business of a good procurer, whoever he procures, female or male, to present someone acceptable to the customers?"

"Absolutely," they said.

"One contribution to acceptability comes from having an attractive hair-do and clothes?"

"Absolutely," they said.

58 "Do we understand also that it's possible to look at people in a friendly way and in a hostile way with the same set of eyes?"

"Absolutely."

"And that it's possible to speak both politely and aggressively with the same set of vocal organs?"

"Absolutely."

"And are there not some things said which incur hatred and some which are conducive to friendliness?"

"Absolutely."

59 "So the good procurer would explain which of these would help towards acceptability?"

"Absolutely."

62

Ἀμείνων δ' ἂν εἴη, ἔφη, ὁ ἑνὶ δυνάμενος ἀρεστοὺς ποιεῖν **(IV)**
ἢ ὅστις καὶ πολλοῖς;

ἐνταῦθα μέντοι ἐσχίσθησαν, καὶ οἱ μὲν εἶπον Δῆλον ὅτι
ὅστις πλείστοις, οἱ δὲ Πάνυ μὲν οὖν.

ὁ δ' εἰπὼν ὅτι καὶ τοῦτο ὁμολογεῖται ἔφη· Εἰ δέ τις καὶ 60
ὅλῃ τῇ πόλει ἀρέσκοντας δύναιτο ἀποδεικνύναι, οὐχ οὗτος
παντελῶς ἂν ἤδη ἀγαθὸς μαστροπὸς εἴη;

Σαφῶς γε νὴ Δία, πάντες εἶπον.

Οὐκοῦν εἴ τις τοιούτους δύναιτο ἐξεργάζεσθαι ὧν
προστατοίη, δικαίως ἂν μέγα φρονοίη ἐπὶ τῇ τέχνῃ καὶ
δικαίως ἂν πολὺν μισθὸν λαμβάνοι;

ἐπεὶ δὲ καὶ ταῦτα πάντες συνωμολόγουν, Τοιοῦτος 61
μέντοι, ἔφη, μοι δοκεῖ Ἀντισθένης εἶναι οὗτος.

καὶ ὁ Ἀντισθένης, Ἐμοί, ἔφη, παραδίδως, ὦ Σώκρατες,
τὴν τέχνην;

Ναὶ μὰ Δί', ἔφη. ὁρῶ γάρ σε καὶ τὴν ἀκόλουθον ταύτης
πάνυ ἐξειργασμένον.

Τίνα ταύτην;

Τὴν προαγωγείαν, ἔφη.

καὶ ὃς μάλα ἀχθεσθεὶς ἐπήρετο· Καὶ τί μοι σύνοισθα, ὦ 62
Σώκρατες, τοιοῦτον εἰργασμένῳ;

Οἶδα μέν, ἔφη, σε Καλλίαν τουτονὶ προαγωγεύσαντα τῷ
σοφῷ Προδίκῳ, ὅτε ἑώρας τοῦτον μὲν φιλοσοφίας ἐρῶντα,
ἐκεῖνον δὲ χρημάτων δεόμενον· οἶδα δέ σε Ἱππίᾳ τῷ Ἠλείῳ,
παρ' οὗ οὗτος καὶ τὸ μνημονικὸν ἔμαθεν· ἀφ' οὗ δὴ καὶ
ἐρωτικώτερος γεγένηται διὰ τὸ ὅ τι ἂν καλὸν ἴδῃ μηδέποτε
ἐπιλανθάνεσθαι. ἔναγχος δὲ δήπου καὶ πρὸς ἐμὲ ἐπαινῶν τὸν 63
Ἡρακλεώτην ξένον ἐπεί με ἐποίησας ἐπιθυμεῖν αὐτοῦ, συν-
έστησάς μοι αὐτόν. καὶ χάριν μέντοι σοι ἔχω· πάνυ γὰρ
καλὸς κἀγαθὸς δοκεῖ μοι εἶναι. Αἰσχύλον δὲ τὸν Φλειάσιον
πρὸς ἐμὲ ἐπαινῶν καὶ ἐμὲ πρὸς ἐκεῖνον οὐχ οὕτω διέθηκας
ὥστε διὰ τοὺς σοὺς λόγους ἐρῶντες ἐκυνοδρομοῦμεν ἀλλήλους
ζητοῦντες; ταῦτα οὖν ὁρῶν δυνάμενόν σε ποιεῖν ἀγαθὸν 64
νομίζω προαγωγὸν εἶναι. ὁ γὰρ οἷός τε ὢν γιγνώσκειν τε
τοὺς ὠφελίμους αὐτοῖς καὶ τούτους δυνάμενος ποιεῖν
ἐπιθυμεῖν ἀλλήλων, οὗτος ἄν μοι δοκεῖ καὶ πόλεις δύνασθαι
φίλας ποιεῖν καὶ γάμους ἐπιτηδείους συνάγειν, καὶ πολλοῦ ἂν
ἄξιος εἶναι καὶ πόλεσι καὶ φίλοις καὶ συμμάχοις κεκτῆσθαι.

"Would the better procurer," he asked, "be one who can make people acceptable to one particular customer or to many?"

At this point they split. Some said, "To lots, obviously," but others said "Absolutely."

60 Saying that that point was also agreed, Sokrates asked, "If someone could produce people acceptable to the whole city, wouldn't that person be right away the perfect procurer?"

"Plainly yes by Zeus," they all said.

"So, anyone able to turn the people he controlled into something like that would rightly be proud of his skill, and he would rightly earn big money?"

61 When they were all in agreement on that too, "That's the sort of person," he said, "that I think Antisthenes there is."

"Are you attributing this skill to me, Sokrates?" said Antisthenes.

"I am by Zeus," he said, "because I see that you have also perfected the skill that follows it up."

"What's that?"

"Pandering," he said.

62 Antisthenes was very cross and asked, "And what do you know that I've ever done like that, Sokrates?"

"I know you were pander for Kallias there and the wise Prodikos when you saw the one passionate for learning and the other in need of money, and I know you did it for Hippias of Elis, who taught him his memory system, and ever since then Kallias has become even more passionate, because he never forgets anything he sees that's good-looking. 63 The other day, if I remember, you were singing me the praises of your visitor from Herakleia, and when you'd got me excited about him you put him right beside me. Not but what I'm grateful: he's a real gentleman, I reckon. And there's Aiskhylos of Phleious: didn't you praise him to me and me to him so that we went looking for each other like bloodhounds, impassioned by what you said? 64 It is seeing your ability to do that which makes me consider you a good pander. The man with the skill to recognise people who can use each other and with the power to make them want each other could in my view make friendships between cities, and he could broker acceptable marriages, and he'd be very much worth getting hold of for communities and friends and allies. Yet you were

σὺ δὲ ὡς κακῶς ἀκούσας ὅτι ἀγαθόν σε ἔφην προαγωγὸν εἶναι, ὠργίσθης.

Ἀλλὰ μὰ Δί᾽, ἔφη, οὐ νῦν. ἐὰν γὰρ ταῦτα δύνωμαι, σεσαγμένος δὴ παντάπασι πλούτου τὴν ψυχὴν ἔσομαι. καὶ αὕτη μὲν δὴ ἡ περίοδος τῶν λόγων ἀπετελέσθη.

Ὁ δὲ Καλλίας ἔφη· Σὺ δὲ δή, ὦ Κριτόβουλε, εἰς τὸν περὶ V τοῦ κάλλους ἀγῶνα πρὸς Σωκράτην οὐκ ἀνθίστασαι;

Νὴ Δί᾽, ἔφη ὁ Σωκράτης, ἴσως γὰρ εὐδοκιμοῦντα τὸν μαστροπὸν παρὰ τοῖς κριταῖς ὁρᾷ.

Ἀλλ᾽ ὅμως, ἔφη ὁ Κριτόβουλος, οὐκ ἀναδύομαι· ἀλλὰ 2 δίδασκε, εἴ τι ἔχεις σοφόν, ὡς καλλίων εἶ ἐμοῦ. μόνον, ἔφη, τὸν λαμπτῆρα ἐγγὺς προσενεγκάτω.

Εἰς ἀνάκρισιν τοίνυν σε, ἔφη, πρῶτον τῆς δίκης καλοῦμαι· ἀλλ᾽ ἀποκρίνου.

Σὺ δέ γε ἐρώτα. 3

Πότερον οὖν ἐν ἀνθρώπῳ μόνον νομίζεις τὸ καλὸν εἶναι ἢ καὶ ἐν ἄλλῳ τινί;

Ἐγὼ μὲν ναὶ μὰ Δί᾽, ἔφη, καὶ ἐν ἵππῳ καὶ βοῒ καὶ ἐν ἀψύχοις πολλοῖς. οἶδα γοῦν οὖσαν καὶ ἀσπίδα καλὴν καὶ ξίφος καὶ δόρυ.

Καὶ πῶς, ἔφη, οἷόν τε ταῦτα μηδὲν ὅμοια ὄντα ἀλλήλοις 4 πάντα καλὰ εἶναι;

Ἂν νὴ Δί᾽, ἔφη, πρὸς τὰ ἔργα ὧν ἕνεκα ἕκαστα κτώμεθα εὖ εἰργασμένα ᾖ ἢ εὖ πεφυκότα πρὸς ἃ ἂν δεώμεθα, καὶ ταῦτ᾽, ἔφη ὁ Κριτόβουλος, καλά.

Οἶσθα οὖν, ἔφη, ὀφθαλμῶν τίνος ἕνεκα δεόμεθα; 5

Δῆλον, ἔφη, ὅτι τοῦ ὁρᾶν.

Οὕτω μὲν τοίνυν ἤδη οἱ ἐμοὶ ὀφθαλμοὶ καλλίονες ἂν τῶν σῶν εἴησαν.

Πῶς δή;

Ὅτι οἱ μὲν σοὶ τὸ κατ᾽ εὐθὺ μόνον ὁρῶσιν, οἱ δὲ ἐμοὶ καὶ τὸ ἐκ πλαγίου διὰ τὸ ἐπιπόλαιοι εἶναι.

Λέγεις σύ, ἔφη, καρκίνον εὐοφθαλμότατον εἶναι τῶν ζῴων;

Πάντως δήπου, ἔφη· ἐπεὶ καὶ πρὸς ἰσχὺν τοὺς ὀφθαλμοὺς ἄριστα πεφυκότας ἔχει.

Εἶεν, ἔφη, τῶν δὲ ῥινῶν ποτέρα καλλίων, ἡ σὴ ἢ ἡ ἐμή; 6

Ἐγὼ μέν, ἔφη, οἶμαι τὴν ἐμήν, εἴπερ γε τοῦ ὀσφραίνεσθαι ἕνεκ᾽ ἐνεποίησαν ἡμῖν ῥῖνας οἱ θεοί. οἱ μὲν γὰρ

cross, as if I'd slandered you in saying you were a good pander."

"By Zeus," he said, "I'm not now. If that's my power, my heart will be absolutely loaded with wealth." And that round of talk came to an end.

V Kallias spoke. "Kritoboulos, aren't you taking Sokrates on in your beauty competition?"

"By Zeus he isn't," said Sokrates; "he can probably see that the pimp is in good favour with the judges!"

2 "Nevertheless," said Kritoboulos, "I'm not withdrawing. You use your cleverness and prove that you're more good-looking than me. Only," he added, "have the lamp brought up close."

"In that case," said he, "as first item in the trial I summon you for preliminary examination; you just answer the questions."

3 "You get on and ask them!"

"Do you consider that good exists only in man, or in other things too?"

"I certainly do by Zeus," he said; "I recognise it in horses and cows and in plenty of inanimate things. I recognise the existence of a good shield and sword and spear, at any rate."

4 "And how is it possible," he said, "for these things that have nothing in common with each other all to be good?"

"If they are well made for the tasks we employ each one for, or if they answer well naturally to what we need them for, then of course they're good," said Kritoboulos.

5 "You know then," he said, "what we need eyes for?"

"Plainly to see," he said.

"In that case my eyes are better than yours already."

"How come?"

"Because your eyes only look straight forward, whereas mine can look sideways as well, because they protrude."

"You mean," he said, "that a crab has the best eyes of any living thing?"

"Of course I do," he said, "because its eyes are the best set up by nature for effectiveness."

6 "All right," he said. "Which of our noses is better, yours or mine?"

"In my view mine," he said, "on the assumption of course that the gods put noses on us to smell with. Now your nostrils look down to the

σοὶ μυκτῆρες εἰς γῆν ὁρῶσιν, οἱ δὲ ἐμοὶ ἀναπέπτανται, ὥστε τὰς πάντοθεν ὀσμὰς προσδέχεσθαι.

Τὸ δὲ δὴ σιμὸν τῆς ῥινὸς πῶς τοῦ ὀρθοῦ κάλλιον; ΅Οτι, ἔφη, οὐκ ἀντιφράττει, ἀλλ' ἐᾷ εὐθὺς τὰς ὄψεις ὁρᾶν ἃ ἂν βούλωνται· ἡ δὲ ὑψηλὴ ῥὶς ὥσπερ ἐπηρεάζουσα διατετείχικε τὰ ὄμματα.

Τοῦ γε μὴν στόματος, ἔφη ὁ Κριτόβουλος, ὑφίεμαι. εἰ 7 γὰρ τοῦ ἀποδάκνειν ἕνεκα πεποίηται, πολὺ ἂν σὺ μεῖζον ἢ ἐγὼ ἀποδάκοις. διὰ δὲ τὸ παχέα ἔχειν τὰ χείλη οὐκ οἴει καὶ μαλακώτερόν σου ἔχειν τὸ φίλημα;

΅Εοικα, ἔφη, ἐγὼ κατὰ τὸν σὸν λόγον καὶ τῶν ὄνων αἴσχιον τὸ στόμα ἔχειν. ἐκεῖνο δὲ οὐδὲν τεκμήριον λογίζῃ, ὡς ἐγὼ σοῦ καλλίων εἰμί, ὅτι καὶ Ναΐδες θεοὶ οὖσαι τοὺς Σειληνοὺς ἐμοὶ ὁμοιοτέρους τίκτουσιν ἢ σοί;

καὶ ὁ Κριτόβουλος, Οὐκέτι, ἔφη, ἔχω πρὸς σὲ ἀντιλέγειν, 8 ἀλλὰ διαφερόντων, ἔφη, τὰς ψήφους, ἵνα ὡς τάχιστα εἰδῶ ὅ τι με χρὴ παθεῖν ἢ ἀποτεῖσαι. μόνον, ἔφη, κρυφῇ φερόντων· δέδοικα γὰρ τὸν σὸν καὶ Ἀντισθένους πλοῦτον μή με καταδυναστεύσῃ.

ἡ μὲν δὴ παῖς καὶ ὁ παῖς κρύφα ἀνέφερον. ὁ δὲ 9 Σωκράτης ἐν τούτῳ διέπραττε τόν τε λύχνον ἀντιπροσενεγκεῖν τῷ Κριτοβούλῳ, ὡς μὴ ἐξαπατηθείησαν οἱ κριταί, καὶ τῷ νικήσαντι μὴ ταινίας ἀλλὰ φιλήματα ἀναδήματα παρὰ τῶν κριτῶν γενέσθαι. ἐπεὶ δὲ ἐξέπεσον αἱ ψῆφοι καὶ ἐγένοντο 10 πᾶσαι σὺν Κριτοβούλῳ, Παπαῖ, ἔφη ὁ Σωκράτης, οὐχ ὅμοιον ἔοικε τὸ σὸν ἀργύριον, ὦ Κριτόβουλε, τῷ Καλλίου εἶναι. τὸ μὲν γὰρ τούτου δικαιοτέρους ποιεῖ, τὸ δὲ σὸν ὥσπερ τὸ πλεῖστον διαφθείρειν ἱκανόν ἐστι καὶ δικαστὰς καὶ κριτάς.

Ἐκ δὲ τούτου οἱ μὲν τὰ νικητήρια φιλήματα ἀπο- VI λαμβάνειν τὸν Κριτόβουλον ἐκέλευον, οἱ δὲ τὸν κύριον πείθειν, οἱ δὲ καὶ ἄλλα ἔσκωπτον. ὁ δὲ Ἑρμογένης κἀνταῦθα ἐσιώπα. καὶ ὁ Σωκράτης ὀνομάσας αὐτόν, ΅Εχοις ἄν, ἔφη, ὦ Ἑρμόγενες, εἰπεῖν ἡμῖν τί ἐστι παροινία;

καὶ ὃς ἀπεκρίνατο· Εἰ μὲν ὅ τι ἐστὶν ἐρωτᾷς, οὐκ οἶδα· τὸ μέντοι μοι δοκοῦν εἴποιμ' ἄν.

Ἀλλ', ὃ δοκεῖ, τοῦτ', ἔφη.

Τὸ τοίνυν παρ' οἶνον λυπεῖν τοὺς συνόντας, τοῦτ' ἐγὼ 2 κρίνω παροινίαν.

ground, whereas mine are flared, so as to take in smells from everywhere."

"But how is a snubness of nose better than straightness?"

"Because it erects no barrier," he said, "and lets the eyes see what they want direct. A high-bridged nose is like a wall, jealously keeping the eyes apart."

7 "As for the mouth," said Kritoboulos, "I surrender. If it was made for biting things off, you'd bite off a much bigger bit than I would. And you imagine your kissing is softer, don't you, because of your thick lips?"

"By your argument," said he, "I apparently have an uglier mouth than donkeys do. Are you calculating that it's no evidence at all of my superior good looks that even the Naiads, who are divine, produce Seilenoi who are more like me than you?"

8 "I cannot argue against you any longer," said Kritoboulos. "Let them cast their votes, so that I can know as quickly as possible what my punishment or fine is. Only let them vote," he said, "in secret. I'm fearful in case that wealth of yours and of Antisthenes may countervail against me."

9 The boy and the girl then voted in secret, and while they did so, Sokrates tried to arrange for the lamp to be put close in front of Kritoboulos, so that the judges should not be misled, and also for the winner to receive from the judges not ribbons but kisses as garlands. 10 When the votes were emptied out, and they were all for Kritoboulos, Sokrates said, "Oh dear! It looks as though your money, Kritoboulos, is not the same as Kallias'. His makes men better, whereas yours has the ability of most money to corrupt both jurymen and other judges."

VI Next, some of them urged Kritoboulos to take his due of victory kisses, and others told him to get the guardian's consent, and there were various other jests. Hermogenes, however, preserved a silence even then. Sokrates picked him out by name. "Hermogenes," he said, "could you tell us what overindulgence is?"

He replied, "If you are asking what it is, I don't know. But I could tell you what I think it is."

"Well, tell us that," he said.

2 "I adjudge overindulgence to be the annoying of company because of drink."

Οἶσθ᾽ οὖν, ἔφη, ὅτι καὶ σὺ νῦν ἡμᾶς λυπεῖς σιωπῶν;   (VI)
Ἦ καὶ ὅταν λέγητ᾽; ἔφη.

Οὐκ ἀλλ᾽ ὅταν διαλίπωμεν.

Ἦ οὖν λέληθέ σε ὅτι μεταξὺ τοῦ ὑμᾶς λέγειν οὐδ᾽ ἂν τρίχα, μὴ ὅτι λόγον ἄν τις παρείρειε;

καὶ ὁ Σωκράτης, Ὦ Καλλία, ἔχοις ἄν τι, ἔφη, ἀνδρὶ 3 ἐλεγχομένῳ βοηθῆσαι;

Ἔγωγ᾽, ἔφη. ὅταν γὰρ ὁ αὐλὸς φθέγγηται, παντάπασι σιωπῶμεν.

καὶ ὁ Ἑρμογένης, Ἦ οὖν βούλεσθε, ἔφη, ὥσπερ Νικόστρατος ὁ ὑποκριτὴς τετράμετρα πρὸς τὸν αὐλὸν κατέλεγεν, οὕτω καὶ ὑπὸ τοῦ αὐλοῦ ὑμῖν διαλέγωμαι;

καὶ ὁ Σωκράτης, Πρὸς τῶν θεῶν, ἔφη, Ἑρμόγενες, οὕτω 4 ποίει. οἶμαι γάρ, ὥσπερ ἡ ᾠδὴ ἡδίων πρὸς τὸν αὐλόν, οὕτω καὶ τοὺς σοὺς λόγους ἡδύνεσθαι ἄν τι ὑπὸ τῶν φθόγγων, ἄλλως τε καὶ εἰ μορφάζοις, ὥσπερ ἡ αὐλητρίς, καὶ σὺ πρὸς τὰ λεγόμενα.

καὶ ὁ Καλλίας ἔφη· Ὅταν οὖν ὁ Ἀντισθένης ὅδ᾽ ἐλέγχῃ 5 τινὰ ἐν τῷ συμποσίῳ, τί ἔσται τὸ αὔλημα;

καὶ ὁ Ἀντισθένης εἶπε· Τῷ μὲν ἐλεγχομένῳ οἶμαι ἄν, ἔφη, πρέπειν συριγμόν.

Τοιούτων δὲ λόγων ὄντων ὡς ἑώρα ὁ Συρακόσιος τῶν μὲν 6 αὐτοῦ ἐπιδειγμάτων ἀμελοῦντας, ἀλλήλοις δὲ ἡδομένους, φθονῶν τῷ Σωκράτει εἶπεν· Ἆρα σύ, ὦ Σώκρατες, ὁ φροντιστὴς ἐπικαλούμενος;

Οὐκοῦν κάλλιον, ἔφη, ἢ εἰ ἀφρόντιστος ἐκαλούμην.

Εἰ μή γε ἐδόκεις τῶν μετεώρων φροντιστὴς εἶναι.

Οἶσθα οὖν, ἔφη ὁ Σωκράτης, μετεωρότερόν τι τῶν θεῶν;   7

Ἀλλ᾽ οὐ μὰ Δί᾽, ἔφη, οὐ τούτων σε λέγουσιν ἐπιμελεῖσθαι, ἀλλὰ τῶν ἀνωφελεστάτων.

Οὐκοῦν καὶ οὕτως ἄν, ἔφη, θεῶν ἐπιμελοίμην· ἄνωθεν μέν γε ὕοντες ὠφελοῦσιν, ἄνωθεν δὲ φῶς παρέχουσιν. εἰ δὲ ψυχρὰ λέγω, σὺ αἴτιος, ἔφη, πράγματά μοι παρέχων.

Ταῦτα μέν, ἔφη, ἔα· ἀλλ᾽ εἰπέ μοι πόσους ψύλλα πόδας 8 ἐμοῦ ἀπέχει. ταῦτα γάρ σέ φασι γεωμετρεῖν.

καὶ ὁ Ἀντισθένης εἶπε· Σὺ μέντοι δεινὸς εἶ, ὦ Φίλιππε, εἰκάζειν· οὐ δοκεῖ σοι ὁ ἀνὴρ οὗτος λοιδορεῖσθαι βουλομένῳ ἐοικέναι;

Ναὶ μὰ τὸν Δί᾽, ἔφη, καὶ ἄλλοις γε πολλοῖς.

"Do you realise that because of your silence you are annoying us here?"

"Even when you are all talking?" he said.

"No: when we leave off."

"So you've really failed to see that not even a hair, never mind a word, could be inserted into your talk?"

3 "Kallias," said Sokrates, "can you bring any help to a man who's losing the argument?"

"I can," he said. "When the aulos plays, we are totally silent."

"So you people really want me to converse with you to the aulos," said Hermogenes, "like Nikostratos the actor reciting tetrameters to its sound?"

4 "By the gods," said Sokrates, "try it, Hermogenes! A song is sweeter to the sound of an aulos, and I think its notes would give a little sweetness to your conversation, especially if you postured as well, like the aulos-girl, to fit what you were saying."

5 "So," said Kallias, "when Antisthenes here starts examining someone in our symposium, what shall the aulos-accompaniment be then?"

"For my victim," said Antisthenes, "I think the appropriate noise would be whistling."

6 As the talk went on like this, and the Syracusan realised that people were ignoring what he had to show and were enjoying their own company instead, in chagrin he said to Sokrates, "Are you the so-called thinker?"

"It's better than if they called me unthinking," he said.

"Not unless you appeared to be a higher thinker."

7 "Do you know anything higher than the gods?" asked Sokrates.

"But the gods are what they say you're not interested in, by Zeus! They say you're interested in utterly futile stuff."

"The gods would be my interest even in those circumstances: they do good by raining from above, and they provide light from above. If I'm being boring," he said, "that's your fault for being a nuisance."

8 "Never mind that," said he. "Tell me instead how many feet away from me a flea is. That's your surveying skill, so they say."

"Philippos," said Antisthenes, "you're good at comparisons. Don't you reckon this fellow here is like someone trying to be rude?"

"Yes by Zeus," said Philippos, "and a lot of others reckon so too."

Ἀλλ' ὅμως, ἔφη ὁ Σωκράτης, σὺ αὐτὸν μὴ εἴκαζε, ἵνα μὴ 9 καὶ σὺ λοιδορουμένῳ ἐοίκῃς.

Ἀλλ' εἴπερ γε τοῖς πᾶσι καλοῖς καὶ τοῖς βελτίστοις εἰκάζω αὐτόν, ἐπαινοῦντι μᾶλλον ἢ λοιδορουμένῳ δικαίως ἂν εἰκάζοι μέ τις.

Καὶ νῦν σύ γε λοιδορουμένῳ ἔοικας, εἰ πάντα τὰ αὑτοῦ βελτίω φῂς εἶναι.

Ἀλλὰ βούλει πονηροτέροις εἰκάζω αὐτόν; 10

Μηδὲ πονηροτέροις.

Ἀλλὰ μηδενί;

Μηδενὶ μηδὲ τούτων εἴκαζε.

Ἀλλ' οὐ μέντοι γε σιωπῶν οἶδα ὅπως ἄξια τοῦ δείπνου ἐργάσομαι.

Καὶ ῥᾳδίως γ', ἂν ἃ μὴ δεῖ λέγειν, ἔφη, σιωπᾷς. αὕτη μὲν δὴ ἡ παροινία οὕτω κατεσβέσθη.

Ἐκ τούτου δὲ τῶν ἄλλων οἱ μὲν ἐκέλευον εἰκάζειν, οἱ δὲ VII ἐκώλυον. θορύβου δὲ ὄντος ὁ Σωκράτης αὖ πάλιν εἶπεν·

Ἆρα ἐπειδὴ πάντες ἐπιθυμοῦμεν λέγειν, νῦν ἂν μάλιστα καὶ ἅμα ᾄσαιμεν; καὶ εὐθὺς τοῦτ' εἰπὼν ἦρχεν ᾠδῆς.

ἐπεὶ δ' ἦσαν, εἰσεφέρετο τῇ ὀρχηστρίδι τροχὸς τῶν 2 κεραμεικῶν, ἐφ' οὗ ἔμελλε θαυματουργήσειν. ἔνθα δὴ εἶπεν ὁ Σωκράτης· Ὦ Συρακόσιε, κινδυνεύω ἐγώ, ὥσπερ σὺ λέγεις, τῷ ὄντι φροντιστὴς εἶναι· νῦν γοῦν σκοπῶ ὅπως ἂν ὁ μὲν παῖς ὅδε ὁ σὸς καὶ ἡ παῖς ἥδε ὡς ῥᾷστα διάγοιεν, ἡμεῖς δ' ἂν μάλιστα εὐφραινοίμεθα θεώμενοι αὐτούς· ὅπερ εὖ οἶδα ὅτι καὶ σὺ βούλει. δοκεῖ οὖν μοι τὸ μὲν εἰς μαχαίρας κυβιστᾶν 3 κινδύνου ἐπίδειγμα εἶναι, ὃ συμποσίῳ οὐδὲν προσήκει. καὶ μὴν τό γε ἐπὶ τοῦ τροχοῦ ἅμα περιδινουμένου γράφειν τε καὶ ἀναγιγνώσκειν θαῦμα μὲν ἴσως τί ἐστιν, ἡδονὴν δὲ οὐδὲ ταῦτα δύναμαι γνῶναι τίν' ἂν παράσχοι. οὐδὲ μὴν τό γε διαστρέφοντας τὰ σώματα καὶ τροχοὺς μιμουμένους ἥδιον ἢ ἡσυχίαν ἔχοντας τοὺς καλοὺς καὶ ὡραίους θεωρεῖν. καὶ γὰρ 4 δὴ οὐδὲ πάνυ τι σπάνιον τό γε θαυμασίοις ἐντυχεῖν, εἴ τις τούτου δεῖται, ἀλλ' ἔξεστιν αὐτίκα μάλα τὰ παρόντα θαυμάζειν, τί ποτε ὁ μὲν λύχνος διὰ τὸ λαμπρὰν φλόγα ἔχειν φῶς παρέχει, τὸ δὲ χαλκεῖον λαμπρὸν ὂν φῶς μὲν οὐ ποιεῖ, ἐν αὑτῷ δὲ ἄλλα ἐμφαινόμενα παρέχεται· καὶ πῶς τὸ μὲν ἔλαιον ὑγρὸν ὂν αὔξει τὴν φλόγα, τὸ δὲ ὕδωρ, ὅτι ὑγρόν

9 "Even so," said Sokrates, "don't you do a comparison, in case you too look like someone trying to be rude."

"But suppose I'm lining him up with gentlemen: the right comparison to make of me then would be with someone being complimentary, not rude!"

"That's exactly the impression you're giving right now: if you say all his attributes are superior, you're being rude."

10 "Do you want me to compare him with someone inferior then?"

"Not even that."

"No one at all?"

"Don't compare him with any of them."

"But I simply don't know how I can operate as the dinner deserves if I say nothing."

"It's easy," said Sokrates, "on condition that you don't say what you shouldn't say." And thus that bout of overindulgence was quelled.

VII Some of them went on trying to get Philippos to do a comparison, and others tried to stop him, and in the din Sokrates spoke again.

"Since we are all keen on having a say, isn't this the moment for us all to sing?" As soon as he had spoken he started a song.

2 When they had sung, a potter's wheel was brought in for the dancing-girl to do some stunts on. Sokrates intervened. "I'm afraid, man from Syracuse, that I really am a thinker, as you say. At the moment I'm considering how this boy and girl of yours can proceed as comfortably as possible while we have the greatest pleasure watching them, and I'm sure that you want that too. 3 My view is that jumping into daggers is a parade of peril, and quite unsuitable for a symposium. Reading and writing on the wheel as it spins is a bit of a stunt too perhaps, but what pleasure even that could give I cannot decide. And watching people twisting their bodies about and imitating hoops is no more enjoyable than gazing at them when they're still, if they're young and good-looking. 4 An encounter with wonders is certainly not something in particularly short supply if that's what you want; there are things for our amazement right here now: why does the lamp produce light by having a bright flame, while its bronze bowl, despite being bright, gives no light but shows other lights reflected on it? And how does oil, which is wet, increase flame,

ἐστι, κατασβέννυσι τὸ πῦρ. ἀλλὰ γὰρ καὶ ταῦτα μὲν οὐκ εἰς
ταὐτὸν τῷ οἴνῳ ἐπισπεύδει· εἰ δὲ ὀρχοῖντο πρὸς τὸν αὐλὸν 5
σχήματα ἐν οἷς Χάριτές τε καὶ Ὧραι καὶ Νύμφαι γράφονται,
πολὺ ἂν οἶμαι αὐτούς γε ῥᾷον διάγειν καὶ τὸ συμπόσιον πολὺ
ἐπιχαριτώτερον εἶναι.

ὁ οὖν Συρακόσιος, Ἀλλὰ ναὶ μὰ τὸν Δί᾽, ἔφη, ὦ
Σώκρατες, καλῶς τε λέγεις καὶ ἐγὼ εἰσάξω θεάματα ἐφ᾽ οἷς
ὑμεῖς εὐφρανεῖσθε.

Ὁ μὲν δὴ Συρακόσιος ἐξελθὼν συνεκροτεῖτο· ὁ δὲ **VIII**
Σωκράτης πάλιν αὖ καινοῦ λόγου κατῆρχεν.

Ἆρ᾽, ἔφη, ὦ ἄνδρες, εἰκὸς ἡμᾶς παρόντος δαίμονος
μεγάλου καὶ τῷ μὲν χρόνῳ ἰσήλικος τοῖς ἀειγενέσι θεοῖς, τῇ
δὲ μορφῇ νεωτάτου, καὶ μεγέθει πάντα ἐπέχοντος, ψυχῇ δὲ
ἀνθρώπου ἱδρυμένου, Ἔρωτος, μὴ ἀμνημονῆσαι, ἄλλως τε καὶ
ἐπειδὴ πάντες ἐσμὲν τοῦ θεοῦ τούτου θιασῶται; ἐγώ τε γὰρ 2
οὐκ ἔχω χρόνον εἰπεῖν ἐν ᾧ οὐκ ἐρῶν τινος διατελῶ,
Χαρμίδην δὲ τόνδε οἶδα πολλοὺς μὲν ἐραστὰς κτησάμενον,
ἔστι δὲ ὧν καὶ αὐτὸν ἐπιθυμήσαντα· Κριτόβουλός γε μὴν ἔτι
καὶ ἐρώμενος ὢν ἤδη ἄλλων ἐπιθυμεῖ. ἀλλὰ μὴν καὶ ὁ 3
Νικήρατος, ὡς ἐγὼ ἀκούω, ἐρῶν τῆς γυναικὸς ἀντερᾶται.
Ἑρμογένη γε μὴν τίς ἡμῶν οὐκ οἶδεν ὡς, ὅ τι ποτ᾽ ἐστὶν ἡ
καλοκἀγαθία, τῷ ταύτης ἔρωτι κατατήκεται; οὐχ ὁρᾶτε ὡς
σπουδαῖαι μὲν αὐτοῦ αἱ ὀφρύες, ἀτρεμὲς δὲ τὸ ὄμμα, μέτριοι
δὲ οἱ λόγοι, πραεῖα δὲ ἡ φωνή, ἱλαρὸν δὲ τὸ ἦθος; τοῖς δὲ
σεμνοτάτοις θεοῖς φίλοις χρώμενος οὐδὲν ἡμᾶς τοὺς
ἀνθρώπους ὑπερορᾷ; σὺ δὲ μόνος, ὦ Ἀντίσθενες, οὐδενὸς
ἐρᾷς;

Ναὶ μὰ τοὺς θεούς, εἶπεν ἐκεῖνος, καὶ σφόδρα γε σοῦ. 4

καὶ ὁ Σωκράτης ἐπισκώψας ὡς δὴ θρυπτόμενος εἶπε· Μὴ
νῦν μοι ἐν τῷ παρόντι ὄχλον πάρεχε· ὡς γὰρ ὁρᾷς, ἄλλα
πράττω.

καὶ ὁ Ἀντισθένης ἔλεξεν· Ὡς σαφῶς μέντοι σὺ μαστροπὲ 5
σαυτοῦ ἀεὶ τοιαῦτα ποιεῖς· τοτὲ μὲν τὸ δαιμόνιον προ-
φασιζόμενος οὐ διαλέγῃ μοι, τοτὲ δ᾽ ἄλλου του ἐφιέμενος.

καὶ ὁ Σωκράτης ἔφη· Πρὸς τῶν θεῶν, ὦ Ἀντίσθενες, 6
μόνον μὴ συγκόψῃς με· τὴν δ᾽ ἄλλην χαλεπότητα ἐγώ σου
καὶ φέρω καὶ οἴσω φιλικῶς. ἀλλὰ γάρ, ἔφη, τὸν μὲν σὸν

while water, which is wet, puts fire out? And yet, even those topics are not as good a stimulant as wine is; 5 but if your people were to dance to the aulos as Graces, Seasons and Nymphs are depicted dancing, I think that they would spend their time much more comfortably themselves and this symposium would be much more enjoyable."

"Now that, Sokrates," said the Syracusan, "is a good idea, by Zeus it is, and I'll bring on a show that you people will enjoy."

VIII Out went the Syracusan, to applause, and Sokrates started on a fresh theme.

"Gentlemen," he said, "we are in the presence of a great spirit, one who is contemporary in time with the gods born for ever, though in appearance he is the youngest, and in influence all-pervasive, ensconced in the heart of man, Eros: is it right for us to ignore him, especially when we are all votaries of the god? 2 For my own part I cannot remember a time when I have not been passionate about someone, and Kharmides here, I know, has had many admirers, while he's been keen on a few himself; Kritoboulos too is still an object of admiration but already keen on others. 3 And then there's Nikeratos, who's in love with his wife, so I hear, and she with him. And there's Hermogenes: whatever being a gentleman is, every one of us knows that he goes liquid for love of it; can't you see how earnest his eyebrows are, how steady his gaze, how measured his speech, how mild his voice, and how merry his disposition? He has the most august gods as his friends, but he doesn't disdain us mere mortals at all, does he? Are you the only one without a passion, Antisthenes?"

4 "By the gods," said he, "I do have a passion, very much so: it's you."

Sokrates pretended to be shattered, and said in jest, "Don't embarrass me please, not at the moment. As you can see, I'm otherwise engaged."

5 "You auto-pimp, you!" said Antisthenes. "You're always doing that sort of thing, quite blatantly. Sometimes you claim it's your 'voice' when you won't talk to me, and sometimes you're after something else."

6 "In the name of the gods," said Sokrates, "just don't slice me up. I put up with the rest of your tempers, and will do, like a friend. But you see," he said, "let's try to conceal this passion of yours; after all, it's not a

ἔρωτα κρύπτωμεν, ἐπειδὴ καὶ ἔστιν οὐ ψυχῆς ἀλλ' εὐμορφίας (VIII) τῆς ἐμῆς.

ὅτι γε μὴν σύ, ὦ Καλλία, ἐρᾷς Αὐτολύκου πᾶσα μὲν ἡ 7 πόλις οἶδε, πολλοὺς δ' οἶμαι καὶ τῶν ξένων. τούτου δ' αἴτιον τὸ πατέρων τε ὀνομαστῶν ἀμφοτέρους ὑμᾶς εἶναι καὶ αὐτοὺς ἐπιφανεῖς. ἀεὶ μὲν οὖν ἔγωγε ἠγάμην τὴν σὴν φύσιν, νῦν δὲ 8 καὶ πολὺ μᾶλλον, ἐπεὶ ὁρῶ σε ἐρῶντα οὐχ ἁβρότητι χλιδαινομένου οὐδὲ μαλακίᾳ θρυπτομένου, ἀλλὰ πᾶσιν ἐπιδεικνυμένου ῥώμην τε καὶ καρτερίαν καὶ ἀνδρείαν καὶ σωφροσύνην. τὸ δὲ τοιούτων ἐπιθυμεῖν τεκμήριόν ἐστι τῆς τοῦ ἐραστοῦ φύσεως. εἰ μὲν οὖν μία ἐστὶν Ἀφροδίτη ἢ 9 διτταί, Οὐρανία τε καὶ Πάνδημος, οὐκ οἶδα· καὶ γὰρ Ζεὺς ὁ αὐτὸς δοκῶν εἶναι πολλὰς ἐπωνυμίας ἔχει· ὅτι γε μέντοι χωρὶς ἑκατέρᾳ βωμοί τέ εἰσι καὶ ναοὶ καὶ θυσίαι τῇ μὲν Πανδήμῳ ῥᾳδιουργότεραι, τῇ δὲ Οὐρανίᾳ ἁγνότεραι, οἶδα. εἰκάσαις δ' ἂν καὶ τοὺς ἔρωτας τὴν μὲν Πάνδημον τῶν 10 σωμάτων ἐπιπέμπειν, τὴν δ' Οὐρανίαν τῆς ψυχῆς τε καὶ τῆς φιλίας καὶ τῶν καλῶν ἔργων. ὑφ' οὗ δὴ καὶ σύ, ὦ Καλλία, κατέχεσθαί μοι δοκεῖς ἔρωτος. τεκμαίρομαι δὲ τῇ τοῦ 11 ἐρωμένου καλοκἀγαθίᾳ καὶ ὅτι σε ὁρῶ τὸν πατέρα αὐτοῦ παραλαμβάνοντα εἰς τὰς πρὸς τοῦτον συνουσίας. οὐδὲν γὰρ τούτων ἐστὶν ἀπόκρυφον πατρὸς τῷ καλῷ τε κἀγαθῷ ἐραστῇ.

καὶ ὁ Ἑρμογένης εἶπε· Νὴ τὴν Ἥραν, ἔφη, ὦ Σώκρατες, 12 ἄλλα τέ σου πολλὰ ἄγαμαι καὶ ὅτι νῦν ἅμα χαριζόμενος Καλλίᾳ καὶ παιδεύεις αὐτὸν οἷόνπερ χρὴ εἶναι.

Νὴ Δί', ἔφη, ὅπως δὲ καὶ ἔτι μᾶλλον εὐφραίνηται, βούλομαι αὐτῷ μαρτυρῆσαι ὡς καὶ πολὺ κρείττων ἐστὶν ὁ τῆς ψυχῆς ἢ ὁ τοῦ σώματος ἔρως. ὅτι μὲν γὰρ δὴ ἄνευ φιλίας 13 συνουσία οὐδεμία ἀξιόλογος πάντες ἐπιστάμεθα. φιλεῖν γε μὴν τῶν μὲν τὸ ἦθος ἀγαμένων ἀνάγκη ἡδεῖα καὶ ἐθελουσία καλεῖται· τῶν δὲ τοῦ σώματος ἐπιθυμούντων πολλοὶ μὲν τοὺς τρόπους μέμφονται καὶ μισοῦσι τῶν ἐρωμένων· ἂν δὲ καὶ 14 ἀμφότερα στέρξωσι, τὸ μὲν τῆς ὥρας ἄνθος ταχὺ δήπου παρακμάζει, ἀπολείποντος δὲ τούτου ἀνάγκη καὶ τὴν φιλίαν συναπομαραίνεσθαι, ἡ δὲ ψυχὴ ὅσονπερ ἂν χρόνον ἴῃ ἐπὶ τὸ φρονιμώτερον καὶ ἀξιεραστοτέρα γίγνεται. καὶ μὴν ἐν μὲν τῇ 15 τῆς μορφῆς χρήσει ἔνεστί τις καὶ κόρος, ὥστε ἅπερ καὶ πρὸς τὰ σιτία διὰ πλησμονήν, ταῦτα ἀνάγκη καὶ πρὸς τὰ παιδικὰ πάσχειν· ἡ δὲ τῆς ψυχῆς φιλία διὰ τὸ ἁγνὴ εἶναι

passion for my soul but for my good looks.

7 "As for your passion for Autolykos, Kallias, all the city knows of it, and I think plenty of foreigners do too. That is because both of you come from famous fathers and you are notable people yourselves. 8 I have always admired you, Kallias, and I do so all the more now when I see you are impassioned for someone who doesn't lounge in luxury or surrender to a soft life, but displays to public view vigour, toughness, courage and self-control. A lover's nature is well demonstrated by his desire for that sort of behaviour. 9 Whether there is one Aphrodite or two, Celestial and Popular, I do not know; after all, Zeus is apparently one and the same though he has many titles; but I do know that each Aphrodite has her own separate altars and temples and sacrifices, which are pretty offhand for Aphrodite Pandemos but reverent by comparison for Aphrodite Ourania. 10 One could suggest that Pandemos sends the passion for bodies and Ourania sends the passion for souls and friendship and fine deeds. It seems to me that you too, Kallias, are in the grip of that passion. 11 I take my evidence from the quality of character in your beloved and from the fact that I see you invite his father to your meetings with him. A proper admirer keeps none of this concealed from a father."

12 "By Hera, Sokrates," said Hermogenes, "I admire you particularly for the fact that in this compliment to Kallias you are also teaching him what sort of man he should be."

"Yes by Zeus," said Sokrates, "and in order to increase his happiness I want to put it on record for him that a spiritual passion is much better than a physically based passion. 13 We all understand that without friendship no company is worth comment. For those who admire character, to be friends is called a pleasurable and willing compulsion, but those who want physical contact in many cases revile the behaviour of their loved ones and hate it; 14 and even if the affection is both physical and spiritual, the flower of youth soon passes its prime, naturally, and when that departs inevitably the friendship withers away too, whereas all the time that the spirit is proceeding to greater good sense, so it gets more and more worth loving. 15 In the exploration of beauty there is actually a certain satiety, so that inevitably you feel for your beloved what over-eating makes you feel for food. Spiritual love, however, is all the more

καὶ ἀκορεστοτέρα ἐστίν, οὐ μέντοι, ὥς γ' ἄν τις οἰηθείη, διὰ (VIII)
τοῦτο καὶ ἀνεπαφροδιτοτέρα, ἀλλὰ σαφῶς καὶ ἀποτελεῖται ἡ
εὐχὴ ἐν ᾗ αἰτούμεθα τὴν θεὸν ἐπαφρόδιτα καὶ ἔπη καὶ ἔργα
διδόναι.

ὡς μὲν γὰρ ἄγαταί τε καὶ φιλεῖ τὸν ἐρώμενον θάλλουσα 16
μορφῇ τε ἐλευθερίᾳ καὶ ἤθει αἰδήμονί τε καὶ γενναίῳ ψυχὴ
εὐθὺς ἐν τοῖς ἥλιξιν ἡγεμονική τε ἅμα καὶ φιλόφρων οὖσα
οὐδὲν ἐπιδεῖται λόγου· ὅτι δὲ εἰκὸς καὶ ὑπὸ τῶν παιδικῶν
τὸν τοιοῦτον ἐραστὴν ἀντιφιλεῖσθαι, καὶ τοῦτο διδάξω.
πρῶτον μὲν γὰρ τίς μισεῖν δύναιτ' ἂν ὑφ' οὗ εἰδείη καλός τε 17
καὶ ἀγαθὸς νομιζόμενος; ἔπειτα δὲ ὁρῴη αὐτὸν τὰ τοῦ παιδὸς
καλὰ μᾶλλον ἢ τὰ ἑαυτοῦ ἡδέα σπουδάζοντα; πρὸς δὲ τούτοις
πιστεύοι μήτ' ἂν παρανοήσῃ μήτ' ἂν καμὼν ἀμορφότερος
γένηται, μειωθῆναι ἂν τὴν φιλίαν; οἷς γε μὴν κοινὸν τὸ 18
φιλεῖσθαι, πῶς οὐκ ἀνάγκη τούτους ἡδέως μὲν προσορᾶν
ἀλλήλους, εὐνοϊκῶς δὲ διαλέγεσθαι, πιστεύειν δὲ καὶ
πιστεύεσθαι, καὶ προνοεῖν μὲν ἀλλήλων, συνήδεσθαι δ' ἐπὶ
ταῖς καλαῖς πράξεσι, συνάχθεσθαι δὲ ἄν τι σφάλμα προσ-
πίπτῃ, τότε δ' εὐφραινομένους διατελεῖν, ὅταν ὑγιαίνοντες
συνῶσιν, ἂν δὲ κάμῃ ὁποτεροσοῦν πολὺ συνεχεστέραν τὴν
συνουσίαν ἔχειν, καὶ ἀπόντων ἔτι μᾶλλον ἢ παρόντων
ἐπιμελεῖσθαι; οὐ ταῦτα πάντα ἐπαφρόδιτα; διά γέ τοι τὰ
τοιαῦτα ἔργα ἅμα ἐρῶντες τῆς φιλίας καὶ χρώμενοι αὐτῇ εἰς
γῆρας διατελοῦσι.

τὸν δὲ ἐκ τοῦ σώματος κρεμάμενον διὰ τί ἀντιφιλήσειεν 19
ἂν ὁ παῖς; πότερον ὅτι ἑαυτῷ μὲν νέμει ὧν ἐπιθυμεῖ, τῷ δὲ
παιδὶ τὰ ἐπονειδιστότατα; ἢ διότι ἃ σπεύδει πράττειν παρὰ
τῶν παιδικῶν, εἴργει μάλιστα τοὺς οἰκείους ἀπὸ τούτων; καὶ 20
μὴν ὅτι γε οὐ βιάζεται, ἀλλὰ πείθει, διὰ τοῦτο μᾶλλον
μισητέος. ὁ μὲν γὰρ βιαζόμενος ἑαυτὸν πονηρὸν ἀποδεικνύει,
ὁ δὲ πείθων τὴν τοῦ ἀναπειθομένου ψυχὴν διαφθείρει. ἀλλὰ 21
μὴν καὶ ὁ χρημάτων γε ἀπεμπολῶν τὴν ὥραν τί μᾶλλον
στέρξει τὸν πριάμενον ἢ ὁ ἐν ἀγορᾷ πωλῶν καὶ ἀποδιδόμενος;
οὐ μὴν ὅτι γε ὡραῖος ἀώρῳ, οὐδὲ ὅτι γε καλὸς οὐκέτι καλῷ
καὶ ἐρῶντι οὐκ ἐρῶν ὁμιλεῖ, φιλήσει αὐτόν. οὐδὲ γὰρ ὁ παῖς
τῷ ἀνδρὶ ὥσπερ γυνὴ κοινωνεῖ τῶν ἐν τοῖς ἀφροδισίοις
εὐφροσυνῶν, ἀλλὰ νήφων μεθύοντα ὑπὸ τῆς ἀφροδίτης θεᾶται.
ἐξ ὧν οὐδὲν θαυμαστὸν εἰ καὶ τὸ ὑπερορᾶν ἐγγίγνεται αὐτῷ 22
τοῦ ἐραστοῦ. καὶ σκοπῶν δ' ἄν τις εὕροι ἐκ μὲν τῶν διὰ

insatiable because of its purity; nor is it, as you might think, any less favoured sexually: patently there is fulfilment of the prayer in which we beg the goddess to grant us both the words and the deeds that bring us her favour.

16 "There is no need to discuss how a soul blooming in the beauty proper to a free man and in behaviour that is worshipful and noble, a soul that is both commanding and also kind to its contemporaries, admires and loves its beloved; I will also show that a love of that sort is likely to find a corresponding return of love from the beloved. 17 First, who could hate a man by whom he knows that he himself is reckoned a gentleman? Or when he sees him more concerned for his beloved's good than for his own pleasure? Or when he's sure that there will be no diminution of friendship, whether he loses his wits or falls ill and loses his looks? 18 When people have friendship in common, isn't it inevitable that they look at each other with pleasure, and talk to each other positively, and establish mutual trust, and take thought for each other, and share enjoyment when their actions prosper and annoyance if some slip intervenes, and sustain their delight when they both share good health, and if either falls ill the relationship they have is more durable, and they mind about each other even more when they're apart than when together? Isn't all that the favour of the goddess? It is action of that sort which brings them into old age still passionate about their friendship and still maintaining it.

19 "But if the man is all dependent on the physical, why should the boy love him back? Because the man grants himself what he wants, but allots the most objectionable role possible to the boy? Because he carefully bars his own household from what he's intent on getting from his beloved for himself? 20 As for him not using force but persuasion, that makes him all the more loathsome. A man who uses violence merely exposes his own nastiness, but one who tries persuasion corrupts the soul of the one being persuaded. 21 And why will a boy who sells his youth for money love the purchaser any more than a tradesman in the market loves his customer? When it's fresh coming face to face with faded, handsome with has-been, unimpassioned with passionate, of course he won't love him. A boy doesn't share the pleasures of sex with a man as a woman does: he's sober, facing a sexual drunk. 22 It's no wonder if as a result he even develops disdain for his admirer. Examination would show

78

τοὺς τρόπους φιλουμένων οὐδὲν χαλεπὸν γεγενημένον, ἐκ δὲ (VIII)
τῆς ἀναιδοῦς ὁμιλίας πολλὰ ἤδη καὶ ἀνόσια πεπραγμένα.

ὡς δὲ καὶ ἀνελεύθερος ἡ συνουσία τῷ τὸ σῶμα μᾶλλον ἢ 23
τῷ τὴν ψυχὴν ἀγαπῶντι, νῦν τοῦτο δηλώσω. ὁ μὲν γὰρ
παιδεύων λέγειν τε ἃ δεῖ καὶ πράττειν δικαίως ἂν ὥσπερ
Χείρων καὶ Φοῖνιξ ὑπ’ Ἀχιλλέως τιμῷτο, ὁ δὲ τοῦ σώματος
ὀρεγόμενος εἰκότως ἂν ὥσπερ πτωχὸς περιέποιτο. ἀεὶ γάρ
τοι προσαιτῶν καὶ προσδεόμενος ἢ φιλήματος ἢ ἄλλου τινὸς
ψηλαφήματος παρακολουθεῖ. εἰ δὲ λαμυρώτερον λέγω, μὴ 24
θαυμάζετε· ὅ τε γὰρ οἶνος συνεπαίρει καὶ ὁ ἀεὶ σύνοικος
ἐμοὶ ἔρως κεντρίζει εἰς τὸν ἀντίπαλον ἔρωτα αὐτῷ
παρρησιάζεσθαι. καὶ γὰρ δὴ δοκεῖ μοι ὁ μὲν τῷ εἴδει τὸν 25
νοῦν προσέχων μεμισθωμένῳ χῶρον ἐοικέναι. οὐ γὰρ ὅπως
πλείονος ἄξιος γένηται ἐπιμελεῖται, ἀλλ’ ὅπως αὐτὸς ὅτι
πλεῖστα ὡραῖα καρπώσεται. ὁ δὲ τῆς φιλίας ἐφιέμενος μᾶλλον
ἔοικε τῷ τὸν οἰκεῖον ἀγρὸν κεκτημένῳ· πάντοθεν γοῦν φέρων
ὅ τι ἂν δύνηται πλείονος ἄξιον ποιεῖ τὸν ἐρώμενον. καὶ μὴν 26
καὶ τῶν παιδικῶν ὃς μὲν ἂν εἰδῇ ὅτι ὁ τοῦ εἴδους ἐπαρκῶν
ἄρξει τοῦ ἐραστοῦ, εἰκὸς αὐτὸν τἆλλα ῥᾳδιουργεῖν· ὃς δ’ ἂν
γιγνώσκῃ ὅτι ἂν μὴ καλὸς κἀγαθὸς ᾖ, οὐ καθέξει τὴν φιλίαν,
τοῦτον προσήκει μᾶλλον ἀρετῆς ἐπιμελεῖσθαι. μέγιστον δ’ 27
ἀγαθὸν ·τῷ ὀρεγομένῳ ἐκ παιδικῶν φίλον ἀγαθὸν ποιήσασθαι
ὅτι ἀνάγκη καὶ αὐτὸν ἀσκεῖν ἀρετήν. οὐ γὰρ οἷόν τε πονηρὰ
αὐτὸν ποιοῦντα ἀγαθὸν τὸν συνόντα ἀποδεῖξαι, οὐδέ γε
ἀναισχυντίαν καὶ ἀκρασίαν παρεχόμενον ἐγκρατῆ καὶ
αἰδούμενον τὸν ἐρώμενον ποιῆσαι.

ἐπιθυμῶ δέ σοι, ἔφη, ὦ Καλλία, καὶ μυθολογῆσαι ὡς οὐ 28
μόνον ἄνθρωποι ἀλλὰ καὶ θεοὶ καὶ ἥρωες τὴν τῆς ψυχῆς
φιλίαν περὶ πλείονος ἢ τὴν τοῦ σώματος χρῆσιν ποιοῦνται.
Ζεύς τε γὰρ ὅσων μὲν θνητῶν οὐσῶν μορφῆς ἠράσθη, 29
συγγενόμενος εἴα αὐτὰς θνητὰς εἶναι· ὅσων δὲ ψυχαῖς
ἀγαθαῖς ἀγασθείη, ἀθανάτους τούτους ἐποίει· ὧν Ἡρακλῆς
μὲν καὶ Διόσκουροί εἰσι, λέγονται δὲ καὶ ἄλλοι· καὶ ἐγὼ δέ 30
φημι καὶ Γανυμήδην οὐ σώματος ἀλλὰ ψυχῆς ἕνεκα ὑπὸ Διὸς
εἰς Ὄλυμπον ἀνενεχθῆναι. μαρτυρεῖ δὲ καὶ τοὔνομα αὐτοῦ·
ἔστι μὲν γὰρ δήπου καὶ Ὁμήρῳ

γάνυται δέ τ’ ἀκούων.

τοῦτο δὲ φράζει ὅτι ἥδεται δέ τ’ ἀκούων. ἔστι δὲ καὶ ἄλλοθί
που

that when people love each other for the way they are, nothing unpleasant has ever arisen, but plenty of nasty things have been done on a basis of intercourse without respect.

23 "I will now demonstrate that the companionship of a man who loves physically rather than spiritually lacks the dimension of freedom. Training in what's right to do and say will rightly receive the honour that Akhilleus gave to Kheiron and Phoinix, but teachers who are physically excited will naturally be treated like the beggars they are: they press close, for ever beseeching and importuning a kiss or some other piece of fondling. 24 Don't be startled if I speak rather grossly: the wine is stirring me, and so is the passion that is ever my companion, goading me to speak out against the contrary passion. 25 I think that the man who pays attention to looks is like a tenant farmer: he's not concerned to make the land worth more, but just to get himself as handsome a profit from it as he can. The man seeking friendship is by contrast like the farmer who owns his land: he brings his beloved whatever he can from every source, and so improves his quality. 26 So too with the beloved: as soon as he knows that mere presentation of good looks will bring his lover under control, he's likely to take things easy in all other respects; by contrast, anyone who realises that he won't keep a friendship unless he too is a gentleman is bound to mind his behaviour. 27 The greatest good that happens to anyone eager to make a true friend of his beloved is the fact that he must practise goodness himself. He cannot display his companion's excellence while acting badly himself; he cannot be immodest and intemperate himself and develop modesty and temperance in his beloved.

28 "I want to go into the myths for you, Kallias, as well," he said. "Not only men but also gods and heroes treat spiritual friendship as more important than a physical relationship. 29 Zeus was enamoured of the beauty of many mortal females, but after sex he allowed them to remain mortal, whereas any male whose soul he admired he made immortal. Among them are Herakles and the Dioskouroi, and there are said to be others too, 30 and I declare that Ganymedes too was brought up to Olympos by Zeus for his soul, and not for his body. The evidence is his name: there is a phrase, I think, in Homer, 'He is glad at hearing it.' That means 'he is pleased at hearing it.' Somewhere else is the phrase 'knowing

πυκινὰ φρεσὶ μήδεα εἰδώς. (VIII)

τοῦτο δ᾽ αὖ λέγει σοφὰ φρεσὶ βουλεύματα εἰδώς. ἐξ οὖν
συναμφοτέρων τούτων οὐχ ἡδυσώματος ὀνομασθεὶς ὁ
Γανυμήδης ἀλλ᾽ ἡδυγνώμων ἐν θεοῖς τετίμηται. ἀλλὰ μήν, ὦ 31
Νικήρατε, καὶ Ἀχιλλεὺς Ὁμήρῳ πεποίηται οὐχ ὡς παιδικοῖς
Πατρόκλῳ ἀλλ᾽ ὡς ἑταίρῳ ἀποθανόντι ἐκπρεπέστατα
τιμωρῆσαι. καὶ Ὀρέστης δὲ καὶ Πυλάδης καὶ Θησεὺς καὶ
Πειρίθους καὶ ἄλλοι δὲ πολλοὶ τῶν ἡμιθέων οἱ ἄριστοι
ὑμνοῦνται οὐ διὰ τὸ συγκαθεύδειν ἀλλὰ διὰ τὸ ἄγασθαι
ἀλλήλους τὰ μέγιστα καὶ κάλλιστα κοινῇ διαπεπρᾶχθαι.

τί δέ, τὰ νῦν καλὰ ἔργα οὐ πάντ᾽ ἂν εὕροι τις ἕνεκα 32
ἐπαίνου ὑπὸ τῶν καὶ πονεῖν καὶ κινδυνεύειν ἐθελόντων
πραττόμενα μᾶλλον ἢ ὑπὸ τῶν ἐθιζομένων ἡδονὴν ἀντ᾽
εὐκλείας αἱρεῖσθαι; καίτοι Παυσανίας γε ὁ Ἀγάθωνος τοῦ
ποιητοῦ ἐραστὴς ἀπολογούμενος ὑπὲρ τῶν ἀκρασίᾳ συγ-
κυλινδουμένων εἴρηκεν ὡς καὶ στράτευμα ἀλκιμώτατον ἂν
γένοιτο ἐκ παιδικῶν τε καὶ ἐραστῶν. τούτους γὰρ ἂν ἔφη 33
οἴεσθαι μάλιστα αἰδεῖσθαι ἀλλήλους ἀπολείπειν, θαυμαστὰ
λέγων, εἴ γε οἱ ψόγου τε ἀφροντιστεῖν καὶ ἀναισχυντεῖν πρὸς
ἀλλήλους ἐθιζόμενοι, οὗτοι μάλιστα αἰσχυνοῦνται αἰσχρόν τι
ποιεῖν. καὶ μαρτύρια δὲ ἐπήγετο ὡς ταῦτα ἐγνωκότες εἶεν 34
καὶ Θηβαῖοι καὶ Ἠλεῖοι· συγκαθεύδοντας γοῦν αὐτοῖς ὅμως
παρατάττεσθαι ἔφη τὰ παιδικὰ εἰς τὸν ἀγῶνα, οὐδὲν τοῦτο
σημεῖον λέγων ὅμοιον. ἐκείνοις μὲν γὰρ ταῦτα νόμιμα, ἡμῖν
δ᾽ ἐπονείδιστα. δοκοῦσι δ᾽ ἔμοιγε οἱ μὲν παρατατττόμενοι
ἀπιστοῦσιν ἐοικέναι μὴ χωρὶς γενόμενοι οἱ ἐρώμενοι οὐκ
ἀποτελῶσι τὰ τῶν ἀγαθῶν ἀνδρῶν ἔργα. Λακεδαιμόνιοι δὲ οἱ 35
νομίζοντες, ἐὰν καὶ ὀρεχθῇ τις σώματος, μηδενὸς ἂν ἔτι
καλοῦ κἀγαθοῦ τοῦτον τυχεῖν, οὕτω τελέως τοὺς ἐρωμένους
ἀγαθοὺς ἀπεργάζονται ὡς καὶ μετὰ ξένων κἂν μὴ ἐν τῇ αὐτῇ
ταχθῶσι τῷ ἐραστῇ, ὁμοίως αἰδοῦνται τοὺς παρόντας
ἀπολείπειν. θεὰν γὰρ οὐ τὴν Ἀναίδειαν ἀλλὰ τὴν Αἰδῶ
νομίζουσι.

δοκοῦμεν δ᾽ ἄν μοι πάντες ὁμόλογοι γενέσθαι περὶ ὧν 36
λέγω, εἰ ὧδε ἐπισκοποῖμεν, τῷ ποτέρως παιδὶ φιληθέντι
μᾶλλον ἄν τις πιστεύσειεν ἢ χρήματα ἢ τέκνα ἢ χάριτας
παρακατατίθεσθαι. ἐγὼ μὲν γὰρ οἶμαι καὶ αὐτὸν τὸν τῷ εἴδει
τοῦ ἐρωμένου χρώμενον μᾶλλον ἂν ταῦτα πάντα τῷ τὴν
ψυχὴν ἐρασμίῳ πιστεῦσαι.

close-packed counsels in his heart.' That means 'knowing wise conclusions in his heart.' Put those two together and Ganymedes' place of honour among the gods comes from his name meaning not bodily sweet but mentally sweet. 31 Now, Nikeratos: Homer has made Akhilleus take that spectacular vengeance for Patroklos because it was his comrade who had died, not his beloved; and Orestes and Pylades, and Theseus and Peirithoos, and many others of the best of the demigods, are celebrated in song for having achieved their great and glorious deeds together not because they slept together but because of their mutual pride and joy.

32 "Frankly, wouldn't you find that all brave deeds nowadays are done by those who don't mind taking on hard work and risk, for the sake of praise, sooner than by people with a habit of opting for comfort instead of glory? And yet Pausanias, admirer of the poet Agathon, speaking in defence of those who wallow in intemperance, observed that out of lovers and their loved ones a most valiant army could be made: 33 he said he thought these people would be the most ashamed of deserting each other, a remarkable thing to say if the people who would be most ashamed of doing something ugly were those in the habit of disregarding censure and of trampling on the other's feelings. 34 He even produced as evidence the fact that both the Thebans and the Eleans were well acquainted with this: at any rate, though they slept with their loved ones, he said, they still put them in line beside them for the fight. But the point he makes bears no comparison: for them that's the usual practice, whereas we think it disgraceful. I think that parading them side by side looks like a lack of confidence, in that if the beloved is not close by, he may not perform as a brave man should. 35 The Spartans, however, who reckon that a man physically excited does no more brave deeds anyhow, train their loved ones so perfectly that they are ashamed to desert their companions even when among strangers and even when not drawn up in the same unit as their admirers. They worship the goddess Shame, and not the goddess Shamelessness.

36 "I think we could all agree with what I'm saying if we looked at it like this: which love should a boy have had for someone to trust him with his money, or children, or acts of favour? I'm sure that even the lover who goes by the looks of his beloved would himself entrust all that to the true soul-mate.

σοί γε μήν, ὦ Καλλία, δοκεῖ μοι ἄξιον εἶναι καὶ θεοῖς (VIII) 37
χάριν εἰδέναι ὅτι σοι Αὐτολύκου ἔρωτα ἐνέβαλον. ὡς μὲν γὰρ
φιλότιμός ἐστιν εὔδηλον, ὃς τοῦ κηρυχθῆναι ἕνεκα νικῶν
παγκράτιον πολλοὺς μὲν πόνους, πολλὰ δ᾽ ἄλγη ἀνέχεται. εἰ 38
δὲ οἴοιτο μὴ μόνον ἑαυτὸν καὶ τὸν πατέρα κοσμήσειν, ἀλλ᾽
ἱκανὸς γενήσεσθαι δι᾽ ἀνδραγαθίαν καὶ φίλους εὖ ποιεῖν καὶ
τὴν πατρίδα αὔξειν τροπαῖα τῶν πολεμίων ἱστάμενος, καὶ διὰ
ταῦτα περίβλεπτός τε καὶ ὀνομαστὸς ἔσεσθαι καὶ ἐν Ἕλλησι
καὶ ἐν βαρβάροις, πῶς οὐκ οἴει αὐτόν, ὅντιν᾽ ἡγοῖτο εἰς
ταῦτα συνεργὸν εἶναι κράτιστον, τοῦτον ταῖς μεγίσταις ἂν
τιμαῖς περιέπειν; εἰ οὖν βούλει τούτῳ ἀρέσκειν, σκεπτέον μέν 39
σοι ποῖα ἐπιστάμενος Θεμιστοκλῆς ἱκανὸς ἐγένετο τὴν
Ἑλλάδα ἐλευθεροῦν, σκεπτέον δὲ ποῖά ποτε εἰδὼς Περικλῆς
κράτιστος ἐδόκει τῇ πατρίδι σύμβουλος εἶναι, ἀθρητέον δὲ
καὶ πῶς ποτε Σόλων φιλοσοφήσας νόμους κρατίστους τῇ
πόλει κατέθηκεν, ἐρευνητέον δὲ καὶ ποῖα Λακεδαιμόνιοι
ἀσκοῦντες κράτιστοι δοκοῦσιν ἡγεμόνες εἶναι· προξενεῖς δὲ
καὶ κατάγονται ἀεὶ παρὰ σοὶ οἱ κράτιστοι αὐτῶν. ὡς μὲν οὖν 40
σοι ἡ πόλις ταχὺ ἂν ἐπιτρέψειεν αὑτήν, εἰ βούλει, εὖ ἴσθι.
τὰ μέγιστα γάρ σοι ὑπάρχει· εὐπατρίδης εἶ τῶν ἀπ᾽
Ἐρεχθέως, ἱερεὺς θεῶν οἳ καὶ ἐπὶ τὸν βάρβαρον σὺν Ἰάκχῳ
ἐστράτευσαν, καὶ νῦν ἐν τῇ ἑορτῇ ἱεροπρεπέστατος δοκεῖς
εἶναι τῶν προγεγενημένων, καὶ σῶμα ἀξιοπρεπέστατον μὲν
ἰδεῖν τῆς πόλεως ἔχεις, ἱκανὸν δὲ μόχθους ὑποφέρειν. εἰ δ᾽ 41
ὑμῖν δοκῶ σπουδαιολογῆσαι μᾶλλον ἢ παρὰ πότον πρέπει,
μηδὲ τοῦτο θαυμάζετε. ἀγαθῶν γὰρ φύσει καὶ τῆς ἀρετῆς
φιλοτίμως ἐφιεμένων ἀεί ποτε τῇ πόλει συνεραστὴς ὢν
διατελῶ.

οἱ μὲν δὴ ἄλλοι περὶ τῶν ῥηθέντων διελέγοντο, ὁ δ᾽ 42
Αὐτόλυκος κατεθεᾶτο τὸν Καλλίαν. καὶ ὁ Καλλίας δὲ παρορῶν
εἰς ἐκεῖνον εἶπεν· Οὐκοῦν σύ με, ὦ Σώκρατες, μαστροπεύσεις
πρὸς τὴν πόλιν, ὅπως πράττω τὰ πολιτικὰ καὶ ἀεὶ ἀρεστὸς ὦ
αὐτῇ;

Ναὶ μὰ Δί᾽, ἔφη, ἂν ὁρῶσί γέ σε μὴ τῷ δοκεῖν ἀλλὰ τῷ 43
ὄντι ἀρετῆς ἐπιμελούμενον. ἡ μὲν γὰρ ψευδὴς δόξα ταχὺ
ἐλέγχεται ὑπὸ τῆς πείρας· ἡ δ᾽ ἀληθὴς ἀνδραγαθία, ἂν μὴ
θεὸς βλάπτῃ, ἀεὶ ἐν ταῖς πράξεσι λαμπροτέραν τὴν εὔκλειαν
συμπαρέχεται.

37 "In your case, Kallias, I think you should give thanks to the gods for giving you a passion for Autolykos. It's obvious that he's jealous of his honour: he puts up with huge strain and pain in order to be declared victor in the pankration. 38 If his intention were not just to distinguish himself and his father, but to make himself competent to help his friends by his bravery and to enrich his country by routing its enemies, and so to become known by sight and name both in Greece and abroad, then you must surely reckon that he would treat with the utmost distinction anyone he thought to be his most effective helper in such deeds. 39 If you want his approval, you must first examine what it was that Themistokles understood that enabled him to liberate Greece, and then what Perikles knew that made him patently his country's best counsellor, and consider too what Solon's wisdom was that let him make such effective laws for his city, and you must search out what the Spartans keep doing to appear such excellent leaders: you are their proxenos, and their top men always stay with you. 40 You can be sure that if you want it, the city will soon put itself in your hands. You have all the advantages: your family has been noble since Erekhtheus, you are a priest of the gods who joined Iakkhos in the campaign against the Persian, and in today's festival you plainly excel your ancestors for reverence of attitude, while physically you are the best looking man in the city and strong enough for anything. 41 If you all think I'm talking more earnestly than is appropriate at drinks, even so, don't be surprised. I never fail to share my city's passion for men of a natural quality who are also aiming ambitiously at excellence."

42 Everyone else began to discuss what he had said, but Autolykos just gazed at Kallias. Kallias looked sideways at him and said, "Sokrates, will you then be my pimp to the city so that I can go into politics and always have her favour?"

43 "I will by Zeus," he said, "provided they see you cultivating excellence for real and not just seeming to. A bogus image is soon exposed under test, but if a man's courage is true, and if no harm is done him by god, then his actions always make his good name brighter."

Οὗτος μὲν δὴ ὁ λόγος ἐνταῦθα ἔληξεν. Αὐτόλυκος δὲ (ἤδη IX
γὰρ ὥρα ἦν αὐτῷ) ἐξανίστατο εἰς περίπατον· καὶ ὁ Λύκων ὁ
πατὴρ αὐτῷ συνεξιὼν ἐπιστραφεὶς εἶπε· Νὴ τὴν Ἥραν, ὦ
Σώκρατες, καλός γε κἀγαθὸς δοκεῖς μοι ἄνθρωπος εἶναι.

Ἐκ δὲ τούτου πρῶτον μὲν θρόνος τις ἔνδον κατετέθη, 2
ἔπειτα δὲ ὁ Συρακόσιος εἰσελθὼν εἶπεν· Ὦ ἄνδρες, Ἀριάδνη
εἴσεισιν εἰς τὸν ἑαυτῆς τε καὶ Διονύσου θάλαμον· μετὰ δὲ
τοῦθ' ἥξει Διόνυσος ὑποπεπωκὼς παρὰ θεοῖς καὶ εἴσεισι πρὸς
αὐτήν, ἔπειτα παιξοῦνται πρὸς ἀλλήλους.

ἐκ τούτου πρῶτον μὲν ἡ Ἀριάδνη ὡς νύμφη κεκοσμημένη 3
παρῆλθε καὶ ἐκαθέζετο ἐπὶ τοῦ θρόνου. οὔπω δὲ φαινομένου
τοῦ Διονύσου ηὐλεῖτο ὁ βακχεῖος ῥυθμός. ἔνθα δὴ ἠγάσθησαν
τὸν ὀρχηστοδιδάσκαλον. εὐθὺς μὲν γὰρ ἡ Ἀριάδνη ἀκούσασα
τοιοῦτόν τι ἐποίησεν ὡς πᾶς ἂν ἔγνω ὅτι ἀσμένη ἤκουσε·
καὶ ὑπήντησε μὲν οὖ οὐδὲ ἀνέστη, δήλη δ' ἦν μόλις
ἠρεμοῦσα. ἐπεί γε μὴν κατεῖδεν αὐτὴν ὁ Διόνυσος, ἐπι- 4
χορεύσας ὥσπερ ἂν εἴ τις φιλικώτατα ἐκαθέζετο ἐπὶ τῶν
γονάτων, καὶ περιλαβὼν ἐφίλησεν αὐτήν. ἡ δ' αἰδουμένη μὲν
ἐῴκει, ὅμως δὲ φιλικῶς ἀντιπεριελάμβανεν. οἱ δὲ συμπόται
ὁρῶντες ἅμα μὲν ἐκρότουν, ἅμα δὲ ἐβόων αὖθις.

ὡς δὲ ὁ Διόνυσος ἀνιστάμενος συνανέστησε μεθ' ἑαυτοῦ 5
τὴν Ἀριάδνην, ἐκ τούτου δὴ φιλούντων τε καὶ ἀσπαζομένων
ἀλλήλους σχήματα παρῆν θεάσασθαι. οἱ δ' ὁρῶντες ὄντως
καλὸν μὲν τὸν Διόνυσον, ὡραίαν δὲ τὴν Ἀριάδνην, οὐ
σκώπτοντας δὲ ἀλλ' ἀληθινῶς τοῖς στόμασι φιλοῦντας, πάντες
ἀνεπτερωμένοι ἐθεῶντο. καὶ γὰρ ἤκουον τοῦ Διονύσου μὲν 6
ἐπερωτῶντος αὐτὴν εἰ φιλεῖ αὐτόν, τῆς δὲ οὕτως ἐπ-
ομνυούσης ὥστε μὴ μόνον τὸν Διόνυσον < ... > ἀλλὰ καὶ τοὺς
παρόντας ἅπαντας συνομόσαι ἂν ἦ μὴν τὸν παῖδα καὶ τὴν
παῖδα ὑπ' ἀλλήλων φιλεῖσθαι. ἐῴκεσαν γὰρ οὐ δεδιδαγμένοις
τὰ σχήματα ἀλλ' ἐφειμένοις πράττειν ἃ πάλαι ἐπεθύμουν.

τέλος δὲ οἱ συμπόται ἰδόντες περιβεβληκότας τε 7
ἀλλήλους καὶ ὡς εἰς εὐνὴν ἀπιόντας, οἱ μὲν ἄγαμοι γαμεῖν
ἐπώμνυσαν, οἱ δὲ γεγαμηκότες ἀναβάντες ἐπὶ τοὺς ἵππους
ἀπήλαυνον πρὸς τὰς ἑαυτῶν γυναῖκας, ὅπως τούτων τύχοιεν.
Σωκράτης δὲ καὶ τῶν ἄλλων οἱ ὑπομείναντες πρὸς Λύκωνα
καὶ τὸν υἱὸν σὺν Καλλίᾳ περιπατήσοντες ἀπῆλθον. αὕτη τοῦ
τότε συμποσίου κατάλυσις ἐγένετο.

IX And there that conversation ended. Since it was now time for him, Autolykos got up and went out into a covered walk, and Lykon his father went out with him. As he did so, he turned to Sokrates and said, "By Hera, Sokrates, in my opinion you're a true gentleman."

2 After that, first a chair was set down in the room, and then the Syracusan came in. "Gentlemen," he said, "Ariadne will enter the bedroom which she shares with Dionysos. Then Dionysos will arrive, having become a little tipsy with the gods, and will go to join her; then they will have some fun with each other."

3 So, in came first Ariadne, decked as a bride, and she sat down on the chair. Without Dionysos appearing yet, the bacchic rhythm was played on the aulos. Then they really did admire the dancing-master, for as soon as Ariadne heard the music she reacted in such a way that anybody would have known she was delighted with what she heard. She didn't go to meet him, and she didn't get up either, but she plainly only just kept still. 4 When Dionysos caught sight of her, he danced up to her as lovingly as one possibly could, knelt down, embraced her and kissed her. Despite looking bashful, she embraced him with affection in return, and seeing it, the drinkers clapped their hands and shouted encore, all at the same time.

5 When Dionysos got to his feet and raised Ariadne with him, then there really were gestures of embracing and kissing to behold! People could see that Dionysos was really good-looking, and that Ariadne was beautiful, and that they weren't just in fun, but were kissing truly mouth to mouth, and everyone watched in eager expectation. 6 They could hear Dionysos asking her if she loved him and her giving him such an assurance back that not only Dionysos < ... > but everyone there could have sworn an oath together that the boy and girl were really in love with each other; they didn't look like people who had been taught the moves, but like people at last allowed to do what they had long been wanting to.

7 Eventually, when the party saw them wrapped around each other and apparently going to bed, the bachelors swore to get married, and the married men mounted their horses and rode away to have the company of their wives. Sokrates and the others who remained went off with Kallias to join Lykon and his son in their walk. And so this symposium broke up.

Commentary

NB lemmata in Greek indicate comment wholly or mostly confined to features of the Greek; X. means Xenophon; his works are cited without attribution (unless confusion might arise); references to the Introduction (Intr.) are to its paragraphs; references to text or notes are either to chapter and section or to section alone within the same chapter; dates are B.C. unless otherwise indicated.

Xenophon's works: *Agesilaus (Ages.)*
                       Anabasis (An.)
                       Apologia (Ap.)
                       Respublica Atheniensium (Ath.) = The Old Oligarch
                       Cynegeticus (Cyn.)
                        Cyropaedia (Cyr.)
                       Epistulae (Ep.)
                       de Equitandi ratione (Eq.)
                       de Equitum Magistro (Eq. Mag.)
                       Historia Graeca or *Hellenica (HG)*
                       Hiero (Hier.)
                       Respublica Lacedaemoniorum (Lac.)
                       Memorabilia (Mem.)
                       Oeconomicus (Oec.)
                       Symposium (Smp.)
                       de Vectigalibus (Vect.)

I

1   **Well**: Ἀλλά by origin means 'alternatively'. Some have thought that X. starts thus in conscious contrast with his earlier Socratic writings, but in some contexts the word is little more than a clearing of the mental throat; hence the translation. See GP 20-21, and 172.

τῶν .. ἀνδρῶν ἔργα .. πραττόμενα: word order allows the information to come in manageable units: gentlemen · deeds - serious - light-hearted.

gentlemen: this is perhaps the least unsatisfactory translation of a phrase which means literally 'men good and good'. The first adjective had connotations of 'good to look at' and the second had connotations of 'good in battle'. In the phrase there is a double yes to the question: 'Is this a man both for my friends and for my enemies to see me with?'

serious moments .. lighter moments: to some extent they need each other, and it was Sokrates' custom to mix the two (*Mem.* I 3.8 and IV 1.1). For the lighter touch elsewhere in X. see especially *HG* II 3.56, on what Theramenes said when forced to drink the hemlock: 'I know (says X.) that these are not distinguished utterances, but I think it an admirable feature of the man that when death was upon him his sense of reason and fun did not desert him.'

the people I was with when: X. appears to be claiming that he was at Kallias' party (Intr. 18). In Pl. *Smp.* 172b, the narrator Apollodoros is asked by his friend, σὺ αὐτὸς παρεγένου τῇ συνουσίᾳ ἢ οὔ; 'Were you yourself at the party or not?', which may mark Plato's criticism of such a claim. But X. never implies his presence in what follows; he is claiming (rather loosely) that from being at parties with them he knew the people concerned.

οἷς .. γιγνώσκω: a relative clause. τίσι or ὅτοις would be proper for an indirect question.

2 **horse-race day at the Great Panathenaia**: the Panathenaia (see Intr. 17) was celebrated just after midsummer, in the first month of the Athenian year (details of the occasion may be found in Parke 33-50). The horse racing took place at Phaleron by the sea.

Kallias son of Hipponikos: Intr. 27. Note the usual omission of υἱός, 'son', in this formal naming.

happened to be courting: Intr. 30.

Autolykos: Intr. 20. He is an almost ideal ἐρώμενος, distinguished for good looks and good behaviour, already an athletic victor, and of age to be taken up.

pankration: see Harris, 105-109 and plates 13-21. It was a sort of all-in wrestling. Apart from biting and gouging, no holds were barred. The aim was to force surrender. The event was popular with spectators and prestigious for participants. Eight pancratiasts, two of them boys, are celebrated in Pindar's surviving victory odes. In Ar. *Wasps* (1190-96) Bdelykleon recommends the event as a good topic for conversation at a dinner party.

νενικηκότα: νικήσαντα, aorist participle, would simply report Autolykos' victory: he won. The perfect participle emphasises the achievement: he has won and is the winner!

ἀπῄει .. συνείπετο: the imperfects of Greek narrative always deserve note. Here they mark actions completed only after interruption, which they anticipate. ἔχων, ἀπῄει and συνείπετο are all head of their phrases, not an uncommon position for the verb.

his house in the Peiraieus: in high summer the city of Athens, some miles inland, becomes very hot. A villa on the south shore of the Peiraieus would be not only closer to the racing but, like today's restaurants there, cooler too.

and the boy's father: Kallias is acting with notable openness (see VIII 11). The relationship intended by Kallias is obviously acceptable to Lykon, and if nearly two years later Eupolis still thought it worth guying, then it was presumably sustained.

Nikeratos: Intr. 21.

3 **Sokrates, Kritoboulos, Hermogenes, Antisthenes and Kharmides**: Intr. 19, 25, 24, 26 and 22 respectively.

the Autolykos party .. the Sokrates group: literally 'those on either side of Autolykos .. of Sokrates'. The person named is seen as central.

4 **What a lucky meeting**: literally 'I have met you for something good.'

entertain: ἑστιᾶν, literally 'to hearth.'

ἂν .. φανῆναι: if οἶμαι were removed or put in parenthesis, the main verb would be φανείη ἄν, with matching optative in the εἰ clause. For conditional sentences in the optative, see GMT 207.

dining-room: the Greek word means 'men's room' or 'men's suite of rooms'; there the men of the family could entertain male friends and guests. It appears from excavations that this was usually the biggest room in a house, and the most lavishly decorated (mosaic floors have been found, but no painted wall-plaster has survived). The room was square or oblong, with its door off centre; the couches were set against the walls, leaving the central space for service of food and drink and for entertainers. The smallest rooms excavated could take 7 couches (two to a wall in a square room minus one for the door); 11 was common. There is a survey by Birgitta Bergquist in Murray (ch. 3); see also J. E. Jones, L. H. Sackett and A. J. Graham, *The Dema house in Attica*, BSA 57 (1962) 75-114 and *An Attic Country House below the Cave of Pan at Vari*, BSA 68 (1973) 355-452, and (for the sort of suite a rich man like Kallias might have had in the

Peiraieus) P. Ducrey and I. R. Metzger, *La maison aux mosaïques à Erétrie*, Antike Kunst 22 (1979) 1-21, all with plates.

men of purified souls: literally either 'men purified as to their souls' (accusative of respect and the verb passive; so LSJ citing Pl. *R.* 527d), or 'men having purified their souls' (verb middle). Kallias adds a humorous challenge to his invitation. A purified soul was important to Pythagoreans and to those who sought initiation into the Eleusinian mysteries, but Kallias intends something more intellectual than spiritual: talking with Sokrates clarified one's thinking.

generals .. political hopefuls: eventually Kallias held high office (Intr. 27); at VIII 39-40 Sokrates encourages him to have such hopes, but the disdain audible here persists in his response there. There is no sign that Kallias had invited any such guests or that if he had he now stood them down; but it is odd if he was relying on chance encounters to make up what is virtually Autolykos' coming-of-age party.

(At *Ach.* 594-5 Aristophanes has ἐγώ .. πολίτης χρηστός, οὐ σπουδαρχίδης, 'I'm a good citizen, not a political hopeful's sprog!' σπουδαρχίδης, a nonce form, is plainly comic; the proper form of X.'s word is unclear. The MSS show σπουδάρχαις, as from σπουδάρχης (for which LSJ cite only this passage), but in Hesychius there is σπουδαρχίαι, κατὰ σπουδὴν ἄρχοντες, as from σπουδαρχίας, and editors have accepted that form.)

5   **big money**: Plato (*Ap.* 20a) has Sokrates speak of Kallias as one who had paid more money to sophists than everyone else put together. Protagoras, the first to profess himself a sophist and to ask a fee (Pl. *Prt.* 348e), is said (D. L. IX 52) to have charged 100 minae; Kallias is said (Pl. *Alc.* 1 119a) to have paid the same sum to Zeno.

Protagoras .. Gorgias .. Prodikos: Protagoras and Prodikos were once present together in Kallias' house (Pl. *Prt.* 314bc); unless Plato is guilty of an anachronism, Kallias was playing host to them at the age of about 20, giving Prodikos a bed in his father's office. Protagoras was born in Abdera in Thrace about 490, and visited Athens often. He taught the art of persuasion, and was agnostic both about the existence of the gods and about abstractions mathematical and moral. Gorgias was of the same generation but from Leontinoi in Sicily. He too taught the art of persuasion (works survive); he stressed the moral neutrality of the art itself. He first visited Athens in 427, on an embassy; his oratory took the city by storm. Prodikos was probably younger, and came from Keos, the nearest of the Kyklades to Athens. He too was often in Athens; in his teaching he concentrated on the precise distinction between words of similar meaning. A fuller picture of the three is available in Guthrie, III1 262-280.

do-it-yourself philosophers: αὐτουργός describes a farmer who works his land himself, neither hiring help nor owning slaves. X. notes the strength of such people at *Oec.* V 4; their independence mattered to them as much as Sokrates' freedom from fee-paying clients mattered to him.

6   **I did conceal from you my ability**: X. uses the imperfect: 'I used to ..'. ἔχειν + infinitive is common for 'to be able to'.

to say plenty of clever things: rich young Athenians sought from sophists the skills that would sustain politically their social advantage. Kallias' σοφά, 'clever things', picks up the σοφία which Sokrates attributed to him; for himself Sokrates used φιλοσοφία, 'a desire for knowledge'. Note the idiomatic καί in πολλὰ καὶ σοφά, literally 'things many and clever'.

ἐὰν .. ἦτε: note the marks of a primary indefinite clause, ἄν + subjunctive. In Greek, clauses of future reference nearly always entail indefiniteness, and they are nearly always so marked. There is no corresponding English idiom.

I shall display: Kallias uses the verb proper for a sophist's performance, an ἐπίδειξις.

7   **at first .. finally**: πρῶτον μέν, 'at first', is answered by ὡς δέ, 'but when'. ἔπειτα δέ, 'and finally', marks a third stage.

politely declined his invitation: for this sense of ἐπαινεῖν, 'to praise', see LSJ *s.v.* III; and compare the use of 'merci' in French.

εἰ μὴ ἔψοιντο: the optative, a historic mood, marks the assimilation of the clause to its historic main sentence; use of the future optative shows that the original clause was εἰ μὴ ἔψονται rather than ἐὰν μὴ ἔπωνται. εἰ + future indicative marks, by contrast with the normal ἐάν + subjunctive (see 6 above), an element of threat or alarm: 'If you don't follow...'

οἱ μέν .. οἱ δέ: in Homer ὁ ἡ τό usually have demonstrative force and operate as words in their own right. The use here with the particles μέν and δέ in support is the main survival in classical Greek of the word's original force as a pronoun.

some freshly oiled .. wash as well: literally, 'some having taken exercise and having oiled themselves and some having also washed'. For washing or bathing as something done at home see Ar. *Birds* 131-2; but it could be done at the palaistra (*ib.* 140). All the guests are in an acceptable state of toilette; the distinction between them reinforces the casualness of Kallias' invitation.

8   **Autolykos .. sat .. the rest reclined**: reclining was the privilege of the adult male; the custom seems to have been adopted by the Greeks from Lydia, in the eighth or seventh century (it is discussed in Murray, 6 and 139). The relative positions of only Lykon and his son are clear from X.'s account; they may share a couch (see 13 below).

naturally regal: both Kyros prince of Persia and Agesilaos king of Sparta, over different lengths of time, made a considerable impact on X. He uses the adjective to describe a good master's authority at *Oec.* XXI 10 and its superlative at *An.* I 9.1 to describe Kyros at his death: 'most regal of Persians since Kyros the Great.'

especially: ἄλλως τε καί, literally 'both in other ways and'. In mentioning other possibilities the first two words also dismiss them by comparison with what then comes. The idiom is common (II 3, IV 45, VI 4, VIII 1 and 12). ἄν (with long α) is for ἐάν, the normal monosyllabic form in X. and in later Attic Greek in general; in earlier Attic the normal form was ἤν.

κεκτῆται: as the accent shows and as ἐάν requires, the form is subjunctive; the periphrastic κεκτημένος ᾖ might have been used instead.

modesty and good sense: αἰδώς and σωφροσύνη are the two qualities (outside those proper to war and other fierce competition) most commendable to a Greek; αἰδώς, always a difficult word to translate, marks especially the capacity to feel bashfulness and awe before gods and before men who deserved such a response.

9   **draws the eyes .. forced the gaze**: the verbs are varied deliberately, to stress Autolykos' greater drawing power. There is a double hyperbaton in the separation of πάντων, 'of all', 'of everyone', from first τὰ ὄμματα, 'the eyes', and then τὰς ὄψεις, 'the gaze'. Thus X. marks the universality of both effects. Note the several imperfectives in this passage: εἷλκε, ὁρώντων, ἔπασχε.

τοῦ Αὐτολύκου τὸ κάλλος: the defining genitive precedes its noun (as in the very first sentence of the work) to match the precedence of πάντων.

οὐδεὶς οὔκ: when a compound negative (e.g. οὐδείς) precedes the simple, both negatives take effect; when the compound follows the simple, the compound adds force to the existing negative.

τὴν ψυχήν: 'to the core'; accusative of respect, as in 4 above. πάσχειν is effectively passive in meaning.

οἱ μέν γε: the connective force of γε in this combination is noted at GP 160. It approximates to that of γάρ.

fell silent: literally 'became comparatively silent'. In a context of contrast comparatives are natural in Greek idiom; English tends to use positives, as in the translation. See 10 below.

reacted by gesture: the comment of LSJ on this, 'of actors, *gesticulate*', is baffling. In modern idiom, the guests were using body language.

10   ἐκ θεῶν του = ἔκ τινος τῶν θεῶν. ἐκ is used to mark the origin of an event without saying that the origin is necessarily the cause, or agent. Agency is marked mostly by ὑπό, sometimes by πρός. κατεχόμενοι is passive.

ἐξ ἄλλων: θεῶν and κατεχόμενοι are to be understood from the previous sentence. ἔνθεοι ὑπό in the next phrase replaces these tentative expressions with an explicit one, as our attention is transferred from Autolykos the admired to Kallias the admirer. ἔνθεοι is effectively a participle, like κατεχόμενοι.

go goggle-eyed: literally, 'are carried towards the being seen <to be> comparatively goggle-eyed' (ὁρᾶσθαι is passive, use of the middle being Homeric and poetical). X. may have drunks, epileptics or maenads in mind, Dionysos, Apollo and Dionysos respectively being the agent gods.

sober passion: oxymoron, if not contradiction in terms. Sokrates attempts to resolve the contradiction in VIII 9-10 by dividing Aphrodite into two. Note the force now of ὑπό with ἔρωτος, and the ambiguity of ἔρως itself: the same word does for both emotion and god (as ancient Greek was written in capital letters only, the distinction we might make was not even available).

like free men: literally 'towards that <condition> more typical of a free citizen'. ἐλευθέριος, formed from ἐλεύθερος used as a noun, means 'typical of one who is free'. The political, and so the social, sense of the word (it occurs five times in this work) is paramount, especially in II 4. The neuter of an adjective in its comparative degree used to make an abstract noun is first recorded in Thoukydides, for instance at II 59.3: τὸ ἠπιώτερον καὶ ἀδεέστερον, 'a gentler and less fearful state of mind'; X. uses the idiom again at II 26.

ἃ δή: the relative pronoun, underlined by δή, is the connecting word. So too at IV 24, 62 and VIII 10, and without δή at IV 45, VII 2, VIII 22 and 29.

initiates of Eros: literally 'of that god', the ambiguity noted above being now resolved. Sokrates counts himself an initiate of Eros, in VIII 2; so too in Pl. *Smp.* 177d.

11   τοῦτο ἐπιτεταγμένον: accusative absolute; literally, 'this being fixed'.

Philippos the laughter-maker: Philippos' contribution is catalytic, and welcome, at least initially, but as the evening proceeds his contributions seem more forced and less successful: gentlemen, it appears, can amuse themselves (III 2); the humour of a professional humorist is different. It is not made clear that Philippos himself is not καλὸς κἀγαθός; he takes part in III and IV in the round of boasting, but Sokrates puts him down firmly at VI 9-10, after which he is silent. X. observed laughter-makers at the court of king Seuthes of Thrace (*An.* VII 3.33), and he records Sokrates' view of them at *Mem.* III 9.9, that they were people who could be doing something better; Plutarch, discussing the topic of what were in his day called 'shadows' (*Mor.* 706f-710a), observed a difference, in that Philippos comes uninvited and he is not obsequious (II 14, 27 and IV 55).

εἶπε .. εἰσαγγεῖλαι: infinitive of indirect command. For indirect statement λέγειν is nearly always followed in Attic prose by ὅτι or ὡς with a finite verb. εἴη and βούλοιτο appear in the optative to accord with εἶπε, as is usual in X.

συνεσκευασμένος τε .. πάντα τὰ ἐπιτήδεια: the participle is middle, πάντα τὰ ἐπιτήδεια being direct object. The case of the participle is in accord with the subject of παρεῖναι, which is the same as the subject of ἔφη. Hence no change from the original nominative. The use here of τε deserves note. Single connective τε is, as Denniston observes (GP 497), rare in prose, and it became rarer. There are two other examples in this work, at IV 22 and 31; all belong in Denniston's I (ii) (c).

dine at someone else's expense .. slave .. under great pressure: neither joke, we may reckon, was very new. Catullus in a later generation elaborated the first (poem XIII); Aristophanes had worked on πιέζεσθαι, 'to be pressed', at the beginning of *Frogs*.

καὶ τὸν παῖδα δέ: καί stresses τὸν παῖδα, and δέ is the connecting particle (it has virtually no other function). But sometimes the connecting force seems to lie rather with καί. The function of δέ is then to set the new phrase apart from the preceding matter. See GP 199-203. καὶ .. δέ became common in the fourth century, especially in X., who (as noted by A. Rijksbaron in NAGP 187-208, arguing for καί as the connecting particle) contributes some three quarters of all instances up to his time.

breakfast: ἄριστον (α is long), to be distinguished from ἄριστος adjective.

12 Ἀλλὰ μέντοι: use of this pair of particles is (GP 410) 'practically confined to Plato and Xenophon'. Denniston classes this as assentient, but Kallias is not speaking to Philippos; he is addressing his guests, some of whom might object to the intruder; Kallias gets the assent he wants by using αἰσχρόν, 'it's a shameful thing': he needs Philippos to stir things up, and the appeal to his own honour as a rich man and as host is persuasive.

δῆλον: with ὅτι it had become adverbial, 'it is obvious that' becoming 'obviously'.

13 ὅτι .. εἰμι ἴστε: precedence of a clause of indirect statement over its main verb should be noted; it is quite a common practice, and is not confined to short clauses like this one.

ἄκλητον .. κεκλημένον: accusative masculine. με (or τινα) needs to be understood as subject of the infinitive: literally, 'it is funnier <for me/a man> to come to the dinner uninvited than having been invited'. The parasite Ergasilus in Plautus' *Captivi*, preparing for a pun, calls himself *inuocatus* (70). Note the word order γελοιότερον εἶναι τὸ .. ἐλθεῖν: as is common in such sentences, the predicate comes first.

Take a couch then: τοίνυν, 'in that case', 'then', is often quite sharp, and the use of the present rather than aorist imperative means 'Get on with it'. X. does not indicate whether there is a couch to spare or Philippos shares one; in Plato's *Symposium* (175c and 213b) they recline two to a couch; vase-paintings offer both arrangements. If Kallias' room is a nine-coucher (see note on **dining-room**, 4 above), Autolykos might now move to share his father's couch. If the room is bigger than that, then they dine with gaps, or else (as explicitly in Pl. *Smp.* 180c) there are also guests unnamed. That possibility is considered at IX 7.

amply fed: μεστός is commonly used of people eating.

14 **always**: Greek distinguishes between ἀεί, continuously, and ἑκάστοτε, repeatedly.

he tried .. meant to be funny: literally 'he wanted to say something else funny'. But as the sequel shows, he did say something. Hence the translation.

promptly: ἐν τῷ μεταξύ, literally 'in the in-between <period>'; within the time, that is, when they should have been laughing but weren't.

lay full length: couches were about 1.80m long; so R. A. Tomlinson (Murray, ch. 6).

15 **Are you in pain?**: Kallias expresses a host's dismay and a rich host's indignation. ἀλλ᾽ ἦ (Denniston's 'certain' correction of ἀλλ᾽ ἤ) gives 'lively expression to a feeling of surprise or incredulity' (GP 27-28).

Philippos groaned: Philippos is represented in the Greek by ὅς, a demonstrative pronoun of little currency after Homer (apart from the set expression ἦ δ᾽ ὅς, 'said he', common in Plato) but quite frequent in this work (11 times, as against only 8 in all *Memorabilia*). But ἀναστενάζειν, 'to groan', is highly poetic, and both ἀπόλωλεν, 'has perished', and ἔρρει, 'is gone', are much commoner in the playwrights than in prose. Philippos is playing it up.

τούτου ἕνεκα: literally 'for this reason'. The phrase gives notice of the purpose clause to come (ἵνα εὐφραίνοιντο, 'so that they should be cheered up') but is redundant in English and omitted in the translation.

ἀντικληθησόμενος: ἀντι- is often used in prefix to mark an action which copies or matches a previous one. It can be found so used at II 12, 14, 20, 22, III 3, V 8, VIII 3, 16, 19 and IX 4.

there's no custom .. of even sending out: οὐδέ means 'not even'. Only in a context already negative may it mean 'nor' or 'nor even'. Delivery of ready-to-eat meals is nothing very new; Charles Dickens attests it often. The subject of νομίζεται, 'it is customary', is the noun phrase δεῖπνον προσφέρεσθαι, literally 'dinner to be brought', 'the bringing of dinner'.

As he spoke, he was: imperfects again. The tense can be used in Greek narrative to draw extra attention to the action, as if to say in this instance 'There he was, talking, snuffling, sounding weepy, all at once.'

κλαίειν ἐφαίνετο: literally 'he appeared to be weeping'. 'He could be seen weeping' would be κλαίων ἐφαίνετο. The infinitive with φαίνομαι tends to mark unreality (GMT 914.5), whereas the participle marks reality. As the teachers' hexameter has it,

φαίνομαι ὤν *quod sum*; *quod non sum* φαίνομαι εἶναι.

16 **broke into a guffaw**: καγχάζειν, or καχάζειν, is probably onomatopoeic, from χὰ χά: so suggest LSJ. Note the switch to the aorist for the action seen for itself, without attention to its duration.

bidding his heart be brave: at the back of this phrase (the tone is still tragi-comic) lies the Homeric τέτλαθι δή, κραδίη, 'be bold, my heart, and endure' (*Od*. 20.18), converted, as Malcolm Willcock suggests, using X.'s words, into θάρσει, ἐμὴ ψυχή.

there would be contributions: in using ἔσονται, 'will be', the original tense and mood, rather than ἔσοιντο, X. invites his readers to overhear Philippos as he makes yet another joke. συμβολαί has several meanings: a specific sense of the plural is 'contributions to a shared meal' (as in LSJ IV1a; IV1b is wrong); also at work is the sense 'encounters': in context that means the verbal sparring to be expected of a competitive occasion like a symposium. But the primary sense contains its own joke, since Philippos' contributions will not be the usual ones of food: he will supply jokes, and others will supply not only the food but also the laughter. On those terms (yet another sense of the word) they will proceed.

II

1 **libation and paean**: libations are a sacrifice of the simplest sort, a pouring to the ground of a liquid in propitiation of the earth that first gave it. Here the libation also consecrates the wine to be drunk. Paeans are choral songs of great variety according to circumstance; here the paean is like a sung grace, giving thanks for the food. Now the

symposium proper can start, the drinking and the exchange of conversation and banter, with occasional song and verse.

a Syracusan: nothing is said, but we may reckon that he and his troupe had been hired for the occasion; Kallias' wealth is on show. Syracuse had a reputation like that of Corinth for costly and sophisticated entertainments. X. does not make the man speak Syracusan dialect.

ἔχων τε αὐλητρίδα: τε is, strictly speaking, one word early.

aulos-player: αὐλός is often translated flute. West, 1-2, exposes the error in this and explains it at 81-85. No modern instrument exactly resembles the aulos; hence no 'pipe' or 'shawm', as recommended by West for translation. They were played in pairs (plates in W. D. Anderson, *Music and Musicians in Ancient Greece*, New York 1994, show this well; it is odd that in Greek the word is usually singular, not plural or dual); they could be kept in the mouth by a strap round the head, as some vase paintings show. Plutarch discusses the presence of aulos-players at symposia at *Mor.* 710b, citing Pl. *Prt.* 347c and *Smp.* 176e.

a very comely boy: the dancing-girl is also comely, as we learn at IX 5, but only the boy's looks command attention here. The canons of male good looks were perhaps better established, and more often discussed, than those for females.

kithara: again the name of a modern instrument is avoided. κιθάρα is probably a loan-word (see Chantraine); from it we get guitar and zither, but it was neither of those, as West explains (49 ff). The boy not only plays the instrument but also sings to it (III 1). Mere players were known, and were called κιθαρισταί, but it was customary to use the kithara in accompaniment to song. Plutarch remarks (*Mor.* 713b), 'If I must express my own view, I wouldn't submit a symposium to the music of aulos or lyre on their own without words and song'. See West 69-70.

ταῦτα: literally 'these things'. At IV 55 the Syracusan calls his troupe νευρόσπαστα, 'puppets', using a neuter plural; they are the referent here.

made a prodigious living: translators differ over the meaning of ὡς ἐν θαύματι. It can be taken either with ἐπιδεικνύς, 'demonstrating them as in a wonder', 'as something to marvel at' ('as at shows, at a fairground' appears to require a plural), or with ἐλάμβανε, 'he used to take money as in a wonder', 'in remarkable sums'. The first possibility repeats an idea already present, but the second makes a new point, incidentally attesting Kallias' wealth, and the phrase is appropriately head of its sense unit: hence the translation offered.

2   ἡ αὐλητρὶς μέν: Lysias, a contemporary, would surely have written ἡ μὲν αὐλητρίς, not only to parallel ὁ δὲ παῖς but also to save hiatus.
Sokrates said: X. usually gives Sokrates the lead. Though he spoke of gentlemen in the plural at the start, it is soon clear that Sokrates is the one most on show. X. plays Boswell to Sokrates' Dr Johnson.

3   **some scent:** in Ar. *Lys.* 938-947 also, scent is the ultimate refinement.
τί οὖν: it could have had its sense completed by something like λέγοις ἄν, but the idiom is intelligible as it is.
and in the same way: literally 'Just as there are clothes .., so there's a scent ..'. The Greek idiom of comparative clause before main sentence is not comfortable in English. Note the chiasmus of 'women .. men .. men .. women' with which X. underlines the comparison.

ἀνδρὸς μέν: μέν is answered by μέντοι. So too at 25 below, IV 49, VI 1 and VIII 9.
want .. in addition: note this force of προσ- as prefix.

4   **as they are**: αὐταί, literally 'themselves', 'by just being themselves'. αὐτός when
headword of a phrase can only be emphatic.
gymnasium oil: there were oils of different qualities for different uses then as now;
some oil was deliberately scented. Jars of best Attic olive oil served as prizes at the
Panathenaia; Autolykos would have collected 30 for his victory (Parke 36). The point
about gymnasium oil, and Sokrates is just about to reach it, is that only free men used
gymnasia, and in practice only free men with free time. Use of such oil thus confirmed a
man's social status.
μύρῳ μέν .. αἱ δ' .. ὀσμαί: in order to get μέν with μύρῳ and both words to the head
of the sentence in anticipation of the contrast with other scents and smells, X. extracts
the noun from its place inside ὁ ἀλειψάμενος. ὀσμαί, being half-anticipated, needs no
similar prominence.
slave or free: there is a tart comment on the difficulty of distinguishing who was who
on the streets of democratic Athens in *The Old Oligarch* = [X.] *Ath.* I 10 (Intr. 8).
the work that free men do: free citizens might be potters, cobblers, masons, smiths:
workmen. Sokrates' conclusion depends upon the work being understood as gymnasium
work: hence the need to qualify ἐπιτηδευμάτων with χρηστῶν: χρηστός, literally
'useful', was commonly used to denote upper-class citizens, 'men of use' (as hoplites in
war). Its antonym, πονηρός, 'man of toil' (literally 'toilsome, laboursome') is a common
term of abuse (see VI 10).
Lykon observed: it is appropriate for Lykon to come in here. He alone of the company
is close in age to Sokrates (Intr. 20), and he best can ask, in effect, what Sokrates
himself smells of and so what his status is. At IX 1 he expresses his total satisfaction.
don't any longer take exercise: Lykon is probably being humorous; μηκέτι rather than
οὐκέτι with the participle shows that he is generalising; hence 'the likes of us' in the
translation. But citizens of Athens had a duty to keep fit because they could be called to
serve in the army up to the age of 59: see [Arist.] *Ath.* 53.4 and J. M. Moore, *Aristotle
and Xenophon on Democracy and Oligarchy*, London 1983, 290. For a similar duty at
Sparta see X. *HG* VI 4.17.
Essence of gentleman: literally 'gentlemanliness'.
Theognis: Sokrates' first answer is apt and witty, but Lykon presses for more, and
Sokrates' recourse to the authority of Theognis is particularly apt in context. Theognis
lived in Megara in the sixth century, when aristocratic control of Greek society was
beginning to weaken; he wrote of it with nostalgia, and was much quoted on occasions
like this. Sokrates' quotation of him is itself a relic of what would have been the main
occupation of symposia in an earlier generation, the exchange of verses (Ezio Pellizer
explores this in Murray, ch. 12). For the text (this couplet is verses 35-36 of Elegies
book I; διδάξεαι is a variant for μαθήσεαι) see D. C. C. Young, ed. *Theognis*, Leipzig
1971² and for discussion of the poet D. A. Campbell, ed. *Greek Lyric Poetry*, Bristol
1967, 343-7.
The couplet contains Homeric words and forms as follows: ἐσθλός is a synonym for
ἀγαθός; ἀπό is at a distance from the genitive it works with; διδάξεαι, 2nd. sing.
future middle, is in its uncontracted form; κακοῖσι is an unabbreviated dative plural.
The stem μισγ- for μιγ/μειγ- is very rare outside Homer (and Herodotos); ἐόντα =
ὄντα; νόον is uncontracted.
5   **goes by it**: literally 'uses it'. The compliment is swift and neat.
upon examining it with you < .. > in turn: most editors (not Thalheim) agree that
some words which X. wrote have gone missing. Bartlett offers the following
supplement: 'When, that is, he wished to carry off the prize for the pancratium, he

considered with you [who would be able to teach him these things, and he associated with him. Similarly, if he wishes to carry off the prize for virtue, he will consult with you] in turn as to who is in his opinion most capable in the practice of these things, and he'll associate with him.' I quote Bartlett to help expose the problem. X.'s Greek starts in historic sequence (ἐβούλετο, imperfect) but finishes in primary (δοκῇ, subjunctive and συνέσται, future indicative). Hence the conclusion of editors that the end of the first sentence and the start of the second have been lost. The presence of αὖ, 'in turn', common in such a context of comparison, helps to confirm the view.

6   ἐνταῦθα δή: demonstratives are well able to serve as connecting words, with or without δή, which is scarcely used in the narrative of this work except to support connecting demonstratives.

a teacher of that: τούτου, 'of that', must refer to something in the lacuna just noted, such as τὸ ἀγαθόν, 'goodness' (Bartlett's 'virtue'). Were this a dialogue of Plato, we would expect the serious discussion to start now; whether goodness is teachable is explored in *Laches* and *Meno*. Instead we have Sokrates' tact in seeing that the occasion is wrong; in X.'s other Socratic works, Sokrates' serious talk is all one-to-one.

it was as learnable a thing as there was: literally 'if indeed anything else <was learnable>, this too <was> learnable'. Note καί twice, stressing first ἄλλο and then τοῦτο.

7   εἰς αὖθις: note εἰς + adverb; so too εἰς ἀεί.

νυνὶ δέ: as usual, νῦν δέ means 'in this situation', 'as things are'. The deictic -ί, common with the demonstratives οὗτος, ὅδε and ἐκεῖνος and their adverbs, can also emphasise some demonstrative adverbs like νῦν and ἐνθάδε.

in position: literally 'standing on <the spot>'. The tables have gone, and the girl is somewhere in the centre of the room.

someone bringing in hoops: if the assistant were the Syracusan or the boy, that could easily have been said. Someone familiar with the act is needed. A possible fifth member of the troupe comes dimly into view.

8   with a whirr: δονουμένους, 'being shaken', 'making a noise', suggests that the rings have attachments, like the moveable parts of a tambourine. All the verbs of this section bar one are in the imperfect.

ὅσον .. ὕψος: hyperbaton; and accusative of distance how far, like the accusative of time how long. Space and time are expressed similarly.

ὡς δέχεσθαι: consecutive infinitive, with ὡς for the commoner ὥστε. The idiom is noted in GMT 608 as quite common in X. among others.

9   Ἐν πολλοῖς μὲν .. καὶ ἄλλοις .. καὶ ἐν οἷς δέ: three idioms already noted are combined in this remarkable phrase, two obvious and one partly suppressed. For πολλοῖς καὶ ἄλλοις see I 6 and for καὶ .. δέ I 11 (μέν is effectively on its own, the force of δέ being largely confined to ἐν οἷς); between these two the basic ἄλλοις τε καί (see I 8) was squeezed into loss of τε. The whole phrase is draped around δῆλον, for which see I 13.

ὥστε: the word is quite common as a connective: so at 11 below, IV 15, 16, 54 and VIII 15.

can instruct her in full confidence: X. shows a husband doing exactly that in *Oec.* VII 4–X 13. That episode is unique in classical literature, and is correspondingly important for our understanding of how the relationship of Greek husband and wife worked. Female competence in male spheres of action is explored by Aristophanes in *Lysistrata* and *Ecclesiazusae*, and tragedy shows much alarming female competence, as well as

self-assertiveness (as in Medea's shocking remark at E. *Med.* 250-1, that she would rather fight three battles as a hoplite than give birth once). Plato discusses the topic in *R.* 451b9 ff.

whatever he'd like her to understand: literally 'whatever he'd like to treat her as understanding'. ὅ τι is direct object of ἐπισταμένῃ, and the sense of χρῆσθαι + dative of the person, 'to use/treat/have to do with', is picked up by Antisthenes.

10 **Antisthenes**: it is plain from his first utterance that considerations of tact are not uppermost in his mind.

Xanthippe: her reputation as a shrew is largely owed to this passage (see also *Mem.* II 2). Modern scholars reckon she had much to complain of; at the end of this party, when the married men go home to their wives, Sokrates does not. Her name suggests upper class origins (Aristophanes comments on names in -hippos in *Clouds*, 60-67). The name of their eldest son, Lamprokles, is also observed to be aristocratic by Guthrie in a long and exhaustive note on Sokrates' marital position (III2 65 note 3).

ὁρῶ .. κτωμένους: note the participle rather than the infinitive of indirect statement. ὁρῶ is a verb of perception here, not of seeing by eye.

people who want to be horse-trainers: literally 'people wanting to become horsy'; ἱππικούς is complement of γενέσθαι and τούς goes with the participle. The analogy which Sokrates makes (provoked by Xanthippe's name) is like many which Plato also has him make, in being drawn from life. The company's familiarity with horses may be seen at IX 7.

I chose my wife because of my desire: in the Greek the order of ideas is 'Wanting to be with people I obtained her'. The weight is in the participle phrase, which comes first.

εἰ ταύτην ὑποίσω the sense of threat or alarm in εἰ + future indicative was noted at I 7, on εἰ μὴ ἕψοιντο. Here Sokrates aims the element of threat at himself.

not far off the mark: thus X. punctuates the progress of the party, and also suggests that Sokrates has not truly answered Antisthenes' question.

11 **swords .. diving in and out of**: in *Mem.* I 3.9 also this sort of act is seen as reckless, like leaping into fire.

she might get hurt: πάσχειν τι, 'to suffer something', is a euphemism for getting killed. The clause verb is primary (πάθῃ, not πάθοι), despite the historic main verb, in virtual quotation of the original 'Let her not suffer!'

12 **Sokrates called to Antisthenes**: καλέσας, 'called', suggests that Sokrates and Antisthenes are not seated side by side; at IV 61 Sokrates uses οὗτος, 'he there', of him, whereas at VI 5 Kallias uses ὅδε, 'he here'.

At least the people watching this: γε, 'at least', by limiting the focus to the watching group helps to force agreement from Antisthenes: he cannot sustain his scepticism before evidence.

ἡ ἀνδρεία διδακτόν: the non-agreement of the complement is idiomatic in generalisations of this sort. So we may say, 'Bravery is a teachable thing'.

13 κράτιστον: understand ἐστιν. καί, 'actually', gives its force to the whole sentence.

εἰπεῖν .. ποιήσειν: λέγειν + infinitive usually expresses indirect command in Attic Greek (as noted at I 11), but that is λέγειν + present or aorist infinitive, not + future infinitive; here, εἰπεῖν virtually means 'to promise': hence the future. An infinitive of indirect statement is nevertheless so uncommon after the aorist εἶπον (GMT 753) that Eric Handley's suggestion of reading ἀνειπεῖν, 'to announce', is very attractive.

charge the enemy spearpoints: ὁμόσε ἰέναι, literally 'to go in one and the same direction'; the phrase is standard Greek for hoplites charging. V. D. Hanson, *The*

Western Way of War, New York 1989, 29 and especially 140-47, exposes the need for hoplites to keep close formation and to move in strict parallel when charging. λόγχαι, 'spearheads', exemplifies the figure of speech called synecdoche, when part of something is named for the whole of it. Quintilian discussing synecdoche (VIII 6.19-22) picks as his first example *mucronem pro gladio,* 'swordpoint for sword'.

14 **said Philippos**: he cannot afford in his rôle to let Antisthenes' wit go unchallenged, but his gibe at a contemporary politician brings something alien into the spirit of this symposium (though it might not be at others: see Murray, ch. 10).
Peisander: Aristophanes attacked the man in *Peace* (395), *Birds* (1553 ff.), *Lysistrata* (490) and elsewhere, as did the other comic poets, for greed, warmongering and cowardice. His position in Athenian politics was set out by Thoukydides (VIII 53 and 68); A. G. Woodhead, AJP 75 (1954) 131-146, partly, and rightly, rescues him from the calumnies of the comedians. In the crisis of 415 at least, Peisander acted vigorously and sensibly to protect the democracy; later, espousing oligarchic politics, he fell foul of it and died in obscurity abroad convicted of treason (Intr. 28).

15 ὅμως: literally 'nevertheless'. ὤν is thus given concessive force.
when he's dancing: literally 'with his figures'.
You might as well praise: literally 'you resemble one praising'.

16 προσενενόησα: προσεννοεῖν does not occur in classical Greek, but neither does προσνοεῖν, the reading of the MSS. προσεννοεῖν is a conjecture, but very plausible: ἐννοεῖν is a common compound, and certain prefixes can be added *ad lib.*, often as second prefixes; for προσ- see 3 above, and for ἀντι- I 15.
arms: literally 'hands', used in synecdoche for everything from shoulders to fingertips.
the way you need to dance if .. fitter: literally 'just as it is necessary to dance for the one meaning to have his body fitter'.
ἐγὼ μέν. μέν goes unanswered. Its original function was merely emphatic (GP 359), any contrast being left implicit.
from you: there is some stress on 'you', as the accent shows (παρὰ σοῦ, not παρά σου). Sokrates anticipates objection from the other gentlemen that he is willing to learn from a hireling a skill which, at symposia at least, had probably been held in increasing disesteem since Hippokleides danced away a marriage (Hdt. VI 129; and Burkhard Fehr in Murray, ch. 13).

17 πότερον: literally 'which one of two'. It has no equivalent in English in a direct question, and is represented in the translation by 'Why?'. In the end there are more than two questions; the original pair is marked by ἐπὶ τούτῳ and ἐπ' ἐκείνῳ (18), but a third is added at τόδε (19). All the possibilities are swept up at ἢ οὐκ ἴστε. The first question of the original pair develops some complexity; Sokrates speaks very earnestly.
ἢ εἰ ἥδιον. this ἢ is in response to μᾶλλον; ἥδιον is adverbial with the infinitives, which depend on βούλομαι. For the comparative ἥδιον (rather than ἡδέως) see note on 'fell silent' at I 9.
ἢ εἰ τοιούτων γυμνασίων ἐπιθυμῶ .. ποιεῖν: this ἢ is not in response to πότερον either, but simply marks an alternative wish within the first limb of the double question. ἐπιθυμεῖν works either with a genitive (represented in the translation by 'to use') or with an infinitive. In this sentence, both constructions occur together, but any sense of anomaly is diminished by the intervening matter.
into balance: ἰσόρροπος, 'balanced', occurs in the Hippocratic corpus as well as in tragedy and Plato. Sokrates expresses the old aristocratic ideal, but the rewards obtainable by athletic success had brought into prominence, even in the fifth century, the sort of specialised physique visible today in tall thin high-jumpers and hulking shot-

putters. R. Wallace makes an illuminating comparison with modern body-building in *Some Neglected Aspects of the Classical Tradition*, Classical Association News 11 (1994) 5-6.

18 **at my advanced age**: he was still under 50 (Intr. 19); he exaggerates for fun.

seven-couch room: Sokrates means something modest. See note at I 4.

in the shade: the virtue of a Greek house in the summer is its coolness. X. quotes Sokrates on ideal housing at *Mem.* III 8.8-10.

19 **a belly larger than it should be**: the jokes in Ar. *Clouds* 392 ff. confirm the picture here. At least gluttony was not to blame. μείζω is the alternative form for μείζονα. καιρός means 'right moment/measure/point' of something.

μὴ μαίνοιο: the optative is attuned to the historic ἔδεισα. Contrast ἐφοβοῦντο μή τι πάθη at 11 above.

ἤκουσα .. ὠρχούμην .. ἔμαθον .. ἐχειρονόμουν: the alternation of aspect between aorist and imperfective is worth note. X. could not have written οὐ μὲν ὠρχούμην: μέν and δέ do not follow οὐ in Attic prose. οὐ bears an accent when it is last word of its unit.

ὅμοια οἷς: literally 'things similar to the things which'. οἷς represents a combination of ἐκείνοις ἅ, called relative attraction; the English 'similar to what' matches it.

do some arm movements: χειρονομεῖν is used for shadow-boxing in Pl. *Lg.* 830c; if Kharmides meant that, there would be no disgrace. Expertise in dancing, as noted in 16 above, aroused social doubts.

20 **said Philippos**: in he comes again.

καὶ γὰρ οὖν: equivalent to τοιγαροῦν, and in this sense unique to X. So GP 112.

well matched: in using ἰσοφόρα Philippos does three things at once: he quotes *Od.* xviii 373 (where it describes two oxen of equal strength), he alludes to Sokrates' ἰσόρροπον (17 above), and (after a fashion) he compliments Kharmides.

δοκεῖς ἐμοί: after φαίνει the phrase is strictly redundant, but X. catches the manner of colloquial conversation.

κἄν = καὶ ἄν. ἄν goes with γενέσθαι (for γένοιο of direct speech). In sentences of some length it is common to find ἄν early and then repeated, especially beside the verb, as here.

weighing out .. loaves of bread: Philippos imports his joke from outside, as at 14 above. It seems to depend upon (i) all loaves (of the same sort and price, no doubt) having to be the same size and (ii) Kharmides exercising his arms to a point where his biceps would match his thigh muscles. The office of market-inspector is described in [Arist.] *Ath.* 51.

Do invite me: there is a light stress on 'me', marked in the Greek by μέν (see on 16 above). Kallias means that he himself would not be ashamed to dance in Sokrates' company, whatever others might feel.

22 **unnaturally comical**: literally 'more comical than nature'; Philippos would look comical dancing anyway, but he accentuates it.

ταὐτά: adverbial; 'in the same way', 'too'.

bending over forwards: easier, but also more comical. Aristophanes has some fun with the posture in *Clouds* 191-4.

they had been praising: note the translation of the imperfect; so too for καμπτομένη and ἐμιμεῖτο.

23 ἀπειρήκει: see under ἀπεῖπον in LSJ, not under ἀπολέγω.

the boy: one of Kallias' slaves, not the Syracusan's boy.

the big bowl: φιάλαι were wide, shallow bowls, about 25cm across, used for libation. Philippos may mean the one just so used (see 1 above). Plato's Alkibiades (*Smp.* 213e) also asks for a large cup (type unspecified: ἔκπωμα is his word) when he enters, but then asks for the wine cooler itself, which would hold nearly half a gallon: an epic touch, suggests Dover (PS 162). The three survivors of that party were eventually drinking from one φιάλη, passing it round (223c). Its shape would not make for easy drinking.

24   **Actually**: Sokrates seems to think that they would expect him not to approve of such drinking. If so, it would be for their sakes rather than his: he could see the rest of them under the table (Pl. *Smp.* 223cd).

Wine irrigates: the metaphorical use of the verb first occurs in Pindar (*I.* 6.64). Plato also puts the verb in Sokrates' mouth, when he speaks of the irrigating effect of symposia (*Phdr.* 276d).

mandragora: a plant with narcotic properties, also called mandrake. Plato (*R.* 488c) compares its power with that of alcohol: a rebellious crew on board the ship of state will 'fetter their honest captain with mandragora or drink or something else, and take control themselves'. So too [D.] X 6: 'We cannot rouse ourselves; we are like men who have drunk mandragora'.

it soothes irritability: λυπή here is passive. For its active sense, the capacity to annoy, see VI 2.

25   **too much to drink all at once**: both climate and geology make Greece a country where the rain can be destructive, falling heavily enough to wash away plants and soil together. Sokrates in using ποτίζειν, 'to give to drink', personifies the plants and prepares for the comparison.

have the air blow through them: literally 'be blown through by the breezes'. So Cicero uses *perflantur* of the hills of Rome (*Rep.* II 11).

to their pleasure and no more: literally 'how much they like, that much they drink'. Note the persistence of the singular verb for the neuter plural subject.

26   **we pour in**: Sokrates takes Philippos' verb (23 above) but uses it in the middle voice, implying that now the stomach is the cup.

never mind talk sense: μὴ ὅτι, 'never mind', is elliptical for something like μὴ εἴπῃς ὅτι, 'don't mention the fact that'. Note λέγειν τι, 'to mean something', 'to speak meaningfully'.

'besprinkle us with little cups and oft': κύλικες, the drinking cups of ancient Greece, were broad and shallow (like those sometimes used for champagne nowadays) but without the long thin stem and held by a handle either side. In diameter they vary from under 10cm to nearly 50; in depth they vary too; capacity varies accordingly.

Gorgias: his language came to seem too high-flown for prose (see note on I 5); Sokrates chooses his words to match that elevation. In ἐπιψακάζειν there is a play upon ἐπιπίνειν, 'to drink after eating'; both ἐπιψακάζειν and πυκνά the adverb are poets' words almost without exception until X.'s time; the whole phrase from μικραῖς happens nearly to form an iambic trimeter. It attracted Cicero's attention: in *Sen.* 46 he says: *pocula delectant me, sicut in Symposio Xenophontis, minuta atque rorantia*, 'I like cups that are small and yield the wine in droplets, as in Xenophon's Symposium.'

comparative merriness: the word reminds us of the purpose which X. declared at the start (παιγ- is akin to παιδ-). For the neuter of a comparative adjective used as an abstract noun see I 10. Note that ὑπὸ τοῦ οἴνου depends on μεθύειν, not on the participles, and that the use of ὑπό indicates some personification: see VIII 21.

27 **Philippos adding**: again he gets the last word in, and X. closes the episode in usual fashion (see Intr. 35, and 10 above). The decision on how to take their wine is a moment of importance in any symposium, when the host, or perhaps a distinguished guest, would establish how much water to add to the wine and how else to order the evening. Murray and F. Lissarrague refer to the topic in Murray, chs 1 and 14 respectively.

drive round the cups: that is, go round filling them. LSJ's 'push the cups round' implies producing new ones every time, which is less likely.

III

1 **tuned his lyre to the aulos**: so in a modern orchestra the oboe sets the pitch. For X. here, lyre and kithara are clearly interchangeable words; the distinction is drawn by West (48-59). Singing at symposia was once the especial contribution of youngsters present: if old customs were to be preserved, Autolykos should have sung (Ar. *Clouds* 1354-72, and Jan Bremmer, Murray ch. 9).

this mixture: Kharmides uses the word proper to their own mixing of wine with water in the κρατήρ, the mixing bowl.

thoughts of sex: Kharmides replaces Sokrates' 'thoughts of friendliness' (II 24) with Aphrodite, who can represent sexual intercourse as Bakkhos can wine. Sokrates intervenes too quickly for anyone to follow Kharmides' line, substituting τέρπειν, 'to cause enjoyment', and then shifting the ground further with ὠφελεῖν καὶ εὐφραίνειν, 'to cause benefit and pleasure'. Symposia could end in sexual intercourse, as vase-paintings show; the topic returns in VIII and IX.

2 εἶπαν = εἶπον. Many forms of εἶπον, especially the second persons, show the alpha of the weak aorist.

ποίων λόγων ἁπτόμενοι: the question lies in the participle phrase in Greek (see II 10): 'grasping what sort of discussion would we..?' In English such phrases are better translated as the main sentence.

3 **the promise that Kallias made**: at I 6. Sokrates tactfully puts his host back in charge. Note ἐγὼ μέν: μέν makes space for others to comment, but, as at II 20, that space does not have to be filled.

εἰ συνδειπνοῖμεν: the historicised version of ἐὰν συνδειπνῆτε, which represents Kallias' ἐὰν παρ' ἐμοὶ ἦτε (I 6).

what you each know about that's good: translation of both ἐπίστασθαι, to know about', and ἀγαθόν, 'good', is difficult because substitutions for each word are made as the dialogue develops. First Sokrates substitutes 'worth most' for 'good'; then Kallias switches to 'what I pride myself on', and (in 5) to what is seen as 'useful'. This is the point at which procedure for the first half of the evening is set; in this section everybody makes a preliminary statement, and in section IV, the longest of all the sections, most of the statements are amplified, in speech or dialogue or both.

ὅ τι ἕκαστος ἐπίστασθε .. ὅ τι ἕκαστος ἡγεῖται: relative clauses, not indirect questions, and treated as definite in context: 'that precise thing which each man ..' Note ἕκαστος singular with ἐπίστασθε 2nd pers. plural: 'you all severally'.

οὐδείς σοι .. ἀντιλέγει τὸ μὴ οὐ λέξειν: literally 'no one is saying the "shan't say"'. τὸ μὴ οὐ λέξειν is the direct object of -λέγει, and in τὸ μὴ οὐ λέξειν, μή has full value as the negative in 'shan't say', while οὐ merely repeats the negative implicit in ἀντι- (for ἀντι-, 'in response', see note on I 15). The idiom can be explored further in GMT 811-14 (with 685); there is an analysis in A. C. Moorhouse, CQ 34 (1940) 70-77. σοι here is ethic dative rather than indirect object dative; 'to you' would overtranslate it.

4   **I will tell you**: literally 'I am telling you'. The present is idiomatic in a context of this
immediacy.

what I most pride myself on: φρονεῖν μέγα, literally 'to think big', is common for 'to
be proud'. ἐπί + dative means 'in terms of', 'upon condition of'. The phrase now recurs
many times.

Antisthenes asked: his intervention here prepares us for his combative further
interrogation of Kallias at IV 2-3.

διδάσκων: the participle depends on an assumed main sentence of βελτίους ποιεῖς,
'You make them better'. Such ellipses are common in dialogue.

If that's what justice is, yes: literally 'If justice is gentlemanliness' (Kallias ignores the
first alternative). In Greek sentences of the form 'A is B' the subject is usually marked
by the presence of the definite article and the complement by the absence of it; the
complement tends to come first.

ἥ γε ἀναμφιλογωτάτη: to be understood are the words already used by Kallias,
'justice is gentlemanliness', to which Antisthenes responds 'The most indisputable
<justice is gentlemanliness>'. γε marks his lively assent, as commonly in dialogue (GP
130).

ἐπεί τοι: a rather colloquial equivalent of γάρ. So too at IV 5 and V 5, but without τοι.

ἀνδρεία μὲν καὶ σοφία .. ἡ δικαιοσύνη: the definite article here generalises
δικαιοσύνη: justice as a whole; in the case of the other two nouns X. has in mind not
bravery and intelligence as a whole but instances of them only; hence the absence of
definite article. βλαβερά is neuter plural (hence δοκεῖ is singular); for a neuter
complement to a feminine subject see II 12.

ἔστιν ὅτε: literally 'there is <occasion> when'; strictly, the rest of the sentence becomes
a dependent clause, but the phrase is used adverbially, like δῆλον ὅτι, sometimes
becoming ἐνίοτε.

οὐδὲ καθ' ἕν: literally 'not even by a single item'. The negative pronoun οὐδείς, 'no
one', comes from combining οὐδὲ εἷς, 'not even one', into one word. They were
sometimes separated for emphasis.

5   **I .. shall be happy**: οὐ φθονεῖν is fairly colloquial; the verb has a strong sense, 'to
begrudge', when positive, but a weak sense when negatived.

Come on, Nikeratos: Kallias turns first to the man who was (apart from Autolykos and
Lykon) his only original guest.

being a brave man: literally 'becoming a good man'. The translation expresses the
standard connotation of the phrase; see I 1, and for example *Il*. 5.529; and X. *Ages*. II 8.
The Homeric sense endured.

I could .. recite .. straight off: Nikeratos' attitude to his skill emerges at IV 7, where he
turns his knowledge into a joke against himself; he probably speaks here more of what
he was famous for than proud of.

6   **rhapsodes**: professional reciters of Homer; prizes for recitation were given at the
Panathenaia. They were not highly regarded; for a further contemptuous view see *Mem*.
IV 2.10, where Sokrates' interlocutor Euthydemos also uses ἠλίθιος of them; see too
Pl. *Ion*.

ὀλίγου: genitive of space within which; literally 'within a little', 'nearly'.

the deep meaning: Sokrates intervenes before Antisthenes can draw the inference that
Nikeratos also is stupid. ὑπόνοια is literally 'subthought'; so Plato for example uses it at
R. 378d.

Stesimbrotos .. Anaximander: Plato mentions Stesimbrotos at *Ion* 530d; it seems he was a rhapsode, and came from Thasos. Of the Anaximander mentioned here we know nothing.

ὥστε .. λέληθε: ὥστε + indicative (negative οὐ) is used for the consequence that does, rather than might, happen (GMT 582).

7   **Good looks**: the claim is made quite straightforwardly. Good looks mattered.

8   **Wealth**: deliberate paradox. Antisthenes means to be funny, and is helped by the fact that Hermogenes takes him at face value.

obol: the smallest unit of currency; there were six to a drachma.

μηδὲ ὀβολόν: understand αὐτῷ εἶναι, from εἴη αὐτῷ (in direct speech ἐστι σοί) in Hermogenes' sentence. Despite the fact that what Antisthenes says is an indirect statement ('I haven't an obol'), μή is the proper negative in oaths in indirect speech (GMT 685).

to dust himself with: wrestlers would cover themselves in oil and then sand themselves; so Lucian, *Anach.* 2. The infinitive, tacked on to explain, is called epexegetic.

9   **You certainly need a hearing**: that is to say, Antisthenes' paradox needs to be justified. Nothing indicates that Hermogenes is not the speaker still, but the response seems a little out of character; perhaps Kallias should have the line.

a very agreeable thing: Sokrates' reputation for comparative poverty makes him a good person to comment here. But his poverty appears to be a feature of his later years (Pl. *Ap.* 38b); in 424, close to the historical date of this work, he had means enough to fight as a hoplite at Delion (Pl. *Ap.* 28e, *La.* 181ab and *Smp.* 220e). See Intr. 19.

causes .. fewest fights: literally 'is least fight-about-able'.

needs no protection to preserve it: literally 'being unwatched is saved'. Sokrates gives his four points rhetorical balance with two pairs of anaphora, using first ἥκιστα twice and then the negative prefix ἀ- twice.

10   **What about you, Sokrates**: Sokrates might have been kept to the end (he is in IV); it is certainly right for Kallias to ask the question.

a very solemn face: Guthrie III2 40 n. 3 collects instances from the comic poets of σεμνός, 'solemn', used abusively particularly of Sokrates. See note on VIII 3.

Procuring: μαστροπεία is first recorded here; its noun of origin, μαστροπός, 'pimp', procurer', is first recorded at Ar. *Th.* 558. There is the same lack of explicitness in the Greek word (whose root means 'seek': see Chantraine under μαίομαι) as in the English. It is Sokrates' fun to choose an outrageous word and to omit the expected 'of partners for sex' - which he never meant anyway, as he eventually reveals at IV 61-62.

11   **σύ .. δῆλον .. ὅτι .. φρονεῖς**: σύ works in hyperbaton with φρονεῖς, δῆλον ὅτι, '<it is> clear that', being virtually adverbial (see I 13). προσειπὼν ὅτι, words not in the MSS, have been added by editors.

Kallippides the actor .. extraordinary airs: he became a byword for overacting. Aristotle refers to him at *Po.* 1461b-1462a; Plutarch mentions him four times. ὑπερσεμνύνεσθαι, 'to be hyperproud', is not otherwise recorded; its cue is in 10 above.

can get .. weeping in their seats: literally 'can seat .. weeping'.

12   **νικηφόρος**: nominative because it refers to the same person as οὗτος.

blushed: ἀνερυθριᾶν, 'to blush up', is recorded only here and at Pl. *Chrm.* 158c. The prefix draws attention to the spread of the blush.

By Zeus: it appears that he was free to swear like his elders.

13   **μήν**: 'μήν adds liveliness to the .. question' (GP 332).

leant up against him: a beautifully perceived moment.

βασιλέως: without the definite article βασιλεύς means the great king of Persia, the standard example of ultimate wealth after the fall of Lydia.

Caught red-handed: literally 'I have been caught in the act of theft itself'; but the phrase had become a cliché.

14 **What's your particular glory**: Nikeratos varies the formula, perhaps to tease Hermogenes, a man of some stolidity (see VI 1-4); in the active the verb had religious connotations (see IV 47-49).

σφίσι: dat. pl. of σφεῖς, 'they'. The nominative seldom occurs; the word is mostly used reflexively.

IV

1 **Sokrates said**: he acts as chairman so that Kallias can lead off.

ἃ ἕκαστος ὑπέσχετο: this clause forms the subject of ἐστιν. ὡς .. ἐστιν is the object clause of ἀποδεικνύναι.

ἀκούοιτ᾽ ἄν: 'you might like to hear'. Kallias uses the polite idiom of optative + ἄν in response to Sokrates' use of it.

what justice is: 'goodness', 'justice' and 'gentlemanliness' were used one for another without discrimination in III 4.

Brilliant: literally, 'O best of men'.

2 **rose at the answer**: in Herodotos (an author whose vocabulary often shows up in X.: Intr. 34), and also in Thukydides, the verb used here can mean 'to react to rebellion'.

once they know .. pay for it: literally 'because of the knowing that there is <that> upon buying at which they shall have their needs'. ὅτου depends on πριάμενοι as the regular genitive of price. With ἔστιν ὅτου compare ἔστιν ὅτε at III 4. Kallias sees the situation exactly as the Old Oligarch (Intr. 8) saw it: ἐν γὰρ τοῖς βελτίστοις ἔνι .. ἀκρίβεια .. εἰς τὰ χρηστά, ἐν δὲ τῷ δήμῳ .. πονηρία. ἥ τε γὰρ πενία αὐτοὺς μᾶλλον ἄγει ἐπὶ τὰ αἰσχρά, καὶ .. ἡ ἀμαθία ἡ δι᾽ ἔνδειαν χρημάτων, 'amongst the upper classes there is a great efficiency for good, whereas the people are in trouble, being drawn to bad behaviour both by their poverty and by the ignorance that comes of poverty' ([X.] *Ath.* 1.5).

3 **And .. actually**: ἦ is little more than the expiration of breath that it sounds like; it commonly expresses some astonishment.

what they get: note that in Greek the clause is indefinite: 'whatever it is that they get.'

οὐ μὲν δή: this is an idiom of response peculiar to X. (GP 392).

4 καί .. μέντοι: another Xenophontic idiom (GP 413).

5 **By Zeus .. let him**: Kallias was getting irritated by Antisthenes, and Sokrates intervenes to lower the temperature. As it happens, his example of soothsayers can be undone from X. himself: at *HG* II 4. 18-19 he tells of a soothsayer at the battle of Munychia in 403 who foresaw and fulfilled his own death.

ἀνεχέσθω: Sokrates uses the present imperative; Kallias used the aorist. The change of aspect deserves note: Kallias' aorist puts it simply; 'just put up with it'. Sokrates' imperfective draws attention to the process of putting up with it.

6 **the improvement that .. can give you**: literally 'at what you will be better if you consort with me'. ἃ depends on βελτίονες: accusative of respect.

has dealt with: literally 'has composed <poetry> about'.

estate management .. Odysseus: the longer the list goes on, the more risible it gets, as Nikeratos intended.

kingship too: Antisthenes, quoting *Il.* iii 179, was probably going to take a cynical line (Intr. 26) and mock the use of such knowledge in a world where kings were obsolete,

but Nikeratos, quoting xxiii 335-7, gives him no chance and carries on even more tongue in cheek, in a world where chariots were owned by the rich but driven by hired professionals.

the right-hand horse: chariots were raced anti-clockwise; the left-hand horse was kept on a close rein so that it rounded the turning-post precisely but with some loss of speed, while the other horse, with further to go, was given its head and encouraged to pull the team round as fast as possible.

αὐτὸν δὲ κλινθῆναι .. ἡνία χερσίν: our texts of Homer show αὐτός for αὐτόν (Homer's infinitive is imperatival whereas Nikeratos' depends on δεῖ), εὐπλέκτῳ ἐνὶ δίφρῳ, 'in a well-woven chariot', for εὐξέστου ἐπὶ δίφρου, and ὁμοκλήσας for ὁμοκλήσαντ᾽. Such variation is commonplace in ancient texts.

There are Homeric forms as follows: κλινθῆναι for κλιθῆναι; εὐξέστου (note the position of the breathing) is quadrisyllabic; δίφρος means 'chariot-board', 'chariot', rather than 'seat'; ἧκα; τοῖιν for τοῖν and used as a pronoun; κένσαι uniquely for κεντῆσαι; ἡνία neuter for ἡνίαι. ἀτάρ, or αὐτάρ, common in Homer with the force of δέ, is common later only in Aristophanes; οἱ, dat. sing. of ἑ, has possessive force with ἡνία: 'the reins to it', 'its reins'.

7   **if I remember**: που, by origin literally 'somewhere', adds a nice touch of self-deprecation.
       An onion adds relish to a drink: Nikeratos quotes from *Il.* xi 630, and gives a wittily unheroic turn to the conversation. ἐπί goes with ποτῷ and κρόμυον is usually κρόμμυον. Onion may be brought in a saucer to accompany a drink in Greece today.
       πίεσθε: the usual future of πίνειν is πίομαι, but the exceeding rarity of a future with neither sigma nor contraction (compare ἔδομαι from ἐσθίειν) may have led X. to 'correct' the anomaly, as later authors did.

8   **μηδὲ διανοηθῆναι μηδένα ἄν**: this is the reflex in indirect speech of οὐδὲ ἂν διενοήθη οὐδείς. μή is for οὐ because the whole phrase is subordinate to a verb appearing in a purpose clause where the negative is naturally μή.
       there's the chance: κίνδυνος, 'danger', had a weakened sense in colloquial Greek. So too the verb κινδυνεύει usually means 'there's a likelihood'.
       season: literally 'sweeten'. Onions have a high sugar content, as shown by the way they caramelise when fried. But 'to season' is the standard sense of the verb ἡδύνειν; Aristotle uses it of the effect of salt (*Mete.* 359a32-34).
       εἰ .. τρωξόμεθα: for εἰ + future indicative see I 7; Sokrates means the threat humorously. τρώγειν, 'to munch', is the verb for humans eating fruit and vegetables; it is especially the verb for herbivorous animals eating.
       after dinner as well: it seems that they had been served onions already; onions were a staple item of food, but if they were served twice in a meal, it would not say much for the variety of Kallias' cuisine.
       ὅπως μὴ φήσῃ: to introduce this phrase a main verb in the imperative, such as φυλαττέσθω, 'let a man take care', may be understood. At *Mem.* I 2.37 the imperative, exceptionally, is present. The idiom is set out in GMT 271-283.
       had a fine time of it: ἡδυπαθεῖν, 'to suffer sweet', allows Sokrates a final punning reference to the onions.

9   **Nibbling**: the force of the prefix ὑπο- is probably diminutive; so LSJ, ὑπό F II. Their interpretation under ὑποτρώγω is mistaken.
       καλῶς ἔχει: 'it's fine'. The idiom of adverb + ἔχειν is very common, and is still in use.

feed .. before a bout: literally 'upon feeding them garlic bring them to a bout'. The more important piece of information is in the participle phrase.

10 **I'll speak .. said Kritoboulos**: the speech he now makes is the longest one so far; Antisthenes exceeds him slightly a little later; Sokrates outdoes both in VIII. Long speeches are unlikely to have been typical of ordinary symposia; Plato's *Symposium* is a special case, and the length of Sokrates' speech in VIII is probably affected by that (Intr. 15). The length of the speeches of Kritoboulos and Antisthenes, however, is to be seen as part of X.'s characterisation of them.

If I'm not .. you .. would .. deserve a 'mixed' conditional, in that the clause verb is primary and the main verb historic. But this sort of thing happens in all languages; and ὑπέχοιτε ἄν is the polite version of ὑπέχετε, 'you deserve'. Kritoboulos makes a challenging and competitive start.

deception: prosecutions for deception of the people did occur. The first notable case concerned Miltiades son of Kimon, in the year after Marathon (Hdt. vi 136). See D. M. McDowell, The Law in Classical Athens (London 1978), 179-181.

11 **μὴ ἑλέσθαι ἄν**: in direct speech οὐκ ἂν ἑλοίμην. μή replaces οὐ as the proper negative after a verb of swearing (see III 8).

12 **Kleinias**: he was probably a cousin of the outstandingly good-looking Alkibiades; Kritoboulos' relationship with him is mentioned at *Mem.* I 3.8. Davies, 600 VI, explores the family.

τυφλός .. τῶν ἄλλων .. Κλεινίου: τυφλός is seldom used as it is here, with dependent phrases; the genitive is that of the area within which there is concern, literal or metaphorical.

13 **τὸν δέ γε σοφόν**: δέ γε here simply tacks on a third item to the first two (GP 155-6; this instance is not noted); τὸν μὲν ἰσχυρόν .. is answered by ὁ δὲ καλός ..

will achieve: the right English here for the optative + ἄν is, as often, the simple future.

15 **perfection**: literally 'all excellence'. Behind Kritoboulos' claim may be dimly seen a concern of Plato's Sokrates, that qualities such as justice, admirable in themselves, are not the whole of goodness.

Because we .. are an inspiration to: literally 'because of the us breathing something into'. A transitive use of ἐμπνεῖν is common in Homer.

what's more: this exceptional use of καὶ μήν within a sentence is largely an idiom of X. (GP 352).

shame and self-control: these qualities were noted in Autolykos at I 8, and Sokrates returns to them in his speech in VIII.

οἵ γε: addition of γε to the relative pronoun gives causal force to the clause.

16 **ἰοίην**: ἴοιμι is much the commoner form of the optative of εἶμι; but other verbs in -μι have present optative active singular in -ιην, -ιης -ιη as a rule.

17 **ἀλλά .. μέντοι**: a progressive use, 'almost confined to Xenophon' (GP 411).

ταύτῃ γε: the adverb looks forward to the participle phrase, which is further interpreted by ὡς, 'on the grounds that'.

go over: the verb παρακμάζειν is first recorded in X.

good-looking old men .. for Athena: the evidence survives, just, on the Parthenon frieze (slab X in particular).

18 **ὧν τις δέοιτο**: the bare optative makes this a historic indefinite clause. The cause of its historicity is hard to see. Perhaps διαπράττεσθαι is to be taken as imperfect rather than present infinitive, which might just be rendered in English as 'it's nice to have been getting people to do what you wanted'. But some editors read ὧν <ἄν> τις δέοιτο: 'what you would like them to do' - apodosis without protasis.

19 **You make this boast**: some editors print this sentence as a statement. We do not know how classical authors punctuated their work; the earliest forms of question mark known are medieval.

uglier than: 'ugliest of ..' says Kritobulus, using a common idiom and also playing with the genitive in Sokrates' phrase ἐμοῦ καλλίων.

all the Seilenoi: Seilenos was a companion of Dionysos and father of the satyrs. Good evidence for them comes in our only whole surviving satyr play, *Cyclops*, by Euripides. Vase paintings of them give us a good idea of what Greeks thought ugly: among other things, a snub nose and protruding eyes, such as Sokrates was said to have (Pl. *Tht.* 143e; comparison of Sokrates with Seilenoi is also made by Alkibiades, Pl. *Smp.* 215a-b).

20 Ἄγε νυν: νυν, not νῦν. So in English there are phrases like 'Well now', 'There now', where 'now' has a much reduced sense.

ὅπως μεμνήσῃ: see 8 above.

διακριθῆναι .. κρινάτω: it is not uncommon for the prefix of a verb soon repeated to be dropped. So too with διαφέρειν at V 8.

Alexander son of Priam: often known as Paris, the judge of the most famous beauty competition of all between Hera, Athena and Aphrodite. For the form of phrase 'A son of B' see I 2.

21 οὕτω σαφές .. ὡς: X. uses οὕτω .. ὡς rather than οὕτω .. ὥστε several times in this work: II 8, and 37 and 39 below.

at him for real: literally 'at himself'. For the force of αὐτός see II 4.

22 **why be .. a nuisance**: literally 'why provide business'. To translate the ethic dative μοι is difficult: 'why, pray,' would once have served; but if Sokrates were stressing the nuisance to himself, he would say ἐμοί. There is great irritation, nevertheless, as is shown by δῆτα (GP 270).

trying to get him where you can see him: use of the future 'you shall see', makes this virtually a purpose clause. For the future so used with a relative (not an uncommon idiom), see GMT 565. The translation offered requires ἄγεις but not παρέχεις to have conative force. Todd, Ollier and Tredennick all suppose Sokrates to be the object of ἄγεις and translate 'bringing me where you can see him' or words to that effect; Todd emends τε to τέ μ᾽.

ἡ μὲν αὐτοῦ ὄψις: αὐτοῦ is again emphatic; otherwise the order of words would be ἡ μὲν ὄψις αὐτοῦ.

23 **Hermogenes intervened**: Hermogenes lacked a sense of humour, as is painfully obvious in VI 1-5. X. has him intervene here to point the humour up; Sokrates is apparently provoked into fantasy.

madly in love: literally 'struck by passion'.

οὐδὲ πρὸς σοῦ ποιῶ τὸ ..: literally 'I don't treat <it> as even issuing from you, the ..', 'I don't put <it> at your door that ..'. πρός + genitive is one way of marking the agent or source of action in Greek (see I 10 on ἐκ).

to look on .. complacently: περιορᾶν, 'to look around', carries the implication 'and do nothing'.

Well, when: for μήν marking the question see III 13.

whiskers .. move down: Kritoboulos appears to be growing sideboards to compensate for lack of beard. LSJ cite ἴουλος, 'down', 'first facial hair', only from the poets, overlooking this instance; καθέρπειν, 'to creep down', is also a rare and poetical word, and is not used elsewhere by X. In the next sentence προσεκαύθη is recorded by LSJ

here alone in a metaphorical sense. Some comical effect was clearly intended; what it was meant to be is not clear. Since hair does not grow immediately behind the ears, Sokrates may be into pure nonsense.

τούτῳ μέν .. Κλεινίᾳ δέ: virtually possessive datives dependent on ἴουλος.

τότε: its function is to pick up the participle: 'while going.., that's when..'

24 **His father .. sent him to me**: one of the two indictments of Sokrates in 399 claimed that he corrupted the young. Here X. attests the confidence which one Athenian father had in him. Others are named at Pl. *Ap.* 33e.

Gorgons: first mention of a Gorgon's head, supposedly able to petrify people, comes at *Il.* v 741, on Athena's shield.

never went away: οὐδαμοῦ is used emphatically rather than literally ('in no place'); so too in 30 below.

blinking: σκαρδαμύττειν is also used by Euripides, in his surviving satyr play *Cyclops*, 626. R. G. Ussher in his edition of it (Rome, 1978) notes the colloquial tone of the word: Sokrates is trying to keep things light.

25 **δοκεῖ μοί γε**: γε marks δοκεῖ; it cannot mark the unstressed μοι. For its position see GP 150. δοκεῖ μοι was perhaps seen as virtually one word.

and we're talking confidentially: literally 'so as to have been spoken among us ourselves'. Plato also uses the idiom: see GMT 777.

has actually kissed: advice from Sokrates on the dangers of kissing was once given to X. himself; he records it at *Mem.* I 3.8-13, Kritoboulos being the example. See note on VIII 1.

οὗ ἔρωτος: not to be taken together. ἔρωτος depends on ὑπέκκαυμα and οὗ, which refers to the kissing, on δεινότερον (genitive of comparison).

26 **ἀφεκτέον**: gerund of ἀπέχειν; literally 'there must be distance kept'. The person by whom the thing is to be done goes in the dative.

the kisses of good-lookers: that is, 'the kisses one might give to good-lookers'. τῶν ὡραίων is objective genitive.

27 **scare**: literally 'bogey-madden'. μορμολύττεσθαι is a slightly comical combination of Μορμώ, a bogey used to scare children (*HG* IV 4.17) and λύττα, 'madness'.

you in person .. the pair of you .. Kritoboulos: Kharmides wittily holds up the name of the other till the end. In using μαστεύειν, 'to search', he may be echoing Sokrates' μαστροπεία, 'procuring' (III 10: μαστεύειν shares a root with μαίεσθαι); note too the chiasmus of 'bare shoulder' (ὦμον γυμνὸν πρὸς γυμνῷ .. ὤμῳ) and the considerable hyperbaton of σε and ἔχοντα. As often, X. uses the participle after the verb of seeing.

at the schoolmaster's: it looks as if a teacher's store could serve as a local library.

28 **so that was the itch .. was it**: literally 'those things then, as if bitten by some small animal, I itched as to the shoulder'. ὦμον is an accusative of respect; ταῦτα, 'those things', stands as pronoun for 'those itchings', and is internal accusative. The physical pain in the shoulder is matched to the emotional pain in the heart by τε with the one and καί with the other.

πλεῖν: the form is common in Aristophanes and later Attic prose for πλέον or πλεῖον.

beastie: θηρίον is in form a diminutive of θήρ, 'wild animal', but it lost any diminutive sense early.

a scratch upon my heart: the Greek is high-flown; καρδία, 'heart', is very rare in prose but very common in poetry, and κνῆσμα, from κνῆν, 'to scrape, scratch', is unique in its metaphorical application here.

your chin .. your head: literally 'you grow your hair long as to your chin equally with your head'. For the acc. of respect in τὸ γένειον compare the Homeric phrase κάρη κομόωντες Ἀχαιοί.

And that was how .. earnest: again X. draws attention to the ending of a phase of conversation.

29 **Your turn, Kharmides**: if order of speaker here followed order of speaker in III, Antisthenes would speak next.

πιστεύεσθαι: a personal passive for a verb taking a dative of the person in the active is surprising, but it is common with πιστεύειν from the fourth century on. The personal passive ἀπειλεῖσθαι, however (31 below), appears to be unique.

30 **when I was a rich man**: in 415, on the eve of the great expedition to Sicily, many statues of Hermes which stood outside people's houses were deliberately vandalised. Kharmides was implicated in the prosecutions which ensued. It is easy to date his impoverishment to that event, but if he had become poor as early as 422 (the dramatic date of this work), some other cause is needed (Intr. 28, and 31 below).

ὅτε μὲν .. πρῶτον μέν: the second μέν is answered by ἔπειτα δέ and the first by νῦν δέ.

αὐτόν τί με κακόν: τι goes with κακόν and με with αὐτόν. In μή τίς μου above and in ἀεί τί μοι below the indefinite precedes the personal pronoun; that precedence may account for the interlacing here (at 40 below, however, we have εἴ μού τις). τί and τίς are not interrogatives; their accents are owed to the enclitics that follow them.

sycophants: in a community with ever increasing use of the courts, with no provision for state prosecution, and with reward in certain cases for those who took on the task themselves, some mischief was likely to arise. X. speaks of it at *Mem.* II 9.

more likely to be hurt by them than vice versa: literally 'competent to suffer badly more than to do them <badly>'.

to spend money: the two best-known services (λειτουργίαι) that rich men could render the state were paying for a tragic chorus at the Great Dionysia and equipping and maintaining a trireme for a year. Other liturgies are mentioned at *Oec.* 2.6.

couldn't get away: Kharmides was not prevented by any law or physical disability. For the sense of ἐξῆν see ἔξεστι in the next sentence, and compare Ar. *Clouds* 530: παρθένος γὰρ ἔτ᾽ ἦν κοὐκ ἐξῆν πώ μοι τεκεῖν, 'I was still unmarried, and I couldn't have a child'.

31 **I'm deprived of my foreign estates**: many Athenians owned land on Euboia, but they were not cut off from that until the Spartan occupation of Dekeleia in 413. ὑπερόριος, 'foreign', literally 'across the border', suggests something close to Attica, which could be territory at Oropos lost after the battle of Delion in 424.

my Attic properties: literally 'the local bits', 'the bits in the land'. This use of the word is without parallel in LSJ. We do not know where in Attica Kharmides' land was. If his properties lay in the north west, they would have been close to the Peloponnesians' path of invasion in 431.

household goods have been sold: the sale will be the penalty for complicity in the mutilation of the Herms (30 above). Fragments survive of the record of the sale of Alkibiades' property after his condemnation.

πέπραται: the root πρα- serves for the perfect and aorist passive of 'to sell'; see LSJ under πέρνημι. πωλεῖν and ἀποδίδοσθαι supply the rest of the verb.

32 εἰμὶ νῦν μέν: νῦν μέν εἰμι would better match τότε δέ .. ἦν, but Kharmides speaks like one who has committed himself to one pattern of utterance before he sees the other. ἦ is commoner than ἦν, but see 30 above.

pay my dues .. contribution: φόρος and ἀποφέρειν are the technical terms for tribute and paying it; this is the language for members of the Athenian empire paying their dues to Athens and Athena. Kharmides is being humorous, first about his own liturgies and then in expression of the upper class view that the poorer citizens were subsidised by the state, for jury service (from *c.* 454) and later for other public business like attendance at assembly (the much disputed diobelia) or at the Dionysia. LSJ do not record this instance of τέλος (here rendered as 'contribution'); it should be *s.v.* in I 8 as a comic perversion.

Σωκράτει: it goes with συνῆν; note the hyperbaton.

οὐκέτι οὐδέν .. οὐδενί: a small modification is now necessary of the rule set forth at I 9: when the first of a string of negatives is itself compound, following compound negatives merely add energy to it, as here.

because of the city: in tax, that is.

33   **never to be rich**: Kallias was to be poor himself one day; here he expresses a polite astonishment at the attitude Kharmides adopts.

the powers of aversion: literally 'the apotropaic ones'. So Aristophanes has his chorus pray at *Knights* 1307; at *Birds* 61 Apollo is identified as the apotropaic god.

have a very foolhardy .. turning up: literally 'abide the outcome like one fond of risks if I'm hoping to get something from somewhere'.

34   **It is because I think**: Antisthenes begins like one raring to go; the Greek even lacks 'It is'. Sokrates' talent for paradox has plainly rubbed off on Antisthenes. Even more important is the impact on him of Sokrates' indifference to physical comfort. Sokrates' actual poverty came later, after the dramatic date of this work (see note on III 9), and for him it was incidental. In Antisthenes we see that indifference turned into an enabling principal.

35   πολλὰ ἔχοντες χρήματα: the smallest possible hyperbaton.

ἐφ' ᾧ .. κτήσονται: a future indicative in this sort of clause is 'sometimes' used by Herodotos and Thoukydides (GMT 610); an infinitive is commoner.

36   **tyrants**: Antisthenes names no names. Tyrants were an intermittent phenomenon of Greek politics; most seized power with popular support, but tended to lose both support and power, in that order.

37   **the net result .. is that I .. reach**: literally 'it survives, is left over, for me to reach'. LSJ quote the impersonal use of περιεῖναι only in the orators.

ἄχρι τοῦ .. μέχρι τοῦ .. ὥστε: X. rings the changes. πεινῆν and διψῆν share with ζῆν and χρῆσθαι the peculiarity of being α-contracting verbs that show η instead of α.

38   γε μήν: this pairing is several times more common in X. than in all other classical literature (GP 347).

thatch: literally 'reeds'; the plural is in common use for 'roof'.

to rouse me: literally 'to rouse'. The object is to be understood: LSJ record no intransitive use of the verb; otherwise, 'to get up' would do.

wants sex: see III 1. Antisthenes treats sex as a merely physical need, comparable with that for food, clothing and housing.

39   πάντα .. ἕκαστα: 'all, taken together' .. 'all, taken separately'.

more pleasurable than is appropriate: the hedonist proposition 'what is good is what is pleasurable' is here close to straight contradiction.

40   **piece**: Antisthenes toys with a paradox: the word implies a piece of property, something solid.

εἰ .. παρέλοιτο: the clause belongs after ὁποῖον (its optative παρέλοιτο matches παρέχοι ἄν in its apodosis) but has been promoted for emphasis to the front of the sentence.

41 προσφέρωμαι: probably middle (see LSJ *s.v.*, C.1). In which case, perhaps τι should be added, as the verb does not appear to be used intransitively. A similar view of food and drink is expressed by Sokrates at *Mem.* I 6.5.

Thasian wine: the quality of wine from Thasos is attested casually at Ar. *Lys.* 196 and *Wealth* 1021.

42 **Frankly, .. much juster**: Antisthenes aims this remark at his host; γε neatly underlines the word 'just' that they were quarrelling over, first at III 4 and then in 2-3 above.

εἰκός: this is the main sentence; understand ἐστι, as is usual. The accusative and infinitive phrase is draped around it in hyperbaton, first the complement δικαιοτέρους, then εἶναι and then the subject τοὺς .. σκοποῦντας, the common order of words for such statements (see I 13 and III 4).

οἷς .. ἀρκεῖ: the relative clause (a definite one) might have been followed by οὗτοι but is short enough not to need it. μάλιστα and ἥκιστα mark the two units adequately.

43 **typically free**: Antisthenes gives a moral turn to a word used earlier in a more political sense (II 4).

Here's Sokrates .. here's me: the sentences are paired by τε .. τε, a pairing rarer in prose than verse (GP 503). The only other occurrence of the pair in this work is on the lips of Hermogenes (49 below).

44 σχολάζων: strictly, the participle should be either in the accusative, in agreement with με, the unspoken subject of the infinitives, or in the dative, harking back to μοι (possible confusion with Σωκράτει prevented that); but the clause ὃ .. τιμῶμαι has broken Antisthenes' thread, and he makes the participle agree with the subject of τιμῶμαι.

45 τά τε ἄλλα .. καί: see I 8. τὰ ἄλλα is accusative of respect.

I'm going to be his debtor, for a loan: literally 'I shall have come from him having borrowed' or 'I shall be here having borrowed from him'; παρ᾽ αὐτοῦ works with either verb. Nikeratos' intervention is witty: in two or three sentences he takes envying and borrowing off Kallias, a Homeric quotation off himself, weighing and counting off Antisthenes, and his own name for fondness of money off everyone.

non-neediness: literally 'the being in need of nothing'.

οὕτω: this looks forward to the quotation from Homer (*Il.* ix 122-3: part of the compensation offered to Akhilleus by Agamemnon); it is represented in the translation by 'so' at the other end of the phrase. In the quotation χρυσοῖο is the old form of χρυσοῦ and ἐείκοσι of εἴκοσι.

46 **to say who your friends are**: literally 'to say your friends who they are'; as often, the subject of the indirect question is made the object of the introducing verb.

47 **Greek and foreign ..**: Hermogenes' whole short speech shows so much patterning that some frigidity creeps in. The opening μέν is irregularly met by καὶ μήν (as at VII 3); after that he uses τε .. καί three times, καί .. καί twice, οὔτε .. οὔτε twice, and μέν .. δέ three times, once with anaphora (πάντα μέν .. πάντα δέ); there is another anaphora in πᾶσαι γοῦν .. πάντες γοῦν .., the pair of sentences subsidiary to the μέν/καὶ μήν pair. For the structure of ὡς .. εὔδηλον see I 13.

our communities .. other peoples: 'πόλεις' and 'ἔθνη' repeat the distinction Hermogenes made between Greek and non-Greek at the start. There is plentiful evidence in Herodotos that Greek oracles were not used only by Greeks; there is a

notable example in I 46.2-56.1. Likewise there was Greek consultation of the oracle of Ammon in Egypt.

48   **never let me out of their sight**: the idea of an all-seeing god was well established, but with reference to divine capacity rather than to divine practice. Hermogenes' idea goes beyond mere capacity.

καὶ ὅ τι .. ἀποβήσεται: the definite nature of the clause is emphasised by the initial καί.

ἀγγέλους: not the object of πέμποντες but in apposition to the following trio of nouns which are its objects.

ὅ τι δεῖ καὶ ἃ οὐ χρή: the variation is idle. χρή, by origin a noun, fell out of favour, being less amenable to conjugation than δεῖ the verb.

49   ἐπαινῶ τε .. ὧν τε.. εὐφημῶ τε .. καὶ ἐφ' οἷς: the repetition of τε is remarkable. καὶ ὧν .. καὶ εὐφημῶ was more to be expected.

their gifts .. I .. return in part: literally 'of what they give (note the definite clause, in contrast with the two in the next two sentences) I always provide <some> back.' Hermogenes refers to the practice of libation and sacrifice.

the gods also: as well as other gentlemen, that is. Sokrates is alluding to the conversation at II 4.

50   **When they arrived at Philippos**: yet to speak are Lykon, Autolykos, Sokrates and Philippos. It is fairly plain that Autolykos will not speak; nor need his father. It also becomes clear that Sokrates is being held back so that what he says is the climax of this section.

You mean I shouldn't be? .. After all: literally 'Isn't it right, since'. ὁπότε can have causal force; the addition of γε confirms it (see 15 above).

for fear .. despite themselves: a claim in keeping with his self-confidence.

52   **you, man from Syracuse .. your boy**: parallels and contrasts with Autolykos are evident, but X. does not interpret Kharmides' question for his readers. Sokrates' contribution is further postponed. παῖς, 'child' (male or female), also meant 'slave'; slaves had the dependent status of children.

his ruin: literally 'to destroy him'. The Syracusan means moral corruption rather than the boy's obsolescence as a dancer and a beauty. Sokrates takes 'destroy' to mean 'murder', in deliberate misunderstanding.

53   **What great .. do they think**: literally '<They plot> thinking what so great'. The question is asked in the participle phrase (see III 2); the main verb is borrowed from the previous speaker.

ἂν διαφθαρῆναι: the reflex of ἂν διαφθαρείη in direct speech, to fit with εἰ γένοιτο.

54   **By Zeus I do**: for economy, we may reckon, at least in principle. The two girls of the troupe would also share a bed .

εὐτύχημα .. τὸ .. φῦναι: first the complement, then the subject, marked by the definite article: the sentence has familiar form. The subject of φῦναι, with which ἔχοντα agrees, is σε, to be understood from σου. The object of ἔχοντα is τὸν χρῶτα.

55   **puppets**: literally 'string-pulled things'. The word occurs elsewhere only in Herodotos (II 48.2) until much later. The apparent contempt, of both audience and troupe, is surprising; in context the Syracusan is probably trying to be funny.

ὅπου ἂν ᾖς: this time X. preserves the primary sequence of the original prayer rather than write ὅπου εἴης to fit with the historic ἤκουον.

abundance .. wits: φρένες, 'wits', is mostly a poets' word; the balance in the phrasing is underlined by the assonance of ἀφθονία and ἀφορία.

56   ἐφ' ᾗ: the gender anticipates that of τέχνη.

εἶπας, εἶπαν: for the α see III 2.

Let us first agree: the language that follows is familiar to us from Plato's dialogues. Sokrates' friends knew it at first hand. There is parody of Plato, especially in the repeated 'Absolutely'; there is surely parody of Sokrates too in the repetitions of οὐκοῦν, μέν without δέ, and τί δέ. This is a fine example of the fun which X. set out to show at the start.

57   τοῦτον: the masculine does service for both genders, picking up both ἥν and ὄν. Partners of either sex could be procured, as is shown by the law which Aiskhines quotes (1.14): νόμον .. τὸν τῆς προαγωγείας, .. ἐάν τις ἐλεύθερον παῖδα ἢ γυναῖκα προαγωγεύῃ ('the law .. on procuring, .. if someone procures a free-born boy or woman').

One contribution to acceptability comes from: literally 'Is there one particular thing aiming at the being pleasing from'.

59   **which of these would help towards**: literally 'of these .. the bits contributing to'. The participle of the Greek is expressed as a clause in the English .

ἀμείνων .. ἂν εἴη .. ὁ .. δυνάμενος: complement, verb 'to be', subject; note the word order again, and the prominence given to ἑνί in preparation for the contrast with πολλοῖς. πολλοῖς in the event is given a relative clause to contain it, whose verb δύναται is to be understood from δυνάμενος.

but others .. "Absolutely": X.'s timing is delightful.

60   **Saying .. agreed**: Sokrates' sense of fun is very evident here; Plato's Sokrates might have pressed for a proper answer.

ὁμολογεῖται: the primary tense of the original is preserved.

to turn .. something like that: literally 'to work, create, people of that sort out of <those> whom he controlled'.

61   **Antisthenes**: his pride was in a different sort of wealth; but that is only part of Sokrates' joke.

ἀκόλουθον: feminine; a two-termination adjective.

Pandering: by root, μαστροπ- words (see III 10) should refer to finding people suitable for sex and προαγωγ- words to presentation of them to clients. That is clearly the distinction Sokrates draws in referring to the skill that 'follows up' procuring. The law quoted by Aiskhines (see 57 above) not surprisingly uses προαγωγ-, registering the point at which something actionable took place. English has pander, pimp and procure (LSJ use all three indiscriminately under both μαστροπ- and προαγωγ-). Pandering comes from Pandarus, who in Chaucer's poem *Troilus and Criseyde* (part of Shakespeare's inspiration for *Troilus and Cressida*) acted as go-between. A pander brings together two people who probably wish to be together; as a translation of προαγωγ- it is not quite right, but it is less offensive than pimp or procure, and may be held to work better in context: Sokrates now uses it three times more, until Antisthenes accepts the idea. The activity is not one to talk about in polite company; Sokrates gets away with it as long as he does because this company trusts him to make sense of his incredible claim in some witty and pertinent fashion.

62   **Prodikos**: see I 5.

passionate .. even more passionate: the language Sokrates uses would be seen by most of the company as metaphorical; for him, however, philosophy was a passion. Nevertheless, he was well aware of the double entendre.

Hippias of Elis: 'I have never found any man who was my superior in anything', he is reported to have said. He certainly tested the field, being a man of very great versatility. Plato bears witness to his memory system (*Hp. Ma.* 285e). See Guthrie III1, 280-285.

ἀφ' οὗ: literally 'from which <time>'; χρόνου is to be understood.

63 **your visitor from Herakleia**: this Herakleia was in Sicily. On the evidence of Plato (*Prt.* 318b-c), the visitor was the painter Zeuxippos, commonly known as Zeuxis.

Aiskhylos of Phleious: unknown. Phleious was a small community south-west of Corinth.

64 **with the skill .. and with the power**: οἷός τε εἶναι and δύνασθαι are not synonymous; δύνασθαι marks a more strictly physical ability.

αὐτοῖς: equivalent to ἀλλήλοις; see LSJ under ἑαυτοῦ III.

could in my view make .. and .. broker: There is a conditional sentence underlying the surface structure: 'If a man were able.., he could, it seems to me, make...' 'Make' and 'broker' have become infinitives dependent upon δοκεῖ the main verb; ἄν goes with them.

communities and friends and allies: the trio covers relationships national, personal and international.

as if I'd slandered you: literally 'as having heard, been spoken of, badly'. The sense 'to be spoken of' is common for ἀκούειν (outside Homer: see LSJ III).

my heart will be .. loaded with wealth: literally 'I shall be loaded in my heart'; τὴν ψυχήν is accusative of respect. With the reference to his wealth Antisthenes wittily returns to his original boast, now justified by Sokrates in a new way.

that round .. came to an end: X. has set up enough leads to continue his narrative, but that is the end of the formal part of the evening, and he marks it.

V

1 **he isn't**: not in the Greek, and to be understood from context.

2 **You use your cleverness and**: literally 'If you have something clever'. The conditional clause is idiomatic; no doubt is cast on Sokrates' cleverness.

have the lamp brought up: some artificial light was likely; the room would have no windows. Use of the definite article does not mean there was only one lamp; Kritoboulos is pointing to the nearest. προσενεγκάτω, 'let <someone> bring', has no subject; one of Kallias' slaves is meant.

as first item .. examination: Sokrates uses the language of the courts. πρῶτον is better taken in apposition to the whole sentence rather than to ἀνάκρισιν; καλοῦμαι is present rather than future, as at III 4.

3 **You get on and ask them**: δέ γε marks the 'lively rejoinder' (GP 153).

good: the basic meaning of καλός, 'good to look at', (see I 1) is present throughout. But the word could be used in the sense 'morally good' and also 'functionally good'. Kritoboulos in replying accepts the common equation 'If good-looking, then good' in the sense at first of 'functionally good', but soon the basic sense comes to the fore again. Wherever 'good', 'well', 'better' and 'best' occur in the translation here, some ambiguity of reference is to be understood.

4 **nothing in common with each other all .. good**: Plato's Sokrates often presses his companions in much the same way. So Meno is challenged to identify the common element in a list of activities which he names as good (*Men.* 72a).

Ἄν .. ᾖ: ἄν is for ἐάν, and ᾖ works with both εἰργασμένα and πεφυκότα to create periphrastic perfect subjunctives (for a natural perf. subj. see I 8).

καὶ ταῦτα .. καλά: literally 'indeed these things are good'; καί stresses the whole apodosis.

5 εἴησαν: εἶεν is the standard form, but εἴημεν, εἴητε and εἴησαν are not rare.

look straight .. sideways: literally 'see the thing along straight .. the thing from flank'. ἐκ πλαγίου, 'from flank', is a military expression.

has the best eyes: εὐόφθαλμος, literally 'well-eyed'. Note the accusative and infinitive after λέγεις, rare in Attic prose for statements. We are close to 'You require a crab to be best-eyed?', virtually indirect command.

6　**ποτέρα**: feminine singular, as the accent shows, agreeing with ῥίς.

ἀναπέπτανται: perfect passive of ἀναπετανννύναι, 'to spread'. The root is πετασ- or πετα-, here in its reduced form, or zero grade, πτα-.

it erects no barrier: painters and sculptors, as vase-paintings and statues show, liked the nose to run straight down from the forehead with little or no depression or change of angle at the bridge.

7　**you imagine .. don't you**: Kritoboulos starts to construct Sokrates' argument for him.

your kissing: literally 'the kissing of you'. The genitive is better taken as subjective than objective, but deliberate ambiguity is possible.

By your argument .. uglier: Sokrates in reply constructs what should be Kritoboulos' objection. 'Ugly', αἰσχρός, has the full range of meaning that its antonym καλός, 'beautiful', has.

ἐκεῖνο: not translated. It gives notice of the clause starting ὅτι.

Naiads .. Seilenoi: Sokrates throws Kritoboulos' jibe at IV 19 straight back at him. Naiads, named from νᾶν, 'to flow', were water spirits.

θεοὶ οὖσαι: θεός is of common gender; θεός fem. is as common as θεά.

8　**διαφερόντων .. φερόντων**: see note on IV 20 for the loss of prefix.

countervail: καταδυναστεύειν is first recorded in X. Perhaps, like many a coinage, it is meant humorously; it caps a passage of notable banter.

9　**voted, and while they did**: literally 'were carrying up'. The imperfect makes space for the actions of Sokrates in the next sentence. This use of ἀναφέρειν is not noted in LSJ; the object 'pebble' is to be understood.

10　**emptied out**: some process involving jars and mimicking the Athenian process of voting was being used, such as Aristophanes makes play with at *Wasps* 987-94.

all for Kritoboulos: all two of them! εἶναι σύν, 'to be on the side of', occurs also in *An.* III 1.21.

both jurymen and other judges: 'other' is not in the Greek. Sokrates uses first the word proper for men judging a court case; the second is more general: it was used, for instance, for people judging plays, as in Ar. *Ach.* 1224, *Clouds* 1115 and *Birds* 445.

VI

1　**the guardian**: κύριος has legal overtones; it is used humorously. In the case of the girl it suggests that a proposal of marriage is in prospect.

overindulgence: the literal sense of παροινία, 'drinking past a certain point', may be seen in Pl. *Euthphr.* 4c: Euthyphro's father committed murder παροινήσας, 'having got drunk'. That sense, however, is rare; usually the word refers to behaviour consequent upon drinking, as shown in X. *An.* 5.8.4: μεθύων ἐπαρώνησα, 'when drunk I behaved badly', and D. 23.114: μεθύων ἐπαρώνει, 'he used to get drunk and misbehave'. The passive regularly means 'to be mistreated'. Hermogenes' response, as Sokrates probably expected, is slightly pedantic. For the use of παρά in παρ' οἶνον see LSJ *s.v.*, C III 7.

what it is, I don't know: Hermogenes denies personal experience of being drunk. Such people would not be easy company at symposia.

2　οὐδέ .. μὴ ὅτι: for 'not even .. never mind' see II 26.

παρείρειε: this is the old Attic form of the 3rd sing. aorist optative active.

3   **Kallias**: Sokrates turns to the man who is not only his host but also Hermogenes' half-brother.

I can: Kallias' answer is fatuous, and irritates Hermogenes further, as is shown in his repetition of the phrase 'So you really'.

σιωπῶμεν: indicative, not subjunctive ('let us be silent'), as shown by λυπεῖς σιωπῶν above and by the sequel here.

Nikostratos .. tetrameters: Nikostratos is mentioned by Plutarch (*Mor.* 348E), with qualified enthusiasm. Tetrameters are long lines, of at least 15 syllables: Hermogenes picks the metre in order to exaggerate his task.

4   **A song is .. and**: literally 'Just as a song is .. so also'. For this translation of a comparative clause see II 3.

sweetened: the same word as that translated 'to season' at IV 8.

if you postured, like the aulos-girl: μορφάζειν, 'to make shapes', is not recorded elsewhere in classical Greek. LSJ misunderstand the context here, offering 'gesticulate', not something an aulos-player could do while playing. I am grateful to M. L. West in correspondence for suggesting 'make faces' or 'adopt postures'. The second would be well within the powers of an aulos-player[1]. If Hermogenes' body language is showing what he thinks about the company, then Sokrates' jibe, too sharp to be merely humorous, is well-aimed. The sharp tone of his teasing is sustained at VIII 3.

5   **For my victim**: the contrasting 'for me..' goes unsaid (see note at II 16).

whistling: συριγμός (the word is first recorded in X.) properly describes the noise of panpipes (σῦριγξ), an instrument likely to cause more distortion of the face than the aulos. Antisthenes means that cross-examination by him will reduce the victim to such a degree of confusion that the onlookers will whistle in derision. The word is wittily kept to the end.

6   **Are you the so-called thinker**: literally 'the one called thinker is you?'. The definite article marks the subject; σύ is complement. For φροντιστής, 'thinker', see Ar. *Clouds* 94, 101, 155 and 215; the label stuck, as Pl. *Ap.* 19c shows. *Clouds* was produced at the City Dionysia of 423, a little over a year before this party; the Syracusan is well up to date. X. may have owned a text of the play; equally, his knowledge could come from friends and hearsay. Sokrates referred to *Clouds* himself in his speech in court in 399; the play had done much, he thought, to prejudice people against him (Pl. *Ap.* 18d and 19c). X. quotes it here as part of his apologetic purpose, giving the lines deliberately to the outsider.

a higher thinker: literally 'a thinker of the things in the air'. The phrase comes from *Clouds* 360: Sokrates quotes as well.

7   οὐ τούτων: literally 'not them'. οὐ negatives the pronoun rather than the sentence as a whole.

utter rubbish: literally 'very unprofitable things'.

do good .. from above: Sokrates' Greek for these two words makes an untranslatable pun on the Syracusan's word for rubbish; first comes 'from above', ἄνωθεν, and then 'do good', ὠφελεῖν.

If I'm being boring: literally 'if I'm speaking cold things'. This use of ψυχρός, 'cold', may be seen in Ar. *Th.* 170 and 848; it underlies the joke in *Ach.* 138-140. In

---

1 Eric Handley draws my attention to Ar. *Poet.* 1461b30-32: 'vulgar aulos-players rolling around if they have a discus throw to represent, and manhandling the chorus-leader if they are playing in *Skylla'*.

apologising for the quality of his pun by chiding the Syracusan, Sokrates may help to provoke what follows.

8 **how many feet away from me a flea is**: the Syracusan refers, with misunderstanding, to *Clouds* 144-52, where Sokrates and Khairephon are said to be investigating how far a flea can jump measured in flea feet.

surveying skill: see *Clouds* 200-205. The Syracusan is confusing various words for measuring which occur in this part of the play.

comparisons: literally 'likening <someone to someone>.' For the game of comparisons as played at symposia see Ar. *Wasps* 1309-21.

λοιδορεῖσθαι βουλομένῳ: λοιδορεῖσθαι is middle (the commoner use), not passive. For βουλομένῳ as 'trying to' rather than 'wanting to', see I 14.

ἄλλοις .. πολλοῖς: Philippos picks up the dative σοι.

9 **in case you too**: noblesse oblige. Sokrates gives the lesson in gentlemanliness. Philippos changes tack at once, but Sokrates is not fooled: to flatter the Syracusan will simply be another way of putting him down.

εἴπερ γε εἰκάζω .. δικαίως ἂν εἰκάζοι μέ τις: not a mixed condition, since the apodosis responds to an unspoken protasis εἴ μέ τις εἰκάζοι ('<if one were to compare me at all ..> one would have to compare me ..'), rather than to the apparent protasis 'if I line him up'.

τοῖς πᾶσι καλοῖς: πᾶσι is dependent on καλοῖς, 'good in all things'. καλοῖς serves for καλοῖς κάγαθοῖς (see I 1).

If you say all his attributes are superior: the text after 'you say' (between εἰ and φῇς) is an emended text; what X. wrote is not recoverable.

10 **someone inferior**: literally 'more troublesome people'. πονηρός is the social antonym of χρηστός, 'useful', 'good' (II 4). It shares the root of πόνος, 'toil', and πένης, 'poor man'.

σιωπᾷς: subjunctive.

bout of overindulgence: X. finishes with the word that he began with. Thalheim observes that the content of this sentence would fit better at the end of VII 1; X. has slightly anticipated his own narrative.

VII

2 **a potter's wheel**: 'the Greek potter's wheel was a heavy, sturdily built disc of wood, terracotta, or stone about two feet in diameter... It was customary practice to have .. an apprentice turn the wheel by hand': so J. V. Noble, *The Technique of Painted Attic Pottery*, London 1966, 7. Figures 73 and 78 in the book show some of what he describes. There is a red-figure bell krater in the National Museum in Athens (12683; I am grateful to Eric Handley for the reference) which shows a girl dancing to an aulos-player on just such a table.

I'm afraid: literally 'I'm in danger', 'I risk'. This colloquial use of κινδυνεύειν is common: see IV 8.

3 τὸ μὲν .. κυβιστᾶν: Sokrates piles up quite a list of undesirable activities before reaching εἰ δὲ ὀρχοῖντο, 'but if they were to dance', at 5 below; the list is summarised by the μέν in the sentence immediately preceding εἰ δὲ ὀρχοῖντο, which repeats and renews the initial μέν with τὸ κυβιστᾶν.

Reading and writing on the wheel as it spins: Sokrates speaks as if it was a familiar stunt.

ἡδονήν .. ταῦτα: the subject of an indirect question or statement is sometimes taken as object of the introductory verb; so at IV 46 (and see V 5). Here, both subject and object are promoted outside the clause.

τό γε διαστρέφοντας .. θεωρεῖν: the articular infinitive, subject of its sentence, is apparently interrupted by its predicate ἥδιον, but there is a θεωρεῖν is to be understood before ἥδιον and a τό after ἤ: the infinitive phrase comes twice, and as is common in comparisons, words that would be repeated are omitted. Here a remarkable hyperbaton is created.

gazing at them when they're still: Sokrates overlooks his enjoyment of the boy moving at II 15; but that was dancing, not circus tricks.

4   οὐ .. σπάνιον τό .. ἐντυχεῖν: note again predicate preceding subject.

why does the lamp: the force of ποτε can be represented by stressing 'does'. According to Plato (*Phd.* 96a6-99c6), any interest that Sokrates once had in natural science gave way to his interest in moral phenomena.

water, which is wet: ὅτι, translated 'which', is ambiguous. The clause could mean 'because it is wet'.

5   **but if your people**: the change of subject is marked in the Greek only by the switch from singular ἐπισπεύδει (subject ταῦτα) to plural ὀρχοῦντο.

Graces, Seasons and Nymphs: they are associated in dance notably in two poems of Horace (*Odes* I 4 and IV 7). R. G. M. Nisbet and M. Hubbard (edd. A Commentary on Horace Odes, Book 1, Oxford 1970) cite h. Hom. 3.194-6: αὐτὰρ ἐϋπλόκαμοι Χάριτες καὶ εὔφρονες Ὧραι Ι Ἁρμονίη θ᾽ Ἥβη τε Διὸς θυγάτηρ τ᾽ Ἀφροδίτη Ι ὀρχεῦντ᾽ ἀλλήλων ἐπὶ καρπῷ χεῖρας ἔχουσαι, 'The Graces with their lovely locks, the kindly Seasons, Ι Harmony, Youth and Aphrodite daughter of Zeus Ι danced with their hands on each other's wrists'.

ἂν οἶμαι .. διάγειν καὶ .. εἶναι: ἂν goes with the infinitives, which stand in for διάγοιεν and εἴη.

VIII

1   **to applause**: the verb is passive. The middle appears not to be in use; otherwise 'began to get himself organised' would be a likely translation. συγκροτεῖν is quite common in X.; before him it is recorded only in Aristophanes (*Knights* 471).

a fresh theme: pederasty (Intr. 30) was inevitably a strand of this work; it comes and goes in prominence. X. has Sokrates give warning of its perils also at *Mem.* 1.3.8-15, where Sokrates' interlocutor is X. himself, and the example Sokrates uses is of Kritoboulos and Kleinias (there called son of Alkibiades, which he probably was not: see note on IV 12). In calling the theme fresh X. may simply be marking a transition,[1] but καινός can also mean 'revolutionary': the length and seriousness of Sokrates' address, despite some lightness in the asides, is anomalous in context; it is an essentially hortatory and epideictic (I 6) speech, and its vocabulary and structures verge on the Gorgianic (II 26, and below).

a great spirit Sokrates uses the word δαίμων. At Pl. *Smp.* 178a7 Phaidros calls Eros god, using θεός. Dover PS discusses the two words at 202d13: δαίμων may be used

---

1 This is the likely point for Thesleff's proposed re-writing (Intr. 15) to begin. The arguments he offers are reinforced by the remarkable incidence in this chapter's opening section of vocabulary (some of which is notable) not used elsewhere in the work: ἀειγενής, ἀμνημονεῖν, δαίμων, ἐξιέναι, ἐπέχειν, θιασώτης, ἱδρύειν, ἰσῆλιξ, καινός, κατάρχειν, μέγεθος, νεώτατος and συγκροτεῖν. μορφή occurs elsewhere only in this chapter. See also on 13 below for the frequency in this chapter of φιλία and ἀνάγκη. Other words occurring more often in the chapter than outside it are ἀρετή, ἀσκεῖν and ὀρέγεσθαι.

'specifically of supernatural beings lower in rank than θεοί'. But at the end of this sentence Sokrates switches to θεός.

contemporary in time: more or less the same point is also made by Phaidros in Plato's *Symposium*.

votaries: X. uses a word particularly associated with worshippers of Bakkhos (Hdt. 4.79.5, and E. *Ba. passim*); he uses it more loosely at *Mem.* 2.1.31.

2   ἐγώ τε .. Χαρμίδην δέ: the sequence τε .. δέ is well established (GP 513-14).

ἔστι δὲ ὧν .. ἐπιθυμήσαντα: literally 'there is of whom <I know> him too having been desirous'. ἔστι rather than εἰσί is usual, despite the plural of ὧν, and is standard when the relative pronoun is not nominative.

3   **and she with him**: literally 'and he is loved back'. For the force of ἀντι- see I 15. In context the word is of more importance than may appear: see Dover GH 52, and 16 below. An attractive story was later told (Hieronymus *adv. Iouinianum* i 310) that when Nikeratos was killed (Intr. 21) his wife refused to survive him. That story could well have grown from this word.

Hermogenes goes liquid: Sokrates maintains the mocking tone of his thrusts in VI. Metaphorical use of τήκειν, 'to melt', is almost entirely poetical.

august: σεμνός is a word with some range of meaning (see note on III 10); Euripides explored it in *Hippolytus*, and there are useful comments on it at 93 and 99 by W. S. Barrett (ed. Oxford 1964).

only .. Antisthenes: Sokrates probably knew what response he would get, and timed his moment of comedy to precede the serious stuff. Only Lykon and Philippos are not given romances of some sort here.

4   **shattered**: θρύπτεσθαι is mostly used metaphorically; so in 8 below.

5   **auto-pimp**: literally 'procurer of yourself'. Antisthenes' jibe has the energy of a man not content to take part in mere banter; he reverts to the more offensive word (see IV 61).

τοτὲ μέν .. τοτὲ δέ: note the accent. τοτέ is an indefinite version of τότε.

your 'voice': the 'voice' was sufficiently notorious for Sokrates to discuss it at his trial (Pl. *Ap.* 31c4-d6), and it is mentioned elsewhere as something familiar (id. *Euthphr.* 3b5, *Phdr.* 242b8, *Tht.* 151a4 and *Euthd.* 272e3 and X. *Mem.* 1.1.2 and *Ap.* 4). On the whole its advice was negative.

ἄλλου του: either 'something else' or 'someone else'. The ambiguity might be deliberate, but in X. the usual object of ἐφίεσθαι is ἀρετῆς or the like.

6   **slice me up**: κόπτειν, 'to chop', is a routine word in comic cook scenes; see Handley on Men. *Dysk.* 398. As Dover (GH 85) says, 'Socrates puts on a delightful act as a conceited and coquettish boy'.

your tempers: literally 'your difficultness'. It is Sokrates' humour to treat Antisthenes' feelings as a little problem better hushed up; admiration for Sokrates' looks (see V) would call Antisthenes' judgment into question.

7   ὅτι γε μήν: γε μήν responds to μέν in the preceding sentence. It is a peculiarly Xenophontic combination, as observed at IV 38, and enjoys a sudden flurry of use, recurring at 13, 18, 37 below and IX 4.

πολλούς: the accusative shows that εἰδέναι is to be understood and that οἶμαι is not parenthetic, as often, but the main verb.

famous fathers: see Intr. 20 and 27.

9   **Celestial .. Popular**: the distinction is also made by Pausanias (Pl. *Smp.* 180d6ff). The epithets appear to be cult titles, and are not confined to Aphrodite. Pausanias and Sokrates each interpret them to suit his own case.

10 ὑφ' οὗ .. ἔρωτος: a remarkable hyperbaton. The passion that embraces Kallias verbally embraces the sentence.

11 **meetings**: in using the plural Sokrates appears to point to occasions in the past when Lykon was present; he may be suggesting that they should continue. Hermogenes' comment seems to confirm the possibility.

A proper admirer: literally 'an admirer who is a gentleman', καλὸς κἀγαθός; see I 1.

12 ἄλλα τε .. ἄγαμαι καὶ ὅτι: literally 'I admire both other things .. and the fact that'. See I 8.

what sort of man he should be: at nearly thirty years of age, Kallias ought to know. Hermogenes is expressing a friendly anxiety (Intr. 24).

to put it on record: Sokrates uses the word for bearing witness as in a court.

13 **friendship**: having used ἔρως, 'passion', and its verb ἐρᾶν as the right words for the feelings of Kallias for Autolykos, Sokrates replaces them almost entirely in the next six sections with softer terms: φιλία, 'friendship' (used nine times in this chapter and only once outside it), and its verb φιλεῖν (which elsewhere, except at IX 6, means 'to kiss'), ἄγασθαι 'to admire', ἐπιθυμεῖν 'to desire' and στέργειν 'to feel affection'. Inequality of relationship between lover and beloved was expected, and it is starkly emphasised in Sokrates' language in 19-22 below. Since ἐρᾶν was so one-sided, Sokrates sought words that allowed him to propose a greater mutuality of feeling, but at the end of section 18 he brings ἐρᾶν and φιλεῖν together in the phrase ἐρῶντες τῆς φιλίας, 'being passionate about their friendship', directing the passion towards what he believes its true end should be. At that point both words could be translated 'love': lovers should love their love.

τῶν .. ἀγαμένων: the genitive depends on ἀνάγκη. ἀνάγκη is used five times in this chapter and not outside it.

willing compulsion: not necessarily oxymoron; what you cannot avoid doing you may also be willing to do: so Iphigenia at Aulis in Euripides' play was willing to be sacrificed.

14 **withers away too**: καί, here translated 'too', is used emphatically ten times in sections 14 and 15. Few can be easily represented in English.

greater good sense: X. may have in mind what Plato has Diotima say (*Smp.* 210a-211c) about the climb from appreciation of particular beauty to appreciation of beauty itself; the idea that the wiser soul is the more loveable is X.'s own.

15 τὰ παιδικά: standard Greek for the beloved youth, but this is its first use in this work.

less favoured sexually: one word in the Greek, a likely invention of X., as is ἀξιέραστος above (but not ἀκόρεστος).

the words and the deeds that bring us her favour: this is very discreet language.

16 **There is no need .. its beloved**: the Greek sentence is elaborately constructed. The noun clause leads, and the main sentence follows, an order first noted at I 13; the order is repeated in the balancing sentence. In the clause the two verbs lead, paired by τε καί; their subject is an extensive noun phrase in which the noun itself, ψυχή, is central and two participles, θάλλουσα and οὖσα, start and finish the phrase; dependent upon θάλλουσα is a pair of nouns paired by τε καί, the second of which is modified by a pair of adjectives paired by τε καί, while οὖσα carries its own pair of adjectives also linked by τε καί.

a corresponding return of love: for the response of Nikeratos' wife to her husband, X. used ἀντερᾶν. Here the word is ἀντιφιλεῖν. See notes on 3 and 13 above. ἀντερᾶν is

used only once of a pederastic relationship, at Pl. *Phdr.* 255d, where the context is heavily qualified.

17　**who could hate a man by whom**: 'a man' is not in the Greek.

εἰδείη .. ὁρῷη .. πιστεύοι: all three verbs take their optative from the main verb δύναιτο. A triple form of sentence is marked by πρῶτον μέν, ἔπειτα δέ and πρὸς δὲ τούτοις. The three subordinate clauses form the triplet, but ὑφ᾽ οὗ which subordinates the first is not repeatable with the other two; the syntax is a little loose, and in the second clause the genitive τοῦ παιδός, 'his beloved's', is awkward when the beloved is the subject of the main verb.

loses his wits: a fragment of papyrus allowed Marchant in his second edition to recommend παρανοήσῃ as the right text. Note that ἄν here = ἐάν.

18　**friendship in common**: the Greek phrase carries an echo of the proverb κοινὰ τὰ τῶν φίλων, 'What friends have, they share.'

ὁποτεροσοῦν: for the effect of -οῦν compare ὁστισοῦν, ὁτιοῦν, 'any at all'.

συνεχεστέραν τὴν συνουσίαν: note the position of the adjective in relation to its noun. Transpose the accusative phrase into the nominative, and the form of statement frequently noted earlier can be seen: complement, verb 'to be' (optional), subject. In such a position the adjective is called predicative: in the sentence συνεχεστέρα ἡ συνουσία, συνεχεστέρα would be the predicate.

19　πότερον: see note on II 17.

ἀπὸ τούτων: the referent is ἅ. In the translation the three words occur as 'from what'.

20　μισητέος: ἐστι is to be understood, as usual with these verbal adjectives.

ἀποδεικνύει: ἀποδείκνυσι is the standard classical form, from ἀποδεικνύναι. X.'s form shows what is called analogical levelling.

21　**tradesman .. customer**: 'loves his customer' is not in the Greek. Trading sex for money is prostitution, but Sokrates' analysis is more uncomfortable for his audience than that: lovers, men with means, made gifts (birds and hares are frequent on vase paintings) to youths without means; even when the relationship was acceptable personally and socially there was a mercenary element in it.

unimpassioned with passionate: for the emotional inequality and its verbal expression see 13 and 16 above.

μεθύοντα: as ὑπό shows, here (as at II 26) the verb is seen as passive; the man is 'made drunk' by his sexual need. The metaphor is stark.

22　**nasty things**: literally 'unholy things', things not sanctioned by divine law. Sokrates still expresses himself strongly; Zeus' pleasure in Ganymedes, used by way of example in 30 below, will need special pleading.

23　**the dimension of freedom**: Sokrates returns to the topic of II 4. The importance of friendship (Intr. 30) gives special point to his remark.

Kheiron and Phoinix: Kheiron the centaur was believed to have run a boarding school for young heroes on Mount Pelion, attended by Akhilleus among others. Phoinix is to be found in *Iliad* ix, explaining how Akhilleus' father had asked him to make the boy μύθων τε ῥητῆρ᾽ ἔμεναι πρηκτῆρά τε ἔργων, 'a speaker of words and a doer of deeds' (443). Mention of the relationship prepares the way for 28-31 below.

teachers who are physically excited: literally 'the one reaching out for the body'. ὀρέγεσθαι is frequent in this chapter.

piece of fondling: 'caress', say LSJ *s.v.*, but X. has picked a word whose basic sense is 'grope'.

24   **the wine is stirring me**: Sokrates was famous for imperviousness to wine (see note on II 24); this remark may be meant to provoke a smile before the seriousness of the next remark.

    the passion that is ever my companion: undefined, but he means the desire to discover right conduct.

    to speak out: literally 'to speak all'. Sokrates uses the word that marks the citizen's privilege among citizens, memorably expressed by Phaidra (E. *Hipp.* 421-3) and comically by Mnesilokhos (Ar. *Th.* 540-1).

25   **a tenant farmer**: literally 'one having hired himself land'. In a society where ownership of land was for most people their most reliable resource, it would not be readily sold but might be available for rent.

26   **mere presentation of good looks**: literally 'the one making provision of good looks'; something of a euphemism. The genitive τοῦ εἴδους is partitive; at *Mem.* I 2.60 X. wrote πᾶσιν ἀφθόνως ἐπήρκει τῶν ἑαυτοῦ, 'he made his resources available to all without stint'. See also IV 43.

    ἄν .. ἄν: the second ἄν is for ἐάν.

27   **anyone eager**: literally 'the man reaching out'. The sense of ὀρέγεσθαι is completed by the infinitive ποιήσασθαι.

    display: the word makes plain the essentially public nature of the relationship. Hence the room for shame to operate.

28   **spiritual friendship .. physical relationship**: literally 'love of the soul' and 'use of the body'. Sokrates puts yet more space between the two things by treating the body as something for mere use. So Antisthenes had spoken (IV 38).

29   Ζεύς τε: literally 'Both Zeus'. X. starts as if he had other gods in mind as well as Zeus, but he fails to complete the pattern. In καὶ ἐγὼ δέ below, καί is connective (see I 11), but only in response to the immediately preceding sentence.

    ἠράσθη .. ἀγασθείη: the indicative marks the first clause as definite, while the optative marks the second clause as indefinite. There seems to be little reason for the variation.

    the Dioskouroi: Castor and Pollux (Polydeukes in Greek).

30   **Ganymedes too**: the tale of Zeus and Ganymedes had become the paradigm of pederasty. Sokrates' attempt to reinterpret the story here is almost perverse.

    a phrase .. in Homer: neither phrase used by Sokrates occurs in our texts of Homer precisely as quoted (see IV 6: modern texts depend upon work begun in Alexandria a century after Sokrates' death); the second is a conflation of πεπνυμένα μήδεα εἰδώς (*Il.* 7.278 and *Od.* 2.38), 'knowing wise counsels', with πυκινὰ φρεσὶ μήδε' ἔχοντες (*Il.* 24.282 and 674 and *Od.* 19.353), 'having close-packed counsels in mind', and the first owes something to *Il.* 13.493: γάνυται δ' ἄρα τε φρένα ποίμην, 'the shepherd is glad at heart'. Accuracy of quotation in Sokrates' day was neither a great concern nor on the whole possible, and etymology was not a science.

    bodily sweet .. mentally sweet: ἡδυσώματος and ἡδυγνώμων are both nonce forms, coined by X. *ad hoc*. The implication that Ganymedes' name was usually taken to mean 'bodily sweet' depends on relating the second element not to μήδεα 'thoughts' but to μήδεα 'genitals'. Both words are used only in the plural and are virtually confined to Homer.

31   **Now, Nikeratos**: but the expert is given no chance to comment.

    Homer has made Akhilleus take .. vengeance: literally 'Akhilleus has been made by Homer to take vengeance'. τιμωρῆσαι depends on πεποίηται.

his comrade .. not his beloved: Sokrates accepts Homer's picture. Aiskhylos was apparently the first to treat the relationship as homosexual, in his play *Myrmidons*, of which a few fragments survive.

καὶ Ὀρέστης δέ .. καὶ ἄλλοι δέ: for the first καὶ .. δέ see on I 11 above; for the second see GP 202: it marks 'the last item of a series' which 'may take the form of an etcetera'.

are celebrated in song for having achieved: literally 'they are sung to have achieved'. διαπεπρᾶχθαι is infinitive of indirect statement after ὑμνοῦνται (LSJ record only finite clauses after ὑμνεῖν). The songs have mostly not come down to us except as reworked in Greek tragedies.

32 **Pausanias .. Agathon**: mention of these two makes it certain that X. knew Plato's *Symposium* before writing this (Intr. 15 and Thesleff 168). They are mentioned without explanatory comment: either X. assumed his readers also knew the work, or the question did not occur to him.

wallow in intemperance: literally 'roll themselves together in lack of self-control'.

a most valiant army: The idea of an army composed of pairs of lovers occurs not in Pausanias' speech but in Phaidros' (Pl. *Smp.* 178e3-179a8), which precedes it. X. was probably not writing with Plato's *Symposium* unrolled in front of him.

33 **disregarding censure .. trampling**: the phrases echo 'wallowing in intemperance'.

34 **Thebans .. Eleans**: the Sacred Band of Thebes (we know nothing about the Eleans in this context) was formed in, or soon after, 378 (Plu. *Pel.* xviii). It numbered 300. It was annihilated at the battle of Khaironeia in 338. Plutarch acknowledges without endorsing it the tradition that it was composed of lovers.

the point he makes bears no comparison: literally 'in saying that, <saying> no comparable instance at all'. λέγων is to be understood a second time. X. speaks for himself here, forgetting that Sokrates was dead before the Sacred Band was formed.

parading .. lack of confidence: literally 'those putting them in the line side by side resemble people not confident'. ἀπιστοῦσιν, dative plural of the participle, depends on ἐοικέναι.

35 **Λακεδαιμόνιοι .. οἱ νομίζοντες**: note the effect of definite article with participle: 'The Spartans, being people who think...'

ἐν τῇ αὐτῇ: understand τάξει from context.

They worship .. Shame: Pausanias the antiquarian records a statue of Shame about four miles along the road north of Sparta (III 20.10). The sort of reference made here and at 39 below to the prowess of the Spartans would be hard to make after their disaster in 371 (Intr. 6).

36 **ὁμόλογοι**: the word is first recorded in X.; it later flourished, but not in X.'s sense.

which love .. someone to trust him: literally 'to the boy who has been loved which way of the two would someone entrust'. The two ways are the physical and the spiritual, treated as mutually exclusive.

acts of favour: χάρις means both the favour conferred by the giver and the gratitude of the receiver. As with the money and children, there is a return to be expected: hence the need for confidence in the one who accepts the care of them.

true soul-mate: ἐράσμιος, literally 'beloved', 'darling', is not common, and is mostly to be found in early lyric poetry. τὴν ψυχήν is acc. of respect.

37 **giving you a passion**: ἐμβάλλειν is common in Homer (*Il.* 3.139, *e.g.*, and *Od.* 19.10) of gods putting feelings in humans.

jealous of his honour: the phrase translates a word which survives in use. τὸ φιλότιμο is still powerful among Greeks today.

νικῶν: Autolykos is subject of all three verbs in the sentence; hence the maintenance of the nominative.

πολλοὺς μέν .. πολλὰ δέ: the similarity in meaning of the two phrases is emphasised by the anaphora; the particles go with the shared adjective rather than with the two nouns.

38 **bravery**: ἀνδραγαθία (used by X. only here and in 43 below) is little removed from καλοκἀγαθία, 'essence of gentleman' (see I 1 and II 4).

routing its enemies: literally 'setting up turn-markers of its enemies'. Turn-markers recorded the place on the battlefield where the enemy line first gave.

39 **Themistokles .. to liberate Greece**: Themistokles is remembered for master-minding resistance to the invasion of Xerxes in 480. Earliest note of his achievement is in Aiskhylos' *Persians*; Herodotos has the larger tale.

Perikles: for over thirty years till his death in 429, Perikles took the lead in the Athenian democracy. His best memorial is in the first two books of Thoukydides.

Solon's wisdom: Solon was elected archon *c.* 592 with a mission to rescue Athens from confusion both social and political. He expressed his aims in verse, some of which survives quoted in Plutarch's *Life*.

Spartans .. excellent leaders: praise of the Spartans comes oddly after mention of the three great heroes of the Athenian democracy, but their way of life attracted much admiration from Athenians of the upper class; in context they bring Sokrates back to Kallias. In this section ἀθρητέον and ἐρευνητέον are merely variants for σκεπτέον. Note how the question is in the participial phrase each time, as observed at III 2.

you are their proxenos: see Intr. 5 note 10 for X. as proxenos and Intr. 27 for Kallias' position.

40 **if you want it**: Sokrates' effort to bring Kallias and Athens together recalls his claim at III 10 to be a good procurer and his explanation of it at IV 62-64. In Kallias' favour he lists items which, for all the democracy, continued to command Athenian respect in choice of leaders. The sheer need for leadership could have been mentioned: in 422 Kleon, Athens' leader more or less since Perikles' death in 429, was killed in battle. Only Nikias, father of the Nikeratos here, commanded much respect among the leaders then available; Alkibiades did not come of age until *c.* 419.

your family .. noble since: literally 'you are of noble birth of those from'. Erekhtheus was one of the last kings of Attica; Athens' oldest families claimed to go back to the time of the kings, before 1000 B.C.

priest of the gods: priesthoods were inherited, and were a prime sign of a family's antiquity. For Kallias' hereditary office of torch-bearer see Intr. 27; the torch was carried in the celebration of the Eleusinian mysteries, a ceremony of great age.

who joined Iakkhos .. against the Persian: Iakkhos was a name of Dionysos; the Persian (literally 'non-Greek, barbarian') is Xerxes. Herodotos records more simply a story that when the Persians had occupied Attica, the Iakkhos song was heard in a cloud of dust over Eleusis (VIII 65). That story had clearly been elaborated, to include the gods more specifically.

σὺν Ἰάκχῳ: by X.'s time σύν had been largely replaced by μετά as the preposition for 'in company with', but X. remained very faithful to σύν. See II 5, 19 and 22, V 10 and IX 7.

in today's festival: ἐν τῇ ἑορτῇ, 'in the festival', is a comment on νῦν, 'now'. Sokrates is referring to the Panathenaia of I 2, not to Kallias' rôle at Eleusis.

the best looking man in the city: and a proper partner therefore for Autolykos, whose good looks were established at the start (I 8-9).

42 **you .. be my pimp**: by using Sokrates' word Kallias recalls Sokrates' claim of III 10 specifically. At IV 56 he called it unseemly; now he makes fun of it. We may doubt how serious he is.

43 **ἂν ὁρῶσί γε**: the force of a verb's aspect is difficult to convey. X. uses the imperfective (present) subjunctive here to indicate that people must see Kallias' behaviour over time. The aorist subjunctive would imply that one sighting was enough.

IX

1 **it was now time for him**: to ease his muscles, that is.

covered walk: the place is named from its chief use; so at *Mem.* I 1.10. LSJ cite this passage not under περίπατος but under ἐξανίστημι II.1.

you're a true gentleman: Lykon's tribute is important for X.'s apologetic purpose (see Intr. 11 and note at IV 24).

2 **After that**: here we might expect to resume X.'s original text (Intr. 15 and note on VIII 1), but the show provided by the Syracusan is not at all what Sokrates suggested at VII 5. Equally, its heterosexuality is in direct contrast with the pederasty so carefully approved by Sokrates in VIII. The edges of X.'s re-writing are not clearly visible.

Ariadne .. Dionysos: the scene is Naxos, where Theseus had left Ariadne after escaping from Crete; the time is her bridal night with the god.

a little tipsy: there is comedy in the very idea of Dionysos himself drunk. For the force of the prefix ὑπο- see note on IV 9.

will have some fun: literally 'they will play'; a euphemism. LSJ record both this meaning and this form of the word only here. At the start we were promised men ἐν ταῖς παιδιαῖς, in their 'child' moments; the last scene is of virtual children miming adult behaviour.

3 **the bacchic rhythm**: as at II 2, there is an instrumental solo. What the bacchic rhythm was is not clear; perhaps ionics, which predominate in E. *Ba.* See West 142-7.

τοιοῦτόν τι .. ὡς: again X. uses ὡς where ὥστε would be commoner.

4 **he danced up to her**: the verb is very rare; the prefix ἐπι- appears to have its literal force.

knelt down: literally 'sat down on his knees'. I am grateful to Malcolm Willcock, citing *Il.* 14.437, for the correct understanding of this phrase.

shouted encore: LSJ note this phrase only here.

5 **gestures**: the word used, σχήματα, is the same as that used for the boy's dancing at II 15 and 16; 'dancesteps', 'figures', 'movements'. σχῆμα shares a root with ἔχειν: literally 'thing held'. See 6 below, and also I 9 and 10.

People there could see: literally 'they, seeing'. οἱ δέ is not definite article with participle, 'the onlookers', but has the pronominal force noted at I 7.

in eager expectation: literally 'upwinged', a vivid and established image: see A. *Ch.* 228 and Hdt. 2.115, for instance.

they had .. been waiting: note the translation of the imperfect; see note on II 22.

6 **if she loved him**: X. uses the present tense, preserving Dionysos' words more closely, as is common in indirect speech in Greek.

not only Dionysos < ... >: the text can be translated as it stands, but the boy would not join in an oath concerning himself and if the god were meant, he would need to be identified as such. Hence the proposal that text has been lost, as it certainly has earlier in the sentence (ὥστε is an editors' addition).

ἦ μήν: the phrase is common at the start of an oath.

ἐφειμένοις: perfect participle middle/passive of ἐφιέναι; literally 'to people let go', 'permitted'.

7   **to have the company of their wives**: literally 'to their wives in order to have them'.
bachelors .. married men .. Sokrates .. others: suddenly there seem to be more people at the party than were named (more are present at *Oec.* 3.1 than talk, and see Pl. *Smp.* 180c); some of them arrived on horseback, apparently, though no horses are mentioned at I 3. X. writes carelessly. The clash between the heterosexual mime and Sokrates' words in VIII is left unresolved, and there are other loose ends. Plato wrote more tidily (*Smp.* 223b6 - end).

Vocabulary

Note: most words in the classes of pronoun, preposition and conjunction are not given, nor are proper names, numerals, or adverbs of straightforward formation; nor are words of great general frequency such as beginners should have learnt. Genitive and gender of a noun are given if not obvious from the form or meaning; verbs are given in the infinitive. The meanings given are not necessarily the whole story of the word. Reference to the text is a recommendation to consult the commentary at that point.

ἁβρός -ά -όν delicate, luxurious
ἁβρότης -ητος luxury
ἀγάλλεσθαι to exult in
ἄγαμος -ον unwed
ἄγαν too much
ἀγαπᾶν to feel affection for
ἄγασθαι to admire
ἁγνός -ή -όν pure
ἀγορανόμος —ου market official
ἀγρός -οῦ field
ἀγών -ῶνος m contest
ᾄδειν to sing
ἄδοξος -ον unseemly
ἀειγενής -ές eternal
ἀζήμιος -ον without penalty
ἀθάνατος -ον immortal
ἀθρεῖν to examine
ἀθρόος -α -ον all together
αἰδεῖσθαι to feel awe, respect
αἰδήμων, -ον bashful, modest
αἰδώς -οῦς f shame, awe, respect
αἴθων glittering
αἰσχύνειν to disgrace, shame
αἰχμητής -οῦ spearman, warrior
ἀκίνδυνος -ον riskless, safe
ἄκλητος -ον uninvited
ἀκόλουθος -ον consequent upon
ἀκόρεστος -ον insatiable
ἀκούειν κακῶς to be slandered

ἀκρασία lack of self-control
ἀκρόαμα thing to be heard
ἀκροᾶσθαι to hear
ἄκων -ουσα -ον unwilling
ἄλγος -ους pain
ἀλεεινός -ή -όν open to the sun, warm
ἀλείφεσθαι to oil oneself
ἀλεκτρυών -όνος cockerel
ἀληθινός -ή -όν true
ἄλκιμος -ον courageous
ἄλλοθι elsewhere
ἀλλότριος -α -ον belonging to another
ἀμελεῖν to neglect
ἄμεμπτος -ον irreproachable
ἀμεταστρεπτί without turning round
ἀμνημονεῖν to forget
ἄμορφος -ον ugly
ἀμφιέννυσθαι to dress oneself
ἀμφίλογος -ον disputable
ἀναγελᾶν to burst into laughter
ἀναγιγνώσκειν to read
ἀνάδημα garland
ἀναδιδόναι to offer upwards
ἀναδύεσθαι to withdraw
ἀναιδής -ές shameless
ἀναιρεῖν to destroy
ἀναισχυντεῖν to behave shamelessly

ἀναισχυντία shamelessness
ἀνακαλύπτειν to uncover
ἀνάκρισις -εως V 2
ἀναμένειν to wait
ἀναμίξ in no order
ἀναμφίλογος -ον indisputable
ἀναπαύεσθαι to rest, take a break
ἀναπείθειν to win over
ἀναπεταννύναι to spread upwards
ἀναπνεῖν to breathe
ἀναπτεροῦν to take wing, excite
ἀνάριστος -ον unbreakfasted
ἀναρριπτεῖν to throw upwards
ἀνασπᾶν to contract
ἀναστενάζειν to groan
ἀναφαίνειν to show up, reveal
ἀναφέρειν to carry up, vote (V 9)
ἀνδραγαθία courage
ἀνδραποδίζεσθαι to enslave
ἀνδρεία bravery
ἀνδρῶν -ῶνος m I 4
ἀνεγείρειν to rouse from bed
ἀνελεύθερος -ον unfree, servile
ἀνεπαφρόδιτος -ον sexually
  unfavoured
ἀνερυθριᾶν to blush
ἀνερωτᾶν to inquire
ἀνέχεσθαι to endure, put up with
ἀνθίστασθαι to stand up
ἄνθος -ους flower
ἀνθρώπινος -η -ον human
ἀνίστασθαι to stand up
ἀνόσιος -α -ον unholy
ἀνταποδεικνύναι to display in
  response
ἀντερᾶν to reciprocate a passion
ἀντιβλέπειν to look in the eye
ἀντικαλεῖν to invite back
ἀντιλέγειν to contradict, deny
ἀντίπαλος -ον matching
ἀντιπεριλαμβάνειν to embrace in
  return

ἀντιπροσφέρειν to bring opposite
ἀντιστοιχεῖν to stand opposite
ἀντιφιλεῖν to love back
ἀντιφράττειν to make a barrier
ἄνωθεν from above
ἀνωφελής -ές useless
ἀξιάκουστος -ον worth hearing
ἀξιέραστος -ον worth loving
ἀξιοθέατος -ον worth gazing at
ἀξιόλογος -ον worth mention
ἀξιομνημόνευτος -ον worth recording
ἀξιοπρεπής -ές worthy of note
ἅπαξ once
ἀπάτη deception
ἀπειλεῖν to threaten
ἀπειπεῖν, ἀπειρηκέναι to be
  exhausted
ἀπελαύνειν to ride away
ἀπεμπολᾶν to sell
ἀπεργάζεσθαι to achieve, create,
  make
ἀπιέναι to come/go away
ἀπιστεῖν to mistrust
ἄπιστος -ον untrustworthy, incredible
ἄπληστος -ον insatiate
ἀποβαίνειν to turn out, happen
ἀποβάλλειν to throw away, waste
ἀποβλέπειν to look sideways
ἀποδάκνειν to bite off
ἀποδεικνύναι, -νύειν to expose,
  show off
ἀποδημεῖν to be away from home
ἀποδιδόναι to give back; (mid.) to
  sell
ἀποδύεσθαι to undress
ἀποκρύπτεσθαι to hide, conceal
  oneself
ἀπόκρυφος -ον hidden
ἀπολαμβάνειν to pick up
ἀπολείπειν to abandon, fade away
ἀπολείπεσθαι to keep distance

ἀπολλύναι to lose; (intrans.) to be lost

ἀπολογεῖσθαι to speak in defence

ἀπομνύναι to swear no

ἀπομύττεσθαι to wipe one's nose

ἄπορος -ον helpless

ἀποτελεῖν to carry out, finish

ἀποτίθεσθαι to put aside

ἀποτίνειν to pay up

ἀποτρέπειν to avert

ἀποτροπαῖος -ον averting ill

ἀποφέρειν to pay (IV 32)

ἅπτεσθαι to grasp

ἄπυρος -ον unfired (unused)

ἀργός -όν idle

ἀργύριον silver, money

ἄρδειν to water

ἀρέσκειν to be pleasing

ἀρεστός -ή -όν acceptable

ἀριθμεῖν to count

ἀριθμός -οῦ number, tally

ἀρίστερος -α -ον left

ἀρκεῖν to suffice

ἁρματηλατεῖν to drive a chariot

ἁρματηλάτης -οῦ charioteer

ἄρτι just now

ἄρτος -ου bread

ἄρχειν to rule, control

ἀσκεῖν to practise

ἄσμενος -η -ον glad

ἀσπάζεσθαι to embrace

ἀσπίς -ίδος shield

ἀσφαλής -ές safe

ἀτιμάζειν to disprize, disesteem

ἀτρεμής -ές motionless

αὐλεῖν to play the aulos (II 1)

αὔλημα aulos-music

αὐλητρίς -ίδος aulos-player

αὐλός -οῦ aulos, pipe (II 1)

αὔξειν to increase, grow

αὔρα -ας breeze

αὐτίκα there and then

αὐτουργός -οῦ independent farmer

αὐτόφωρος -ον self-detected in crime

ἀφαιρεῖν to remove

ἀφθονία abundance

ἀφιστάναι to weigh out

ἀφορία dearth

ἀφροδίσια n.pl sexual activity

ἀφροδισιάζειν to have sexual intercourse

ἀφροδίτη sex

ἀφροντιστεῖν to be heedless of

ἀφρόντιστος -ον unthinking

ἄφρων -ον stupid

ἀφύλακτος -ον unguardable

ἄχθεσθαι to get cross

ἄχρι up to, until

ἄψυχος -ον inanimate

ἄωρος -ον ugly

βακχεῖος -α -ον bacchic

βαλλάντιον purse

βαναυσικός -ή -όν typical of artisans

βασιλεύειν to be king

βασιλικός -ή -όν kingly

βιβλίον book

βλαβερός -ά -όν damaging

βλάπτειν to damage

βλέπειν to look

βοᾶν to shout

βούλευμα plan, resolution

βοῦς βοός c cow

βραχύς -εῖα -ύ short

βωμός -οῦ altar

γάμος -ου marriage

γάνυσθαι to be glad

γαστήρ -τρός f belly

γελᾶν to laugh

γελοῖος -α -ον funny

γέλως -τος m laughter

γελωτοποεῖν to cause laughter

γελωτοποιία creation of laughter

γελωτοποιός -οῦ laughter-maker
γενεαλογεῖν to trace a pedigree
γένειον chin
γεωμετρεῖν to measure land, survey
γῆρας γήρως n old age
γλυκύς -εῖα -ύ sweet
γόνυ γόνατος n knee
γοργός -ή -όν goggle-eyed
γραμματιστής -οῦ school-teacher
γυμνάζεσθαι to take exercise
γυμνάσιον place of exercise
γυμνός -ή -όν bare, naked
γυναικεῖος -α -ον female

δαίμων -ονος c god, divine being
δαιμόνιον VIII 5
δάκνειν to bite
δανείζειν to lend; (mid.) to borrow
δαπανᾶν to spend
δαπανή expenditure
δεδοικέναι to be afraid
δειπνεῖν to dine
δεῖπνον dinner
δεῖσαι to fear
δεῖσθαι to need, require, ask
δημηγορικός -ή -όν political
δημηγόρος -ου (popular) politician
διάγειν to carry on, proceed
διακρίνειν to judge
διαλέγεσθαι to make conversation
διαλείπειν to leave a space
διανοεῖσθαι to think of, intend
διαπνεῖν to blow through
διαπονεῖν to toil through, exercise
διαπράττειν, -εσθαι to do, arrange,
    achieve
διαστρέφειν to twist
διατειχίζειν to build a wall between
διατελεῖν to continue
διατιθέναι to dispose
διαφέρειν to bring across, differ
διδακτός -όν teachable

διδασκαλεῖον school
διιέναι to go through
δικαιοσύνη justice
δικαστής -οῦ juryman
διορύττειν to dig through
διττοί -αί -ά two
δίφρος -ου chariot-board
διψῆν to be thirsty
δολιχοδρόμος -ου distance-runner
δονεῖν to shake
δόρυ -ρατος n spear
δουλεύειν to be a slave

ἔγγειος -ον native, in/on the land
ἐγγίγνεσθαι to occur in
ἐγγύς near
ἐγείρειν to arouse, waken
ἐγκλίνεσθαι to lean on
ἐγκονίεσθαι to get dusty in
ἐγκρατής -ές self-controlled
ἐγχεῖν to pour in
ἐθελούσιος -α -ον voluntary
ἐθίζειν to accustom
ἔθνος -ους group, tribe
εἶδος -ους appearance, looks
εἴδωλον image, likeness
εἶεν all right, OK
εἰκάζειν to liken, compare, estimate
εἴκειν to yield, give way
εἰκός n reasonable, likely
εἰκότως reasonably, naturally
εἴργειν to shut in/out, bar
εἰσαγγέλλειν to announce
εἰσάγειν to bring in
εἰσβλέπειν to stare at
εἰσιέναι to come/go in
εἰσφέρειν to carry in
ἑκάστοτε on every occasion
ἐκκαγχάζειν to guffaw
ἐκκαθαίρειν to purify thoroughly
ἐκκυβιστᾶν to somersault out
ἐκλέγειν to select

ἐκπίπτειν to fall out
ἐκπλαγῆναι to be astonished
ἐκποδών out of the way
ἐκπρεπής -ές outstanding
ἐκτείνειν to stretch out
ἑκών -οῦσα -όν willing
ἔλαιον olive oil
ἐλεγκτικός -ή -όν typical of a cross-examiner
ἐλέγχειν to cross-examine
ἐλευθέριος -α -ον like someone free
ἐλευθεροῦν to liberate
ἕλκειν to drag
ἐμβάλλειν to put in, implant
ἐμπιμπλάναι to fill full
ἐμπνεῖν to breathe in, inspire
ἐμποιεῖν to cause, create
ἔμπροσθεν in front
ἐμφαίνειν to show
ἔναγχος lately
ἐνδεής -ές in need of
ἔνδεια need
ἐνδεῖσθαι to lack, be in need of
ἔνδον inside
ἐνέγκαι, ἐνεχθῆναι - φέρειν
ἐνεῖναι to be in
ἔνθα then, there, when, where
ἔνθεος -ον possessed, inspired
ἐνιδροῦν to work up a sweat in
ἔνιοι -αι -α some
ἐννοεῖν to consider
ἐνταῦθα at that point
ἐντεῦθεν from that point
ἐντυγχάνειν to happen upon, meet
ἐνύπνιον dream
ἐξανδραποδίζεσθαι to sell into slavery
ἐξανίστασθαι to get up
ἐξεργάζεσθαι to make, construct
ἐξηγεῖσθαι to give a lead, explain
ἐξιέναι to come/go out
ἐξίστασθαι to stand out of the way

ἐοικέναι to resemble, be likely
ἑορτή festival
ἐπάγεσθαι to bring in
ἔπαινος -ου praise
ἐπανίστασθαι to get up at
ἐπαρκεῖν to make available
ἐπαφρόδιτος -ον favouring sex
ἐπερωτᾶν to ask
ἕπεσθαι to escort, attend
ἐπέχειν to extend over
ἐπηρεάζειν to be insolent
ἐπιβουλεύειν to plot against
ἐπίδειγμα display, demonstration
ἐπιδεικνύναι, -νύειν to display
ἐπιδεῖσθαι to need extra
ἐπιδημεῖν to be/stay at home
ἐπιέναι to approach
ἐπιθυμεῖν to desire
ἐπικαλεῖν to nickname
ἐπικύπτειν to bend over
ἐπιμελεῖσθαι, -εσθαι to care for, mind about
ἐπιπέμπειν to despatch
ἐπιπόλαιος -ον on the surface, prominent
ἐπισκοπεῖν to observe
ἐπισκώπτειν to jeer at, mock
ἐπισπεύδειν to urge things on
ἐπιστήμη knowledge
ἐπιστρέφεσθαι to turn round
ἐπιτάττειν to fix, appoint
ἐπιτελεῖν to fulfil
ἐπιτηδεύειν to practise
ἐπιτήδευμα practice, exercise
ἐπιτρέπειν to entrust
ἐπιφανής -ές famous
ἐπίφθονος -ον objectionable
ἐπίχαρις charming, agreeable
ἐπιχειρεῖν to try
ἐπιχορεύειν IX 4
ἐπιψακάζειν to drip
ἐπομνύναι to swear in response

ἐπονείδιστος -ον reprehensible
ἔπος -ους word, utterance, verse
ἑπτάκλινος -ον seven-couched
ἐπωνυμία name, title
ἐρᾶν to be passionate about, in love with
ἐράσμιος -ον beloved, darling
ἐραστής -οῦ lover, admirer
ἐρευνᾶν to search out
ἔρρειν to be gone to waste
ἔρως -ωτος passion, love
ἐρωτικός -ή -όν amorous, passionate
ἐσθής -ῆτος f dress, clothes
ἐσθίειν to eat
ἐσθλός -ή -όν good
ἑστιᾶν to entertain at home
εὔδηλος -ον very obvious
εὐδοκιμεῖν to be thought well of
εὐθύ straight
εὔκλεια glory, good name
εὐμορφία beauty
εὐνή bed
εὐνοϊκός -ή -όν well-intentioned
εὔξεστος -ον well-carpentered
εὐόφθαλμος -ον having good eyes
εὐπατρίδης -ου nobleman
εὐπειθής -ές obedient
εὐτέλεια cheapness
εὐτελής -ές cheap
εὐτύχημα piece of luck
εὐφημεῖν to avoid ill words
εὔφορος -ον fit, well
εὐφραίνειν to make happy
εὐφροσύνη pleasure
εὐχάριτος -ον agreeable
εὔχεσθαι to pray
εὐχή prayer
εὐωδία fragrance
ἐφεστρίς -ίδος cloak
ἐφιέναι to permit; (mid.) to desire
ἐφίστασθαι to stand on
ἕωθεν at dawn

ζηλοῦν to envy
ζῆν to live
ζωγραφικός -ή -όν skilled at painting
ζῷον living thing, animal

ἡγεῖσθαι to be guide, think
ἡγεμονικός -ή -όν authoritative
ἡδονή pleasure
ἡδυγνώμων -ον sweet of mind
ἡδύνειν to sweeten, season
ἡδυπαθεῖν to experience pleasure
ἡδυσώματος -ον sweet of body
ἦθος -ους custom, character
ἦκα slightly
ἠλίθιος -α -ον silly
ἡλικία age, time of life
ἧλιξ -ικος c person of the same age, contemporary
ἡμίθεος -ου demigod
ἡνία n.pl. reins
ἠρεμεῖν to keep still
ἥρως -ωος hero
ἥττων -ον less, fewer, inferior

θᾶκος -ου seat
θάλαμος -ου bedchamber
θάλλειν to flourish
θαλλοφόρος -ου olive-shoot bearer
θαρρεῖν to take heart
θάττων -ον quicker
θαῦμα wonder, stunt
θαυμάσιος -α -ον wonderful
θαύμαστος -ον wonderful
θαυματουργεῖν do stunts
θέα -ας sight, spectacle
θέαμα thing to see
θεᾶσθαι to behold, gaze at
θεραπεύειν to serve, tend, cultivate
θεωρεῖν to behold
θιασώτης -ου votary, worshipper
θνητός -ή -όν mortal
θόρυβος -ου confused noise, din

θρασύς -εῖα -ύ bold
θρίξ τριχός f hair
θρόνος -ου chair
θρύπτεσθαι to be enfeebled, coy
θυμοειδής -ές high-spirited,
    mettlesome
θυσία sacrifice

ἰδιώτης -ου private individual
ἱδρύειν to settle, establish
ἱέναι to let go, send
ἱερεύς -έως priest
ἱεροπρεπής -ές appropriate to things
    religious
ἱκανός -ή -όν adequate, sufficient
ἱλαρός -ά -όν glad, merry
ἴουλος -ου down, first beard
ἵππαρχος -ου cavalry commander
ἱππικός -ή -όν to do with horses
ἱπποδρομία horse-race
ἰσῆλιξ -ικος of the same age,
    contemporary
ἰσόρροπος -ον evenly balanced
ἴσος -η -ον equal
ἰσοφόρος -ον equivalent
ἰσχύς -ύος f strength

καθάπερ just like
καθέζεσθαι to sit down
καθέρπειν to creep down
καθεύδειν to sleep
καθίζειν to seat
καθορᾶν to catch sight of
καινός -ή -όν new, new-fangled
καιρός -οῦ right point, right moment
κακουργεῖν to do wrong
κάλλος -ους beauty, good looks
καλοκάγαθία I 1 and II 4
κάμνειν to grow weary
κάμπτειν to bend
καρδία heart
καρκίνος -ου crab

καρπογονία fruitfulness
καρπός -οῦ harvest
καρποῦσθαι to harvest
καρτερία endurance
κατάγεσθαι to seek lodging
καταδυναστεύειν to prevail against
καταθεᾶσθαι to gaze at
κατακεῖσθαι to lie flat
κατακλίνεσθαι to recline
καταλαμβάνειν to come upon, catch
καταλέγειν to recite a list
κατάλυσις -εως dissolution, end
κατάρχειν to begin
κατασβεννύναι to quench, suppress
κατασκευή arrangement, preparations
κατατήκεσθαι to melt down
κατατιθέναι to put in place
καταφρονεῖν to despise
κατέχειν to hold down, control
καῦμα heat, hot weather
κεντεῖν, κεντρίζειν to goad, urge on
κεραμεικός -ή -όν of potters
κιθαρίζειν to play the kithara (II 2)
κινδυνεύειν to be at risk, be likely
κινεῖν to move, stir, provoke
κλαίειν to cry, weep
κλῆσις -εως invitation
κλίνειν to incline, lean
κνῆσμα scratch, bite
κοιμίζειν to put to sleep
κοινῇ in common
κοινός -ή -όν common, shared
κοινωνεῖν to share, take part in
κολάζειν to check, punish
κομᾶν to grow one's hair long
κομπάζειν to boast
κόρος -ου surfeit
κοσμεῖν to equip, arrange, adorn
κρᾶσις -εως mixture
κρατερός -ά -όν strong
κρέμασθαι to hang
κριτής -οῦ judge

κρόμμυον onion
κροτεῖν to clap
κρούειν to knock
κρύπτειν to hide
κρύφα, κρυφῇ in secret
κτῆμα possession, property
κυβιστᾶν to somersault
κύκλος -ου wheel, circle
κύλιξ -ικος f wine-cup
κυνοδρομεῖν to hunt with dogs
κύριος -α -ον having authority
κῶμος -ου revel

λαγχάνειν to obtain as one's portion
λαμπρός -ά -όν bright
λαμπτήρ -ῆρος m lamp
λαμυρός -ά -όν gross
λέβης -ητος m cauldron
λεπτύνειν to thin
λήγειν to leave off
λίθινος -η -ον stony
λογίζεσθαι to calculate, reckon
λόγχη spearpoint
λοιδορεῖν to revile, abuse
λοιπός -ή -όν left, remaining
λούεσθαι to wash
λυπεῖν to vex, irritate
λύπη irritation, irritability
λύρα -ας lyre (III 1)
λύχνος -ου light, lamp
λῷστος -η -ον best

μαθητός -ή -όν learnable
μαίνεσθαι to go mad
μαλακία softness
μαλακός -ή -όν soft
μανδραγόρας -ου mandrake,
　　mandragora
μαντική art of prophecy
μάντις -εως c seer
μαρτυρεῖν to bear witness
μαρτύριον evidence

μάρτυς -υρος witness
μαστεύειν to search for
μαστροπεία pimping, procuring
μαστροπεύειν to procure
μαστροπός -οῦ pimp, procurer
μάχαιρα -ας knife, dagger
μέγεθος -ους size, importance
μεθύειν to be drunk
μειοῦσθαι to diminish, dwindle
μειράκιον youth
μέλειν to be a matter of concern
μεμνῆσθαι to remember
μέμφεσθαι to reproach, blame
μέρος -ους part, share
μέσος -η -ον middle
μεστός -ή -όν full
μεταδιδόναι to give a share of
μεταμέλειν to change concern, cause
　　regret
μεταξύ in between
μετέωρος -ον high in the air
μέτριος -α -ον moderate, reasonable
μέχρι up to, until
μηδέ not even, nor even
μήδεα n.pl. VIII 30
μιμεῖσθαι to imitate
μισεῖν to hate
μισθοῦν to hire
μισθωτός -ή -όν hired, rented
μνημονικόν memory system
μόλις with difficulty
μορμολύττεσθαι to scare
μορφάζειν to grimace
μορφή shape
μόχθος -ου toil, labour
μυθολογεῖν to discuss by myth
μυκτήρ -ῆρος m nostril
μύρον scent
μυροπώλης -ου perfume-seller

ναός -οῦ temple
νέμειν to distribute

νέος -α -ον new, young
νευρόσπαστος -ον pulled by strings
νήφειν to be sober
νικητήριος -α -ον belonging to
  victory
νικηφόρος -ου prize-winner
νόμιμος -η -ον customary
νύμφη bride, young wife

ξίφος -ους sword

ὀβολός -οῦ obol (III 8)
ὀδάξειν to itch
ὀδύνη pain
ὄζειν to smell
οἰκεῖος -α -ον domestic
οἴκημα room
οἰκία house
οἰκοδόμος -ου builder
οἰκονομικός -ή -όν good at household
  management
οἰκτίρειν to pity
οἰκτισμός -οῦ pity
οἶνος -ου wine
οἰνοχόος -ου wine-pourer
οἷόν τε it is possible
οἷος -α -ον of what sort
οἰωνός -οῦ omen
ὀκνεῖν to hesitate
ὁμιλεῖν to consort with, be in contact
ὁμιλία contact, company, converse
ὄμμα eye, sight, look
ὀμνύναι to swear
ὅμοιος -α -ον like, similar
ὁμοκλᾶν to shout
ὁμολογεῖν to agree
ὁμόλογος -ον in agreement
ὁμόσε in the same direction
ὁμοῦ in the same place, together
ὄναρ dream
ὀνομάζειν to name
ὀνομαστός -ή -όν famous

ὄνος -ου c ass
ὄντως, τῷ ὄντι in reality
ὄπισθεν behind
ὁποτεροσοῦν whichever of the two
ὀρέγεσθαι to reach for, grasp at
ὀρθός -ή -όν straight, upright
ὀρθοῦσθαι to straighten
ὁρκίζειν to make swear
ὁρμᾶσθαι to be started, go
ὄροφος -ου reed; pl. thatch
ὀρχεῖσθαι to dance
ὄρχημα dance
ὄρχησις -εως dancing
ὀρχηστοδιδάσκαλος -ου dancing-
  master
ὀρχηστρίς -ίδος dancing-girl
ὀσμή smell
ὅσοι -αι -α how many, as many as
ὅσος -η -ον how big, as big as
ὀσφραίνεσθαι to smell
οὐδέ not even, nor even
οὖς ὠτός n ear
ὀφθαλμός -οῦ eye
ὀφρῦς -ύος f eyebrow
ὄχλος -ου crowd
ὄψις -εως sight, eye
ὄψον cooked food

παγκράτιον I 2
παιανίζειν to sing a paean
παιγνιώδης -ες playful
παιδεύειν to train, educate
παιδιά child's play, fun
παιδικά n.pl. one's beloved
παίζειν to play
παντάπασι altogether
παντελής -ές entire
πάντοθεν from all sides
παπαῖ exclamation of pain
παραγίγνεσθαι to be present at
παραδιδόναι to hand over
παραιρεῖν to take away

παρακαλεῖν to invite along
παρακατατίθεσθαι to entrust, lay up
παρακελεύεσθαι to recommend
παρακμάζειν to pass one's peak
παρακολουθεῖν to press close upon
παραλαμβάνειν to take also
παραμυθεῖσθαι to console
παρανοεῖν to lose one's wits
παρατάττεσθαι to draw up alongside
παρατιθέναι to put beside
παρείρειν to insert
παριέναι to go also
παρίστασθαι to stand beside
παροινία overindulgence in wine
παρορᾶν to look sideways
παρρησιάζεσθαι to speak freely
παχύνειν to thicken
παχύς -εῖα -ύ thick
πεινῆν to be hungry
πεῖρα -ας attempt
πένεσθαι to be poor
πενία poverty
πεπρᾶσθαι to be sold
περιβάλλειν to embrace
περίβλεπτος -ον admired all round
περιδινεῖσθαι to spin round
περιεῖναι to be around, left over
περιελαύνειν to drive round
περιέπειν to manage
περιιέναι to come round, to an end
περιλαμβάνειν to embrace
περιμάχητος -ον worth fighting over
περίμεστος -ον crammed full
περιοδός -οῦ f sequence
περιορᾶν to look on and do nothing
περιπατεῖν to walk round
περίπατος -ου walk, colonnade
περιττεύειν to exceed
πιέζειν to squeeze, oppress
πίνειν to drink
πλάγιος -α -ον oblique, sideways on

πλαστικός -ή -όν skilled at shaping, carving
πλησμονή satiety
πλουτεῖν to be rich
πλοῦτος -ου wealth
ποθεινός -ή -όν desirable, wanted
πόθος -ου desire, yearning
ποιητής -οῦ poet
ποῖος -α -ον of what sort
πολιτικά n.pl politics
πολυτελής -ές expensive
πολυχρηματία high spending
πονεῖν to toil
πόνος -ου toil, labour
πόσοι -αι -α how many
πόσος -η -ον how big
πότερος -α -ον which one of two
ποτίζειν to water
ποτόν drink
πότος -ου drinking party
πρᾶξις -εως action, doing
πρᾶος πραεῖα πρᾶον mild
πρέπειν to befit
πρεσβύτης -ου senior person
πρίασθαι to buy
προαγορεύειν to foretell
προαγωγεία pandering
προαγωγεύειν to pander
προαγωγός -οῦ pander
προγίγνεσθαι to be born before
προειδέναι to know in advance
πρόθυμος -ον eager
προκεῖσθαι to lie before
προνοεῖν to think ahead
προξενεῖν to be proxenos (Intr. note 10)
προορᾶν to foresee
προσάγειν to attract
προσαιτεῖν to beg, importune
προσβλέπειν to look towards
προσδεῖσθαι to need, request in addition

προσδέχεσθαι to receive in addition
προσειπεῖν to address
προσεννοεῖν to think of in addition
προσέχειν to apply
προσήκειν to befit, belong
πρόσθεν previously
προσιέναι to come/go towards
προσκαίεσθαι to get extra burnt
προσλαμβάνειν to take in addition
προσορᾶν to look at
προσπίπτειν to befall
προστατεῖν to be in control of
προστάττειν to appoint, require
προστιθέναι to add
προσφέρειν to bring to
πρόσωπον face
προφασίζεσθαι to plead in excuse
πρώην the other day
πτωχός -οῦ beggar
πυκνός/πυκινός -ή -όν frequent
πύκτης -ου boxer
πώποτε ever yet

ῥᾳδιουργεῖν to take things easy
ῥᾳδιουργός -όν idle, casual
ῥηθῆναι - λέγειν
ῥῆμα word
ῥιγοῦν to be cold
ῥιπτεῖν to throw, hurl
ῥίς ῥινός f nose
ῥυθμός -οῦ rhythm, sequence
ῥώμη strength

σάττειν to pack full
σατυρικά n.pl. satyr plays
σαφής -ές clear, obvious
σεμνός -ή -όν solemn, proud, haughty
σημαίνειν to inform, indicate
σημεῖον mark, sign, instance
σιμός -ή -όν snub-nosed, concave
σιτίζειν to feed
σιτία n.pl. food

σιωπᾶν to be/fall silent
σιωπή silence
σιωπηρός -ά -όν silent
σκαρδαμύττειν to blink
σκέλος -ους limb, leg
σκία shadow
σκοπεῖν to look at
σκοπός -οῦ mark, target
σκόροδον garlic
σκῶμμα jest
σκώπτειν to jest
σοφία learning, wisdom
σοφιστής -οῦ (professionally) learned
 person
σπάνιος -α -ον scarce, infrequent
σπένδειν to make libation
σπεύδειν to make haste
σπουδάζειν to be in earnest
σπουδαιολογεῖν to talk seriously
σπουδαῖος -α -ον serious
σπουδαρχίας -ου would-be politician
σπουδή seriousness
σταθμός -οῦ weight
στέγη roof, house
στέργειν to feel love, affection for
στέρεσθαι to be without
στήλη marker-stone
στρατεύειν to wage war
στράτευμα army
στρατηγικός -ή -όν typical of a
 general
στρωμνή bedding
συγγένεια kinship
συγγίγνεσθαι to be with (for sex)
συγγυμναστής -οῦ partner at exercise
συγκαθεύδειν to sleep with
συγκαλύπτεσθαι to wrap oneself up
συγκυλινδεῖν to roll together
συγκόπτειν to chop up
συγκροτεῖν to clap (hands)
συκοφαντής -οῦ blackmailer
συμβάλλειν to bring together, match

συμβολή I 16
σύμβουλος -ου adviser
συμμανθάνειν to learn together
συμμιγνύναι, -μίσγειν to mix with
συμπαρέχεσθαι to associate in
  providing
συμπαρομαρτεῖν to accompany
συμπόσιον symposium
συμποτής -οῦ fellow drinker
συμφέρειν to be advantageous
συμφοιτᾶν to go (to school) with
συνάγειν to contract
συνακολουθεῖν to follow along with
συναμφότεροι -αι -α both together
συνιστάναι to make stand up too
συναπομαραίνεσθαι to fade away at
  the same time
συναρμόζειν to tune
συνάχθεσθαι to share displeasure
συνδειπνεῖν to dine with
συνδιημερεύειν to spend the day with
συνειδέναι to know mutually
συνεῖναι to be with
συνεξιέναι to come/go out with
συνεπαίρειν to share in rousing
συνέπεσθαι to go along with
συνεραστής -οῦ sharing a passion
συνεργός -όν sharing in work
συνεχής -ές lasting, continuous
συνήδεσθαι to share pleasure
συνιστάναι to introduce
σύνοικος -ον dwelling with
συνομνύναι to swear together
συνομολογεῖν to agree together
συνουσία being together, company
συντεκμαίρεσθαι to calculate
συντυγχάνειν to meet
συριγμός -οῦ whistling
συσκευάζεσθαι to equip oneself with
συστρατεύεσθαι to go on campaign
  with
σφάλλειν to make slip, stumble

σφάλμα slip
σφοδρός -ά -όν vehement
σχεδόν almost
σχέσις -εως state, arrangement
σχῆμα posture, figure
σχηματίζεσθαι to take a posture
σχίζειν to split
σχολάζειν to be at leisure
σχολή leisure
σωφρονεῖν to be self-controlled
σωφροσύνη self-control

ταινία ribbon, headband
τάλαντον talent (of money)
ταμιεύεσθαι to dispense, deal out
τάττειν to appoint, fix, draw up
τεκμαίρεσθαι to judge, estimate
τεκμήριον token, proof
τέκτων -ονος carpenter
τελεῖσθαι to be initiated
τέλεος -α -ον perfect
τέρπειν to delight, give pleasure
τέρψις -εως delight, pleasure
τετράμετρον tetrameter
τίκτειν to give birth
τίμιος -α -ον valuable, costly
τιμωρεῖν to seek redress for
τοῖιν - ὁ ἡ τό (Homeric gen./dat.
  dual)
τοιοῦτος -αύτη -οῦτο such
τοῖχος -ου wall
τοιχωρυχεῖν to break and enter,
  burgle
τολμηρός -ά -όν daring
τοσοῦτοι -αῦται -αῦτα so many
τράπεζα -ης table
τράχηλος -ου neck
τρέφειν to feed, sustain
τρίπους -ποδος m tripod
τρίχες - θρίξ
τροπαῖον VIII 38
τρόπος -ου behaviour

τροφή nourishment
τροχός -οῦ hoop, wheel, disc
τρώγειν to munch, eat vegetables
τυφλός -ή -όν blind

ὑγιαίνειν to be healthy
ὑγρός -ά -όν wet, fluid
ὕειν to rain
ὑμνεῖν to celebrate in song
ὑπακούειν to answer the door
ὑπανίστασθαι to rise in respect
ὑπαντᾶν to meet
ὑπάρχειν to be available
ὑπέκκαυμα tinder, stimulus
ὑπερασπάζεσθαι to welcome warmly
ὑπερορᾶν to disdain
ὑπερόριος -ον foreign
ὑπερσεμνύνεσθαι to be high and
  mighty
ὑπέχειν to undergo, incur
ὑποδύεσθαι to take on, endure
ὑποκριτής -οῦ actor
ὑπολαμβάνειν to take up a remark
ὑπομένειν to wait patiently
ὑπόνοια underlying meaning
ὑποπεπωκέναι to be a little drunk
ὑπόσχεσις -εως promise
ὑποτρώγειν to nibble
ὑποφέρειν to endure
ὕστερος -α -ον later
ὑφίεσθαι to give way
ὑψηλός -ή -όν high
ὕψος -ους height

φαῦλος -η -ον cheap, poor
φέγγος -ους light, beacon
φήμη prophecy
φθέγγεσθαι to utter
φθόγγος -ου sound, voice
φθονεῖν to begrudge
φιάλη bowl (II 23)
φιλεῖν to love, kiss

φίλημα kiss
φιλία friendship, love
φιλικός -ή -όν friendly
φιλόκαλος -ον fond of glory
φιλοκίνδυνος -ον fond of danger
φιλόπονος -ον fond of hard work
φιλοσοφεῖν to love knowledge
φιλοσοφία love of knowledge
φιλότιμος -ον fond of one's honour
φιλοφροσύνη friendliness
φιλόφρων -ον friendly
φιλοχρήματος -ον fond of money
φλόξ φλογός f flame
φοβερός -ά -όν fearsome
φόρος -ου tax, tribute
φράζειν to say, speak
φρένες φρενῶν f mind, heart
φρονεῖν to think
φρόνιμος -ον sensible
φροντιστής -οῦ thinker
φύεσθαι to grow
φωνεῖν to speak
φῶς φάους n light

χαλεπότης -ητος nuisance
χαλκεῖον vessel of bronze
χαρίζεσθαι to favour, gratify
χεῖλος -ους lip
χειρονομεῖν to exercise the arms
χείρων -ον worse, inferior
χιτών -ῶνος m tunic, coat
χλιδαίνεσθαι to luxuriate
χρῆσις -εως use
χρηστός -ή -όν useful, good
χρίειν to anoint
χρῖμα ointment
χρυσίον, χρυσός -οῦ gold
χρώς χροός/χρωτός m flesh
χωρίς apart
χῶρος -ου land

ψεύδεσθαι to deceive

ψηλάφημα   cuddle, grope
ψῆφος -ου f   pebble, vote
ψόγος -ου   reproach
ψύλλα -ης   flea
ψυχρός -ά -όν   cold

ᾠδή   song

ὦμος -ου   shoulder
ὠνεῖσθαι   to buy
ὥρα -ας   season, time of bloom
ὡραίος -α -ον   in season, blooming
ὦτα - οὖς
ὠφελεῖν   to help
ὠφέλιμος -ον   helpful

Indexes

Index of gods, heroes, people, places, and topics

(NB references to the Introduction are by its numbered paragraphs; references to the text and commentary are by the sections and sub-sections: to text alone thus, III 4, to commentary alone thus, III 4n; to both thus, III 4 + n. No references are made to the summary of the text in paragraph 10 of the Introduction)

Linguistic Index

(NB references are to Introduction or to Commentary)

ARIS & PHILLIPS CLASSICAL TEXTS
Published and forthcoming books

AESCHYLUS: EUMENIDES ed. A.J. Podlecki, PERSIANS ed. E. Hall

ARISTOPHANES ed. Alan H. Sommerstein: ACHARNIANS, BIRDS, CLOUDS, FROGS, KNIGHTS, LYSISTRATA, PEACE, THESMOPHORIAZUSAE, WASPS, ECCLESIAZUSAE

ARISTOTLE: ON THE HEAVENS I & II ed. S. Leggatt, ON SLEEP AND DREAMS ed. D. Gallop

AUGUSTINE: SOLILOQUIES *and* IMMORTALITY OF THE SOUL ed. G. Watson

CAESAR: CIVIL WAR I & II ed. J.M. Carter, CIVIL WAR III ed. J.M. Carter

CASSIUS DIO: ROMAN HISTORY Books 53.1-55.9, ed. J.W. Rich

CATULLUS: POEMS 61–8 ed. J. Godwin

CICERO: TUSCULAN DISPUTATIONS I ed. A.E. Douglas, TUSCULAN DISPUTATIONS II & V ed. A.E. Douglas, ON FATE with **BOETHIUS** CONSOLATION V ed. R.W. Sharples, PHILIPPICS II ed. W.K. Lacey, VERRINES II ed. T.N. Mitchell, ON STOIC GOOD AND EVIL ed. M.R. Wright, LAELIUS ON FRIENDSHIP and THE DREAM OF SCIPIO ed. J.G.F. Powell, LETTERS (Jan– Apr. 43 B.C.) ed. M. Willcock

EURIPIDES: ALCESTIS ed. D. Conacher, ANDROMACHE ed. M. Lloyd, BACCHAE ed. R. Seaford, ELECTRA ed. M.J. Cropp, HECUBA ed. C. Collard, HERACLES ed. S. Barlow, HIPPOLYTUS ed. M.R. Halleran, ION ed. K.H. Lee, ORESTES ed. M.L. West, PHOENICIAN WOMEN ed. E. Craik, TROJAN WOMEN ed. S. Barlow, FRAGMENTARY PLAYS VOLUME I eds C. Collard, M.J. Cropp & K.H. Lee

GREEK ORATORS: I ANTIPHON, LYSIAS ed. M. Edwards & S. Usher, III ISOCRATES PANEGYRICUS and TO NICOCLES ed. S. Usher, IV ANDOCIDES ed. M. Edwards, V DEMOSTHENES On the Crown ed. S. Usher, VI APOLLODORUS Against Neaira ed. C. Carey

HELLENICA OXYRHYNCHIA ed. P.R. McKechnie & S.J. Kern

HOMER: ODYSSEY I & II ed. P.V. Jones, ILIAD VIII & IX ed. C.H. Wilson

HORACE: SATIRES I ed. P. Michael Brown, SATIRES II ed. Frances Muecke

JOSEPH OF EXETER: THE TROJAN WAR I-III ed. A.K. Bate

LIVY ed. P.G. Walsh: Book XXXVI, Book XXXVII, Book XXXVIII, Book XXXIX, Book XL

LUCAN: CIVIL WAR VIII ed. R. Mayer

LUCIAN: A SELECTION ed. M.D. McLeod

LUCRETIUS: DE RERUM NATURA III ed. P.M. Brown, DE RERUM NATURA IV ed. J. Godwin, DE RERUM NATURA VI ed. J. Godwin

MARTIAL: EPIGRAMS V ed. P. Howell

MENANDER: SAMIA ed. D.M. Bain, THE BAD-TEMPERED MAN ed. S. Ireland

OVID: AMORES II ed. J. Booth, METAMORPHOSES I-IV ed. D.E. Hill, METAMORPHOSES V-VIII ed. D.E. Hill, METAMORPHOSES IX–XII ed. D.E. Hill *(for 1999)*

PERSIUS: THE SATIRES ed. J.R. Jenkinson

PINDAR: SELECTED ODES ed. S. Instone

PLATO: APOLOGY ed. M. Stokes, MENO ed. R.W. Sharples, PHAEDRUS ed. C.J. Rowe, REPUBLIC V ed. S. Halliwell, REPUBLIC X ed. S. Halliwell, STATESMAN ed. C.J. Rowe, SYMPOSIUM ed. C.J.Rowe

PLAUTUS: BACCHIDES ed. J.A. Barsby

PLINY: CORRESPONDENCE WITH TRAJAN FROM BITHYNIA ed. W. Williams

PLUTARCH: LIVES OF ARISTEIDES AND CATO ed. D. Sansone, LIFE OF CICERO ed. J.L. Moles, MALICE OF HERODOTUS ed. A.J. Bowen, THEMISTOCLES ed. J. Marr

THE RUODLIEB ed. C.W. Grocock

SENECA: LETTERS: A SELECTION ed. C.D.N. Costa, FOUR DIALOGUES ed. C.D.N. Costa

SOPHOCLES: AJAX ed. A. Garvie, ANTIGONE ed. A.L. Brown, PHILOCTETES ed. R.G. Ussher

SUETONIUS: LIVES OF GALBA, OTHO & VITELLIUS ed. D.C.A. Shotter

TACITUS: ANNALS IV ed. D.C.A. Shotter

TERENCE: THE BROTHERS ed. A.S. Gratwick, THE SELF-TORMENTOR ed. A.J. Brothers, THE MOTHER-IN-LAW ed. S. Ireland

THUCYDIDES: HISTORY Book II ed. P.J. Rhodes, HISTORY Book III ed. P.J. Rhodes, HISTORY Book IV–V ed. P.J. Rhodes, PYLOS BC: Book IV, 2-41, ed. J. Wilson

WILLIAM OF NEWBURGH: THE HISTORY OF ENGLISH AFFAIRS I ed. P.G. Walsh & M. Kennedy

XENOPHON: HELLENIKA I-II ed. Peter Krentz, HELLENIKA II–IV ed. Peter Krentz, SYMPOSIUM ed. A.J. Bowen, ON HUNTING with **ARRIAN** eds A.A. Phillips & M.M. Wilcock *(for 1999)*